Tea

Elementary Matters

GILLIE CUNNINGHAM
with JAN BELL
and ROGER GOWER

Pearson Education Limited
Edinburgh Gate, Harlow, Essex CM20 2JE England.
and Associated Companies throughout the world.

www.longman-elt.com

First published 1997
Fifth impression 2001

Set in Adobe ITC Garamond Light 10/12 pt
and Frutiger Light 8.5/10 pt

Printed in Spain
by Gráficas Estella

ISBN 0582 273595

Photocopying
The Publisher grants permission for the photocopying of those pages marked 'photocopiable' according to the following conditions. Individual purchasers may take copies for their own use or for use by classes they teach. School purchasers make may copies for use by their staff and students, but this permission does not extend to additional schools or branches.
Under no circumstances may any part of this book be photocopied for resale.

Authors' Acknowledgements
We would like to thank the following:
- Those people who reported on the material: Sarah Ellis and Mick Lawson.
- Those people who piloted the material in Poland : Ursula Ginter-Ożóg, Ewa Jackiewicz, Marzenna Kaperska, Marzenna Kobierzycka, Barbara Krawiec, Teresa Kubale, Elwira Marciniak, Arkadiusz Mucha, Jolanta Okonek, Andrzej Pałubicki, Urszula Rydz, Agnieska Steć, Elżbieta Wąsowicz and Ewa Wrześniewska.
  In Slovakia: Vlasta Bilaninova, John Boyd and Ewa Kuchárová.

Photo Acknowledgements
We are grateful to the following for permission to reproduce copyright photographs.

Rex Features for page 146.

Illustrated by Kathy Baxendale, Anna McLaughlin, Chris Pavely, Kevin White, and Celia Witchard.

Photocopiable section designed by Nicola Witt.

Text Acknowledgements
We are grateful to the following for permission to reproduce copyright material:
Music Sales Ltd for words to the song 'Sailing'. Words and music by Gavin Sutherland.© Copyright 1972 by Island Music Ltd, 42 British Grove, London W4. All Rights Reserved. International Copyright Secured; Kenneth R Thomson for words of the song 'Lady in Red' by Chris de Burgh pubd. Rondor/IMP Music.

Contents

Contents chart (Students' Book)

Talking about people	People doing things
Names, addresses and telephone numbers *Has/ have got* Possessive *'s* and possessive adjectives *Whose* Numbers over 20	*There is a* ... and *There are some* ... Present Continuous with *He/ she/ they* positive, negative and questions *This/ that/ those/ these*

Skills	Social English/Review
Reading and listening: Liverpool and Dublin **Vocabulary: using dictionaries** **Writing: punctuation**	**Social English** **Dates and times**
Reading and listening: quiz Vocabulary: keeping records Writing: combining sentences – pronouns, *and* and *but*	**Review** Vocabulary: crossword Using your grammar: asking for travel information
Listening: the weather forecast and the song, *Singin' in the rain* Reading: holiday questionnaire Vocabulary: opposites of adjectives Writing: a postcard	Social English Money and shopping for food
Reading: Stephen Spielberg's films Vocabulary: meaning from context Listening: people talking about films Writing: a film review	**Review** Vocabulary: wordsearch Using your grammar: bingo; letter to a pen friend
Vocabulary: opposites of adjectives and negatives with *un-* Reading and listening: continuation of the story Writing: linking words (*and, but, because* and *so)* Listening and speaking: the end of the story	Social English Directions
Reading: Rudolph Valentino Vocabulary: phrasal verbs Writing: biographies of famous people	**Review** Vocabulary: word game Using your grammar: a sound and picture story

Introduction

Who is *Elementary Matters* for?

Elementary Matters begins the *Matters* series for adult and young adult learners of English. It is followed by *Pre-Intermediate Matters, Intermediate Matters* and *Upper Intermediate Matters* and aims to meet the needs of *post-beginners* (students who have completed a course for absolute beginners) as well as *false beginners* (students who have previously studied English, but appear weak because they have not used it for some time). It also recognises that many adult elementary classes contain some absolute or near-absolute beginners and provides resources for that situation. It recognises that there are some fast elementary classes who may simply need to work with the core units and some slow elementary classes who need extra practice activities.

The course contains twelve core units, a CHECK YOUR ENGLISH 'starter unit' and four PRACTISE AND CHECK sections (one every three units). It provides approximately 90-120 hours of classroom material and can be used by students studying in Britain or in their own countries. The flexible structure of the course makes it suitable for students on intensive courses as well as those on part-time courses for an academic year.

Components

1 Students' Book and Class Cassettes

The Students' Book has twelve units, each providing approximately six to eight hours of classroom work, depending on the abilities of the class. There is also an optional CHECK YOUR ENGLISH unit at the beginning, with six to eight hours of work, which aims to review and revise the language taught in a beginners' class. There are four PRACTISE AND CHECK sections, one every three units. On the PRACTISE page (of the PRACTISE AND CHECK section) there are some discrete grammar practice exercises which can be used to supplement and consolidate the practice activities in each of the three previous units. This is particularly useful for slower classes. On the CHECK page there are some check activities which bring together and review the main language points (grammar and vocabulary) of the previous three units and enable the students and the teacher to assess progress. If all of the activities are completed then there is approximately one hours' work on each page (two hours per section).

Each unit consists of the following sections: FOCUS ON VOCABULARY, FOCUS ON GRAMMAR, SKILLS, SOCIAL ENGLISH and REVIEW and *Language reference*.

LANGUAGE REFERENCE

The *Language reference* section provides a concise summary of the language covered in each unit.

Support material at the back of the Students' Book includes:

- a Word list of what we consider to be the most useful new words in each unit.
- Tapescripts of the recordings used in the Students' Book, if they are not already printed in the relevant unit.
- a Pronunciation chart.
- a list of the Modal verbs most used at this level and their communicative functions.
- an Irregular verbs list.

The two Class Cassettes contain all the recordings used in the Students' Book, recordings of the longer reading texts in the Students' Book and two extra songs which have photocopiable exploitation in the Teacher's Book.

2 Workbook and Workbook Cassette

The Workbook consolidates the language practised in the Students' Book. It can be used for homework, for further practice in class, or as material to be worked on in a self-access centre.

Each Workbook unit consists of a GRAMMAR section which revises work done in the Students' Book; a VOCABULARY section which revises and extends work done in the Students' Book; and a WRITING section which gives practice of some important areas of written English such as punctuation, informal letters, spelling and linking words. Most units have a PRONUNCIATION section, which practises important areas of English pronunciation such as word stress and sound/spelling relationships.

The Workbook is available with or without a key to the exercises.

The Workbook Cassette contains all the recorded material needed for the listening and pronunciation exercises. It allows students to listen to material in their own time, using their own cassette recorders.

3 Teacher's Book

The Teacher's Book is designed to benefit teachers with a range of experience. For the more experienced teacher, it provides extra material and ideas to use in the classroom and for the less experienced teacher, it gives guidance in how to use the Students' Book. Each unit of the Teacher's Book opens with a summary of the material covered in the Students' Book and Workbook. The Teacher's Book then goes on to provide support for each section in the following areas:

A = the Aims of the section; L = useful notes on the Language areas covered; = useful methodological support for many of the exercises in the Students' Book; = ideas for visual presentations on the board; = the Tapescripts of any Listening material; = an Answer Key.

Extra material and ideas

Extra material and ideas are found at the end of each section. At the end of the Teacher's Book there are photocopiable materials for further practice and these are signalled P in the relevant exercise.

There is a section of Prepositions and everyday expressions containing the most important of these, unit by unit. These can be used for revision or to check students' knowledge. There are also photocopiable progress Tests for every three units of the Students' Book covering grammar and vocabulary.

Guiding principles

1 Confidence-building

Our assumption at this level is that learners are usually motivated to learn the language. The role of *Elementary Matters*, therefore, is to keep that motivation alive and not to defeat students by making them feel the task of learning the language is too great. At elementary level this is particularly difficult because slow learners are likely to be in the same class as fast learners; post beginners with their restricted beginners' knowledge and skills in the same class as false beginners with a lot of passive knowledge, and occasionally complete beginners alongside genuine elementary students.

Many students at this level are not used to learning a foreign language and have different (often non-communicative) expectations of a classroom. Many also have different learning styles. There are students who prefer to analyse the language and compare it with their own and are reluctant to lose face by trying to use it and make a mistake. These students like to seek the shelter of their mother tongue. At the other extreme there are students who press ahead and try and communicate fearlessly without fully understanding what they are saying or trying to get it right! They usually do not expect to use their mother tongue in a foreign language class (often impossible anyway in a multi-lingual class situation). *Elementary Matters* provides a wealth of extra controlled practice activities in the Workbook and the PRACTISE AND CHECK sections which teachers can integrate into classwork when students need more accuracy work; and it provides a resource bank of photocopiable activities in the Teacher's Book for classes that need more communicative activities. In these different ways *Elementary Matters* takes into account the needs of mixed-ability classes.

A guiding principle of *Elementary Matters* is to build students' knowledge in achievable measures, in order to prevent any loss of confidence and to give confidence to those in whom it is naturally lacking. The course aims to build confidence by providing the following:

COMPONENTS

- A CHECK YOUR ENGLISH starter unit designed to give support to students who are not fully up to the elementary level. (This section also allows the teacher to assess the strengths and weaknesses of the whole class.) The teacher can also give slower students extra practice from the REVISION AND EXTENSION at the end of the CHECK YOUR ENGLISH unit either in class or for homework. The teacher can move quickly or slowly through this starter unit according to the abilities of the class.
- PRACTISE AND CHECK sections every three units. On the PRACTISE page there are extra practice activities linked to individual units.

VOCABULARY

Simple labelling and matching tasks that help students build their vocabulary in a particular topic area, together with word stress and phonetic support where appropriate.

GRAMMAR

- Paradigms to illustrate structural patterns.
- Yellow grammar boxes for on the spot support.
- Clearly presented *Language reference* sections at the end of each unit.
- A clear presentation and practice approach for the main grammar points, with each activity building on the previous one.
- A lot of practice opportunities within the unit as well as optional extra practice in the PRACTICE AND CHECK sections.
- Visual support for difficult vocabulary.
- Constant recycling and revision.
- Many 'Listen and check' exercises, which reinforce the grammar and gently help build the listening skill.

LISTENING

- A lot of short, integrated listening activities.
- Textual support and a variety of non-linguistic tasks for most listening texts.
- Tapescripts at the back of the Students' Book.

READING

- Not only accessible but interesting texts, each with a restricted number of tasks. Teachers with a weak class (or short of time) might choose to restrict the activity even more and omit some tasks.
- Listening support on the cassette for the longer texts which helps build the listening skill in a non-threatening way.
- Warm-up visuals and personalised discussion questions before students are asked to read a text.

WRITING

Integrated writing tasks that do not defeat the students: both restricted and controlled writing tasks and guided communicative tasks.

SPEAKING

- Achievable integrated speaking tasks.
- Opportunities for students to talk about themselves in a semi-controlled communicative way.
- Controlled speaking tasks to develop students' accuracy.
- Integrated pronunciation tasks in every part of the lesson.

The underlying principle, therefore, behind all the encouraging, confidence-building measures is that elementary students, more than students at other levels, need to be helped to succeed.

2 Recycling and revision

At elementary level, it is important not to give too much new language at one go or students feel defeated. Therefore, language that has been introduced should be recycled and activated. In the FOCUS ON VOCABULARY section, 'known' grammar is activated in a communicatively functional way in a section focusing on 'new' vocabulary. Also 'known' grammar and vocabulary is brought in through subsequent practice and skills activities.

Moreover, at this level, in our view it is important that language is not only recycled but overtly revised. This is why we have included a REVIEW section every two units and a CHECK section every three units.

The overall message is 'a little and often'.

3 Focusing on vocabulary

Clearly at all levels grammar is important. However, at elementary level the quickest way students will be able to communicate in a foreign language is through vocabulary. This is why each unit opens with an important topic area of vocabulary, where the students are not only expected to remember and recall a group of new words but are expected to use them in an active communicative situation, using and revising 'known' grammar at the same time. Many of the initial exercises in the activity sequences are of the labelling and matching kind which students at this level find motivating and memorable.

The importance of fixed phrases at this level (*What does ... mean? Can I help you?*) has also not been overlooked. These phrases provide students with ready-made tools for use in communicative situations.

4 English for communication

Elementary Matters assumes that students may at some time need their English for communication. This is why there are sections that help students in a number of social situations, with words and phrases as well as the kind of communicative strategies we use when, for example, we buy a ticket, or want to try on some clothes in a shop.

Equally we believe that while adult learners need to learn about both grammar and vocabulary they also need practise using them. In the FOCUS ON VOCABULARY and FOCUS ON GRAMMAR sections there are many opportunities for use in a semi-controlled and achievable way.

5 Texts

We believe that elementary students can learn a lot from reading short interesting texts in the foreign language. Not only will they see the language items they have been working on in a natural setting but they will have the opportunity to learn and acquire other features of the language. Students will learn by example how to spell, how to shape and structure a sentence and how to shape and structure discourse. This in turn will help them acquire and develop their own writing skills. The longer texts are also recorded on the cassette which gives students an opportunity for further exposure to native-speaker pronunciation.

An 'added-value' of *Elementary Matters* is that most students will not need to buy supplementary skills books.

6 Integration

In order to build up students' confidence we believe it is useful to integrate skills work into many activities, so Listening is integrated into Vocabulary and Grammar as well as Reading.

Pronunciation is integrated into vocabulary work in the FOCUS ON VOCABULARY sections as well as the vocabulary skills work in the SKILLS section; it is also integrated into the FOCUS ON VOCABULARY and SOCIAL ENGLISH sections. Speaking is integrated into every section. Following the 'little and often' principle, students are given integrated tasks which contain small amounts of practice of a number of skills. This helps develop the skills in parallel and gives students confidence to work with them.

We also believe in the need to lay the foundations for good language learning skills, such as dictionary work, keeping vocabulary records, word-building and deducing the meaning words from the context. In *Elementary Matters* attention is paid to this in the SKILLS sections.

7 Flexibility

As we said earlier, there are many kinds of learner in an elementary class and many kinds of elementary classes. We believe therefore that teachers will want to adapt any coursebook to their teaching situation. The sections within each unit have been clearly labelled and signposted to enable you to move activities around (for example to suit the needs of a school examination), omit them (for example on short courses) or supplement them (if some students need further practice) all according to the needs of your teaching programme and the class.

We also believe there are fast track and slow track learners. While the core material is more fast track than slow track (giving the students a sense of progress) there is a lot of support for slow track learners and slow track classes, both in the Students' Book PRACTISE section and REVIEW section and in the extensive controlled practice activities in the Workbook and the wealth of extra ideas and photocopiable materials in the Teacher's Book. These provide valuable extra material for slow learners who need more consolidation and fast learners who want extension material.

Elementary Matters also allows you to omit whole sections if this is appropriate to your teaching situation. For example, in a fast grammar and vocabulary focused course, you may choose to omit the SKILLS section.

Overall, we aim to make teachers feel that they are in charge of the materials and not vice versa. See the Unit organisation section for further ideas on how to exploit the flexibility of the course.

Teaching with *Elementary Matters*

1 Unit organisation

In each unit there are four sections followed by the *Language reference.* The first three sections have a double-page spread for each, the third section has a single page.

The sections can obviously be worked through in the order they appear. Each unit begins with a FOCUS ON VOCABULARY section, goes on to a FOCUS ON GRAMMAR section, then a SKILLS section and ends with a REVIEW OF SOCIAL ENGLISH section. However, there is no reason why you can't start with the FOCUS ON GRAMMAR or the SKILLS or the SOCIAL ENGLISH if you prefer. For example, you could start with the FOCUS ON GRAMMAR section, go on to the SOCIAL ENGLISH section, then move to the FOCUS ON VOCABULARY section and the finish with (or indeed omit if you are a grammar-intensive situation) the SKILLS section. On some occasions it may be necessary to bring the grammar and vocabulary exercises in the Workbook into the classroom, or to use some extra ideas from the Teacher's Book in place of a Students' Book activity.

Also you may choose to break up the sections, depending on the length of your classes, to do part of one section in one lesson, then continue or move on to part of another section in another lesson. The FOCUS ON VOCABULARY and FOCUS ON GRAMMAR sections can usually be divided into those exercises which focus on learning something new and those which focus on using what has been learned; the SKILLS sections fall into three parts; the REVIEW sections have two parts and the SOCIAL ENGLISH sections can usually be divided. You might, for example, choose to set as homework some of the practice activities in the FOCUS ON GRAMMAR section and the writing activities in other sections.

2 The Check Your English unit

The CHECK YOUR ENGLISH unit is optional and teachers may prefer to start the course at Unit 1. The unit has different aims depending on your class. It can be used as a check for assessing the strengths and weaknesses of your class, as revision of the language taught at beginner level, or as teaching material for students who are beginners or near-beginners. It can be used in class time to deal with the different levels in a mixed-ability class or to build confidence in students who 'know' the grammar already but would benefit from going over it again before they start something new.

3 The different sections of the core units

FOCUS ON VOCABULARY

The FOCUS ON VOCABULARY section presents an area of vocabulary based around a particular everyday topic, such as clothes or food. This combined with the visuals and the labelling and matching exercises aims to make the words more memorable. Attention has been paid to their pronunciation through the Listen and check exercises and the word stress symbols on the page, and although at this level the words are often concrete nouns, attention has been paid where possible to the verbs and adjectives with which they collocate.

The section is called FOCUS ON VOCABULARY rather than just VOCABULARY because there is also an aim to recycle and activate 'known' grammar the students will have had presented at beginners' level or in previous units of the course. This is done through such techniques as listening to dialogues, personalised speaking tasks, communication gap activities, cued story-telling and simple free writing tasks. Each of the tasks is limited, interesting and achievable. We feel it is probably important not to correct too much in some of these freer activation exercises to help students build their confidence and learn to communicate meaning.

In FOCUS ON VOCABULARY the unfamiliar vocabulary is usually in the first exercises in the sequences and is often integrated with 'known' words, giving opportunities for revision as well as giving the students a degree of comfort. You might want students to refer to their dictionaries (bi-lingual or a simple mono-lingual) to find out the meaning of unfamiliar words when they do the exercises or you might want to get the students to make guesses which you confirm or correct at the appropriate stage of the exercise.

It is important at this level that students are given the opportunity to say new words (either as word repetition or in sentences) and get the pronunciation right. This means not only sounds but the correct syllable stress in words of two or more syllables. *Elementary Matters* helps in this through the use of phonetic and stress symbols, the listening activities, and the practice activities. However, you might find it beneficial to show on the board how words are formed: for example by dividing the word into syllables (Spa■|nish) and showing where it is stressed. In *Elementary Matters* we use a small box as a stress symbol for both word and sentence stress because we feel it is clearer and cannot be confused with other symbols. It is important to use one system of stress marking and stick to it. *Elementary Matters* also shows students the dictionary convention of a (') mark but in our experience this symbol can sometimes be confused on the board with the apostrophe.

Notice too that reference is made to phonetic symbols and there is a chart of English phonemes on page 144, which you might want to enlarge and put up in your classroom. The aim is not to confuse the students with an extra alphabet but to give them some tools to help them with their pronunciation and to make full use of dictionaries (where the system is often used). The aim, therefore, is to build *recognition* of the symbols but we do not expect students to be able to write them. If you refer to the chart regularly, students will start to gain confidence in being able to work out the pronunciation for themselves. *Elementary Matters* encourages students to see its relevance in dictionary work in the SKILLS section.

In Unit 2 skills we also encourage students to keep vocabulary notebooks and suggest ways of doing this. You may wish to encourage notebooks earlier. As the FOCUS ON VOCABULARY section focuses on a topic area, a ready-made topic grouping of words is provided. You might want students to organise their records according to topic at this level rather than alphabetically. We feel it is important that students are given opportunities to update and organise their notebooks regularly. You might want to collect them in from time to time so that students realise how important they are. Students should be encouraged to add any words/expressions at any time, from their own reading and listening.

At the end of the book, there is a Word list, which includes the most useful words (including phrasal verbs) from each unit. You may like to go over this with students at the end of each unit, or give it for homework, perhaps getting students to add a translation and an example sentence. It is useful for students to look at the lists regularly and try to use the words. They could also add them to their personal vocabulary notebooks and try to group them according to topic.

FOCUS ON GRAMMAR

Students have many different learning styles and we believe that teachers should integrate different ways of presenting and practising grammar into their lessons. In *Elementary Matters* students are sometimes asked to work out the rules from examples or a short text, but it also provides on the spot grammar instruction and highlighting in the form of yellow grammar boxes on the page.

The Teacher's Book gives lots of ideas for highlighting form on the board and provides easy-to-copy visuals. Making the form and rules clear to students allows them to concentrate on when and how the language is used. The Teacher's Book also provides a lot of ideas for lifting the grammar presentation and practice off the page and making it work in the classroom.

It is important to encourage students to refer to and to use the *Language reference* either at the end of a practice activity or as homework. Many adult students also find it useful to keep their own personal grammar notes based on these pages, perhaps contrasting the use and form with their own language.

After each grammar presentation there is oral and written controlled practice, including relevant pronunciation work. Obviously, students at this level benefit from repeating examples aloud (either individually or together), or subvocalising them and gaining confidence in manipulating the form, including the pronunciation. The Students' Book focuses on oral communication work for the classroom and extra ideas are given in the Teacher's Book. There are many more mechanical practice exercises in the Workbook and the PRACTISE AND CHECK sections.

It is useful for students to work on controlled practice activities in pairs or to compare their answers. However, in the FOCUS ON GRAMMAR section we also include oral communicative activities. It is a good idea for teachers to monitor these activities and give some feedback at the end of the lesson, not just on accuracy of form, but on the communicative success of the activity. Note that the grammar is revised in the REVIEW section every second unit.

Every three units there is a PRACTISE AND CHECK section. The PRACTISE part provides extra practice for the grammar of each unit and can be integrated into the lesson with that unit or alternatively set for homework. The CHECK part brings together and revises the grammar and vocabulary of the previous three units and is best done at that point at the end of the three units, either as revision or assessment. (Note there are more formal tests at the back of the Teacher's Book.)

SKILLS

The aim of this section is to develop confidence in reading English, to provide exposure to familiar and unfamiliar sentence structures and vocabulary in a natural 'global' context and to practise vocabulary and writing skills. The longer texts have been recorded for those teachers who like to get the students to listen and read at the same time, or read and then listen, or listen and then read. Each approach has its advantages but linking listening and reading helps students acquire the links (not always obvious!) between sound and spelling in English. In this section (as in the other sections) other listening work is also sometimes integrated (see for example, Unit 5).

READING

The topics in the Reading are often not linked (or only loosely linked) to the other sections. In our experience, students at this level can easily become bored and demotivated if they spend too long on one topic. The texts have been chosen from authentic sources according to their interest value and adapted to provide 'comprehensible input' for elementary level (i.e. just above the students' productive level). There will obviously be vocabulary and grammar that will be unfamiliar to the students but much of this is for 'receptive' purposes. The students are only asked to use what is useful and appropriate to their level. Some difficult vocabulary is illustrated in the supporting photographs and illustrations; others are linked to exercises which either encourage and develop dictionary skills or the skills of deducing the meaning of unfamiliar words in context. Every effort has been made to stretch the students linguistically, with the intrinsic interest of the text carrying them along without destroying their confidence.

Before students read a text there is often an activity which gets them to relate to the text personally and provides an opportunity for them to speak in a less controlled way. There are often further 'warm-up' suggestions in the Teacher's Book. By doing this, and by focusing on some of the key vocabulary which comes up in the text we hope to make the reading process easier for students.

VOCABULARY

We believe that if students have a reasonable range of vocabulary at this level they can at least make themselves understood (not necessarily accurately in terms of grammar) in a communicative situation. We have therefore given vocabulary a high priority in *Elementary Matters*. Where there is a separate sub-section of VOCABULARY after the readings its aim is mainly to focus on developing the vocabulary *skills*. In this way it is different from the FOCUS ON VOCABULARY section, which introduces and practises specific lexical areas.

The main aims of a vocabulary sub-section after the Reading are to help students:

1 To deduce the meaning of words in context. To do this, we suggest that you encourage students to make intelligent guesses and defend these guesses in pairs or groups (in their own language, if necessary). It is important to remember that you are teaching a skill, not testing it, and that the process is as important as, if not more important than, the answer. For this reason, if necessary, students could give their guesses in their own language.

2 To learn to use monolingual dictionaries efficiently and confidently. There are small extracts from monolingual dictionaries and practice exercises in *Elementary Matters*. If possible, recommend a specific dictionary that all students can work from, or take in class sets. We also feel that it is very useful to help students at this level to choose and use a good bilingual dictionary.

When new words come up in the lesson write them on the board and mark the stressed syllable. Make sure you give students plenty of practice in the correct pronunciation.

In general, it is useful for you to keep a record of new vocabulary as it comes up, perhaps on one side of the board, so that students can easily see it, and copy it down. Some teachers like to transfer this new vocabulary to paper or card at the end of each lesson and keep it in a box or bag in the classroom. This is useful for future recycling activities and games, as well as testing.

LISTENING

Listening tasks are often integrated into this and other sections. The aim is to make listening (which is often the most difficult skill at this level) more achievable and less defeating.

With Listening you might like to provide even more support by playing the cassette as often as you feel is necessary (without becoming boring!), pausing the cassette at regular intervals, and accepting answers in the first language if necessary.

The tapescripts for the SKILLS section are at the back of the Students' Book as well as in the Teacher's Book. We feel that as a final activity students can often benefit from reading the tapescript at the same time as they listen to the cassette. If students have not had much listening practice this could, of course, also be done as a first stage. Once again, as with the listening and reading activities mentioned above, it helps build students' confidence in sound/spelling relationships.

It should not be forgotten that the teacher can be an important resource as listening input and not only in general classroom language like instructions. For example, some teachers might like to read the reading texts aloud or act out dialogues to give students extra listening practice. The teacher as listening input is usually less threatening than a cassette containing disembodied voices!

WRITING

As in the other sections Writing is integrated with other activities. The tasks are either personal and achievable (in, for example, paragraph writing linked to a previous activity) or cued. In the SKILLS section there is also work on the Writing skills, for example, focusing on punctuation, linking words and combining sentences as well as freer writing.

We suggest that the marking of students work should focus on what they have been asked to practise and that they are encouraged to monitor their own work, or each other's work before handing it in.

If you ask students to do more creative and 'fun' writing tasks you can simply respond to the material they write as communication, maybe by putting the writing on the wall for other students to read.

Alternatively, rather than correct and mark it you might want to use more guided self-correction approaches, for example, correction symbols. If you do, we suggest that correction symbols are agreed on with the class (for example: G = a grammar mistake; WO = a word order; V = Vocabulary; VF = verb form and so on). This helps you to indicate the type of error and encourage the student to correct his/her own work.

There is more writing in the Workbook which you may want to integrate into your lessons.

SPEAKING

As in other sections Speaking is integrated into many of the tasks and great care has been given to provide lots of opportunities for speaking practice. Don't forget many of the activities in the course can be done as pair or group work. It is true that in a monolingual situation that most students will slip into their mother tongue. In our view this is not necessarily a bad thing (pair work and group work anyway helps encourage co-operation and builds confidence) provided that some of the speaking is in English. After all if all the speaking is done when the teacher is 'up-front' then usually only one student can speak at any one time – an average which is usually improved on even in the most undisciplined of pair and group work.

We also believe that at this level pronunciation work should be integrated into learning grammar and vocabulary and should not be given a separate section. Students are therefore frequently asked to focus on sounds, stress and intonation as part of a sequence of activities.

REVIEW

This section (in Units 2, 4, 6, 8, 10, 12) revises areas of grammar and vocabulary in that and the previous unit(s). In general they are interaction activities or games, which lead on to further revision if necessary (for example, from the PRACTISE AND CHECK section, the Workbook or the Teacher's Book).

SOCIAL ENGLISH

This section (in Units 1, 3, 5, 7, 9, 11) presents and practises an important area of language linked to everyday social situations (such as giving directions and buying clothes). Language (including grammar) is presented within a functional and situational framework. So that, for example, modals such as *can* and *will* are illustrated for what function they perform communicatively in a situation (i.e. asking for permission and making a decision at the moment of speaking) rather than their grammatical value.

There are several pair work, interactional activities with the stimulus material on different pages in the Additional material at the back of the book.

Jan Bell and Roger Gower

ABBREVIATIONS

L = Language T = Teacher SS = Students
SB = Students' Book WB = Workbook
TB = Teachers' Book GW = Group work
PW = Pair work OHT = Overhead projector transparency

Check your English

Students' Book

Unit topic: revision of basic language.

IN THE CLASSROOM: classroom vocabulary; the alphabet; numbers; singular and plural nouns; classroom language; pronunciation and word stress.
HELLOS AND GOODBYES: greetings and farewells; introductions; *to be, a/an*; irregular plural nouns; word stress patterns.
TALKING ABOUT PEOPLE: names, addresses and telephone numbers; *has/have got*; possessive *'s* and possessive adjectives; *whose*; numbers over 20.
PEOPLE DOING THINGS: *There is a .../There are some* with singular and plural countable nouns; Present Continuous with *he/she/they* positive, negative and inverted questions; *this/these*.
REVISION AND EXTENSION: *a/an*; plural nouns: regular/irregular; *to be*; numbers; possessive adjectives/pronouns; possessive *'s*; *whose*; *has(n't)/have(n't)*; *there is a/some*; Present Continuous; *this/that/these/those*; subject/object pronouns.

Workbook

GRAMMAR: *to be*; *a/an*; possessive pronouns; possessive adjectives or *'s*; object pronouns; Present Continuous; questions and short answers; *this/these/that/those*.
VOCABULARY: numbers; classroom language; singular and plural nouns.
WRITING: spelling.

General introduction

This unit is an optional pathway into Unit 1. It serves as a teaching unit for SS who are beginners and as a revision unit for SS who are post or false beginners. If you feel your SS are familiar, though not necessarily accurate, with the language presented in this unit, you may choose to go immediately to Unit 1. In which case you could use this unit and the REVISION AND EXTENSION exercises for homework, concentrating on accuracy of form. If you have a mixed level class, you could equally use these exercises during class time to cater for the difference in levels, with some SS working on the basic exercises in this unit and the more able SS working on the extension exercises which accompany each section. However you choose to use this material, it should be understood that Unit 1 is based on the assumption that SS are familiar with the language points covered in CHECK YOUR ENGLISH and the accompanying REVISION AND EXTENSION exercises.

IN THE CLASSROOM

- Explore and extend vocabulary already familiar to SS.
- Practice of the alphabet.
- Numbers 1–20.
- Useful classroom language.
- Pronunciation: introduction to the phonemic script and word stress.
- Revision of *there is/there are*.

- Some of the vocabulary will be familiar because the words are the same or very similar in S's L1, e.g. *'taxi, 'video*.
- To help SS with pronunciation the alphabet is not only written in alphabetical order but also grouped according to vowel sounds on the cassette, e.g. *a j k h* all incorporate the vowel /eɪ/.
- Numbers 1 to 100. Note that in the REVISION AND EXTENSION exercise *thousands* are introduced. The use of *a* or *one* before the words *hundred, thousand* and *million* is quite complex for this level. We recommend you encourage the SS to use *a* if using round figures *a hundred, a thousand* etc.

The following may be helpful as a simple but useful guideline: *A* is used more often in spoken English, e.g. *We need about a hundred chairs*; *one* is used when we want to be precise e.g. *we need exactly one hundred chairs*. *A* is only used when *hundred, thousand* etc. is used at the beginning of a number, e.g. *a hundred and seven* (107), but (4,160) *four thousand, one hundred and sixty*; *one* is used with *thousand* when it precedes a number of hundreds e.g. *one thousand, four hundred and six* (1,406).

Pronunciation Expect problems in differentiating between numbers such as 13/30, 14/40, 15/50 etc. In isolation the following stress pattern is common *thir'teen, 'thirty*. However, in sentences this differentiation is lost e.g. *They had 'thirteen eggs*. Interestingly, native speakers often have to ask for clarification concerning these numbers.

- **Plural** *-s* is highlighted but limited to regular nouns.
- **Classroom language** focuses on phrases which will help SS to access language and ask for equipment they might need in the classroom, e.g. *What does X mean? Have you got a pen?*
- **General pronunciation** An introduction to the phonemic script. SS are only expected to recognise part of the script. The word syllable focus is on two-syllable words. It is most

important to know where the Pronunciation Chart is (on page 144 of the SB) and how to use it.

Students' Book (page 6)

If this is a new class or if new SS have joined an existing class, there should be some form of S to S introduction and learning of names. It is felt that such activities are more effective when they are not book based and therefore, have not been included in the SB. However, here are some possible activities which will no doubt have a familiar ring.

• Using a ball or orange, begin by saying your name and then throwing the ball to a S who says his/her name. This S then throws it to another S who says his/her name etc. When everyone has introduced themselves, the rules change. The person throwing the ball must say the name of the S he/she is throwing to. If they are wrong, the ball is returned to them and they try again etc.

• Hand each S a list of all the SS' names in your class with two extra names not in your class. SS mingle and say, *"I'm X. What's your name?"* They continue until they have finished ticking off the names of SS in the class, or when you stop the activity. The objective is to find which SS are not in the class (the two extra names).

• A very simple, *Find someone who/whose* activity. This could practise the alphabet, e.g. *Find someone whose name begins with A.* If it's a multilingual class it could be *Find someone who is from Morocco* etc.

Exercise 1a) Note that this exercise aims to get SS to give the English words they know for the objects and people in the photograph. You might want them to add any other words they know. One way of approaching this activity is to ask SS to write as many words as they can on the classroom board. This should immediately establish that you expect the SS to help each other towards a common goal; you expect them to be active learners; you have confidence in their ability; the board is their property too and it's all right to get out of their chairs during a lesson. Correct spelling mistakes as they occur but only indicate the error to the person who made the mistake. Then focus on the photograph in the book. If SS have already identified some of the vocabulary, put a tick next to the word on the board and acknowledge their achievement even if the word is the same in their language. Then let them work individually to identify as many of the other words as they can. Allow SS to use dictionaries if they want and let them work at their own pace for a while.

Exercise 1b) Ask the pairs to add any new words they have found to the list on the board.

Exercise 2a) Establish the meaning of the word *alphabet* before you begin. Ask SS to compare it with their own language: *Does it have the same number of letters?, How many vowels does it have?, Is it written the same?* etc. (See WB page 9.) Ask SS to try to say the letters to see how much they already know. Then play the cassette.

[0.1]
a b c d e f g h i j k l m n o p q r s t u v w x y z

Exercise 2b) Write the following phonemic symbols on the board to represent the vowels used when pronouncing the letters: /eɪ/, /iː/, /e/, /aɪ/, and /uː/. This is how the exercise has grouped the letters to practise the pronunciation: a j k h, b c d e g p t v, f l m n s x z, i y and q u w. The letters *r* and *o* don't have a sound mate. Ask SS which letters are not included in the chart. Practise the letters according to these groupings. If SS don't know the pronunciation of the alphabet, you can expect them to need a lot of review practice for both recognition and production in future lessons. The L1 interference is usually very strong indeed when the alphabet is similar but pronounced differently. Point out that the handwritten ɑ and the printed **a** may look different but are in fact the same letter. It's also worth pointing out any individual touches you may have in your own handwriting and do the odd check here and there by pouncing on a word you have written on the board and asking them to spell it out.

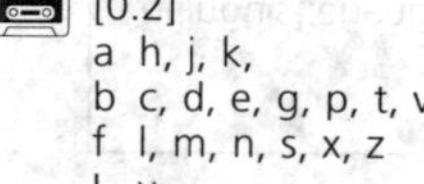

[0.2]
a h, j, k,
b c, d, e, g, p, t, v
f l, m, n, s, x, z
I y
q u, w

Exercise 2c) After you have established the answers with SS ask them to spell the words back to you or a partner. You could then find extra words from the photograph and write them on the board for students to spell to you e.g. *person, watch.*

[0.3]
b - u - s
t - a - b - l - e
v - i - d - e - o
g - u - i - t - a - r
s - a - n - d - w - i - c - h
c - a - s - s - e - t - t - e
m - a - p

bus, table, video, guitar, sandwich, cassette, map

Exercise 2d) To provide more practice, this could be a mingle activity where SS stand up in the middle of the room and ask each other to spell their names.

Exercise 3a) Write the word numbers on the board and illustrate its meaning with some numbers. Again ascertain what the SS already know before you begin. This will help you measure how much time you need to devote to the exercise. If SS are not very familiar with numbers, it is worth highlighting patterns to help SS assimilate. E.g. apart from numbers ***thir**teen* and ***fif**teen* the numbers for teens are the same as the numbers one to nine, e.g. ***four**teen*, ***six**teen* etc. This is again reflected in the decimal numbers ***for**ty* (note the spelling change) ***sixty***, ***seven**ty* etc. The odd ones out are ***twen**ty*, ***thir**ty* and ***fif**ty*. If SS arrange numbers according to these patterns it often helps to assimilate them faster. Note that numbers between 20–999 and the contrastive stress between, e.g. 14 and 40, is dealt with in the section TALKING ABOUT PEOPLE pages 10 and 11.

Exercise 3b) SS could dictate numbers to their partner. They shouldn't dictate them in numerical order.

[0.4]
1, 2, 3, 4, 5, 6, 7, 8, 9, 10, 11, 12, 13, 14, 15, 16, 17, 18, 19, 20

Exercise 3c) Focus attention on the structure, *There is/are*, and the plural form *-s* of the noun. These are all regular plural forms with no spelling changes occurring because of the *-s*. Do the first two with the whole class to establish the meaning of *true* and *false* and the objective of the exercise. When the SS have finished, ask them to check with a partner.

1 F – There are 4 tables.
2 T
3 F – There are 4 pens.
4 T
5 F – There are 5 posters.
6 T
7 F – There is 1 guitar.
8 F – There are 7 books.
9 T

Exercise 3d) If your SS aren't familiar with the game of Bingo, you may need to demonstrate the activity for the whole class before they begin.

Exercise 4a) Give the SS time to look at the pictures before you play the cassette.

[0.5]
1
MALE STUDENT: **Excuse** me, Luis.
TEACHER: Yes?
MALE STUDENT: How do you pronounce this word?
TEACHER: *Niña*. Try it.
MALE STUDENT: *Niña*.
TEACHER: Excellent.
MALE STUDENT: What does **it mean**?
TEACHER: It means ***girl***.

2
FEMALE STUDENT: **How** do you **say** *house* in Spanish?
TEACHER: *Casa*.
FEMALE STUDENT: **Can** you **repeat** that, please?
TEACHER:Yes, **of course**, *casa*.
FEMALE STUDENT: And how do **you spell** it?
TEACHER: C - a - s - a. I'll write it **on the board**.

3
MALE STUDENT 2: **Sorry** I'm **late**.
TEACHER: That's **OK**. **Why don't** you **sit** over here?
MALE STUDENT 2: What page **are we** on?
FEMALE STUDENT: Page **23**. Unit **one**.
MALE STUDENT 2: Thanks. **Have** you **got** a pen?
FEMALE STUDENT: **Here** you **are**.

1C, 2B, 3A

Exercise 4b) Pause the cassette to allow SS time to write the answers. Let them dictate the number of times they need to listen to the cassette and ask them to check their answers with a partner.

Exercise 4c) Write up any sentences that illustrate consonant vowel soundlinking at word boundaries as SS practise saying them e.g. *How do you spell‿it? Have you got‿a pen?* It might be confusing at this point to illustrate intrusive soundlinking which happens at word boundaries where two vowels occur e.g. *Here you‿(w)‿are*. You could focus on the sound by practising /wɑː/ then /jʊwɑː/ then the whole phrase /hɪəjʊwɑː/.

[0.6]
How do you pronounce this word?
What does *house* mean?
How do you say *casa* in English?
Can you repeat that, please?
How do you spell it?
Sorry I'm late.
Have you got a pen?
Here you are.
Sorry, I don't understand.
I don't know.

Exercise 4d) Check the pronunciation of the target words before SS begin.

B guitar, C cassette, D camera, E sandwich

Exercise 5a) To convince SS of the value of phonemics show them a dictionary or phrase book extract which includes phonemic transcriptions. The message being, if you can read these, you will always have access to the pronunciation of English words. If SS aren't familiar with the phonemic script, you will need to do this exercise with the whole class and write the phonemics of at least three of the words in the exercise on the board to focus attention. Point out the symbols that the SS should be able to understand because they follow the same written form as they have in the alphabet (e.g. *b, s, m*). Then focus on the written form of the consonants and vowels which don't have the same symbols. Keep pointing to these and ask SS to repeat the sounds until they are fairly fluent. Then let them try to work out the remaining words in the exercise. Spend sufficient time so that the idea of phonemics becomes familiar and they don't feel overwhelmed. Practice of phonemics can always form the basis of quick warmer or ending activities to lessons. SS don't have to be symbol perfect immediately nor do they ever have to produce the symbols, only recognise them. Refer to the phonemic chart in the SB on page 144.

1 bus 2 camera 3 book 4 teacher 5 student

Exercise 5b) and c) Again, you will probably need to demonstrate what constitutes a syllable (e.g. talxi. If you don't want to use the words in the exercise to do this demonstration, you can use SS' names. Highlight the pronunciation of *camera.* This gives you the opportunity to show that a word that looks as if it has three syllables is commonly pronounced as a two-syllable word. Demonstrate what a stressed syllable is by emphasising it. Again you can use SS' names to practise before doing the exercise in the SB. The two-syllable words in the SB all have first syllable stress. This is a common pattern for two-syllable nouns in English. It would be useful for SS to know this.

 [0.7]
taxi
camera
teacher
student

 'camera 'teacher 'student

Extra material and ideas

1 WB page 5, Exercise 3 and page 9, Exercises 18–20.

2 REVISION AND EXTENSION page 14, Exercise 2, plural nouns.

3 S to S number dictation Tell SS to write 10 numbers between 1 and 20. They dictate these to their partner who writes the numbers down. They then check each other's answers. You could end the activity by asking each SS to dictate one number from their list to you and you write them on the board.

4 Sum dictation You dictate simple sums but SS only write down the answers, e.g. 12 and 24, 6 times 7. You need to preteach *minus* and *times*. (See also SB page 15, Exercise 5.)

HELLOS AND GOODBYES

A
- Extension of basic vocabulary.
- The verb *to be.* There is a review of *to be* focusing on question forms and negatives in Unit 1.
- Basic greetings include informal and more formal styles.
- Taking your leave.
- Introductions: *This is . . . She's from . . .*
- *a* vs. *an.*
- Irregular plural nouns.

L
- The verb *to be* is presented in positive sentences and questions beginning with *Where* and *How.* It's used for introducing oneself and one's place of origin and enquiring about others.
- Highlight the relationship between the speakers to show levels of language formality. All conversations are polite but 1 and 3 show informal and more formal introductions while 2 illustrates a greeting between friends. Highlight the following comparisons;

- *Hello* vs. *Good morning.*
- *Hello* vs. *Pleased to meet you.*

The final conversation is two friends saying goodbye.

Pronunciation It's important that SS use an appropriate pitch range with these phrases. Demonstrate the difference between a low pitch range and a mid to high pitch range. The higher range sounds more polite, interested, friendly etc. To accompany the demonstration you could draw the following faces on card so that you can use them again or make them a permanent feature of your classroom.

One idea is to give them names, e.g. Mary and Jane, and whenever SS begin to sound bored, uninterested, rude etc. because they're using a low pitch range, mention that Mary (the grumpy one) is here and could we have Jane (friendly and polite). Obviously, if a S is intending to sound bored, uninterested or rude, that's a different matter!

Help SS to recognise and encourage the use of contracted forms of the verb *to be.*

A contrastive sentence stress occurs in the greeting: *How are you? Fine thanks. And you?*

Consonant vowel links occur in the greetings *Good‿evening, Good‿afternoon.*

Contrast the weak and strong form of the preposition *from.* The weak form is used in: *I'm from* /aɪm frəm/, and the strong form occurs when *from* is in the final position of a sentence, *Where are you from?* /frɒm/.

Encourage the use of schwa whenever it occurs in vocabulary e.g. *are, evening, afternoon, and, a, to* etc.

Word stress recognition and production is continued, focusing on two- and three-syllable words, e.g. *telephone, apple.*

Main sentence stress is highlighted and practised.

- Irregular plurals include: words ending in *-y* and *women.*
- *a/an.* SS will need to identify which words begin with a *vowel sound* to understand when *an* is used. (Remember having a vowel at the beginning of a word does not necessarily mean we use *an* e.g. *university* begins with a vowel but not a vowel sound, so it's preceded by *a* and not *an.*)

Students' Book (page 8)

Exercise 1a) Focus on the photographs. As a preview for Exercise 3 you could quickly ask SS to name as many things as they can from the photographs. However, don't spend much time on this, just enough for SS to take in the visual information which will enable them to do the matching exercise. Do this as a whole class exercise. After each conversation ask SS to say which photograph they think it matches. If they agree and are correct, continue to the next conversation. If they disagree, play that section again to ascertain the correct answer.

[0.8]
1
TOM: Hello, I'm Tom. What's your name?
MARIA: Maria.
TOM: I'm from Warsaw. Where are you from, Maria?
MARIA: Madrid.
2
JEAN: Hi, Nick.
NICK: Hi, Jean.
JEAN: How are you?
NICK: Fine, thanks. And you?
JEAN: I'm OK.
3
TINA: Good morning, John.
JOHN: Morning, Tina.
TINA: John, this is Mr Bell. He's from New York.
JOHN: Good morning, Mr Bell.
MR BELL: Pleased to meet you.
4
SALLY: Goodbye.
MAN: Bye, Sally. See you tomorrow.
SALLY: Yes. Have a nice evening.
MAN: Thanks. See you.

2c, 3a, 4b

Exercise 1b) Establish the relationship between Tom and Maria. They are not friends, they are strangers, they don't know each other. Refer back to this as you continue through conversations 2, 3 and 4 to highlight the informal and more formal nature of the language which reflect the relationship. In the second conversation establish that Nick and Jean are friends; in the third that Tina knows John and Mr Bell but that John and Mr Bell are strangers. The business setting in the third conversation should help clarify the need for more formal language.

The final conversation is between friends. Practise some of the phrases in the boxes in isolation before asking SS to practise the conversations. Highlight and encourage SS to use weak forms and appropriate sentence stress and pay particular attention to pitch range (see L above).

Exercise 1c) and d) You could focus on the way main sentence stress is signalled in the SB (e.g. *morning*). Ask SS to identify the main sentence stress and mark it on the board. Ask them to copy the same symbol in their books. If they offer the incorrect stress, model the stress they have given and the correct one so they can compare. Then write the words *are*, *from*, *a* and *later* on the board. Play the cassette again and ask SS to listen to how these words are pronounced. Ask them to say the words and when the correct pronunciation is established, write the phonemic transcription on the board. Use this to highlight the schwa /ə/. Tell the SS that schwa is a very common sound in English.

[0.9]
1 Where are you from?
2 I'm from Washington.
3 Have a nice day.
4 See you later.

are = /ə/ from = /frɒm/ a = /ə/ later = /'leɪtə/

Exercise 2a) The gapped conversations focus on the correct form of the verb *to be*.

Exercise 2b) Demonstrate by adopting a new name and city of origin yourself. Ask SS to introduce themselves to as many other SS as they can.

Exercise 2c) Ask two SS to help you demonstrate this activity. After you have introduced the two SS, establish an appropriate greeting *Hello, Nice to meet you,* or *Pleased to meet you*.

Exercise 3a) If you feel SS need a rest from speaking, allow them to do this individually. You could, of course, offer them the choice.

2 bag = 5, books = 10
3 coat = 4, cassette = 9, clock = 2, cupboard = 3
4 door = 6, dictionary = 8
5 envelopes = 1

Exercise 3b)

[0.10]
1 apple
2 bag, books
3 coat, cassette, clock, cupboard
4 door, dictionary
5 envelopes

Feed back with the whole class and correct any pronunciation mistakes as they occur but don't indicate whether they are the right words or not before playing the cassette. The elision of /p/ in *cupboard* /kʌbəd/ may cause problems. It would be beneficial to create an atmosphere from the beginning that suggests to SS that mistakes are OK, and they will be corrected if correction is appropriate to the activity. With this acceptance, you should be able to establish a healthy approach to correction. There is a growing body of evidence which supports the effectiveness of immediate correction. The suggestion is that connections within the brain are more likely to be established if there isn't a delay. This does not, however, mean that one correction of a mistake is ever enough. Delayed correction is always possible in more communicative activities.

Exercise 3c) Illustrate the rules for when to use the indefinite articles *a* and *an*. Copy the following on the board and ask SS to copy it in their books at the same time.

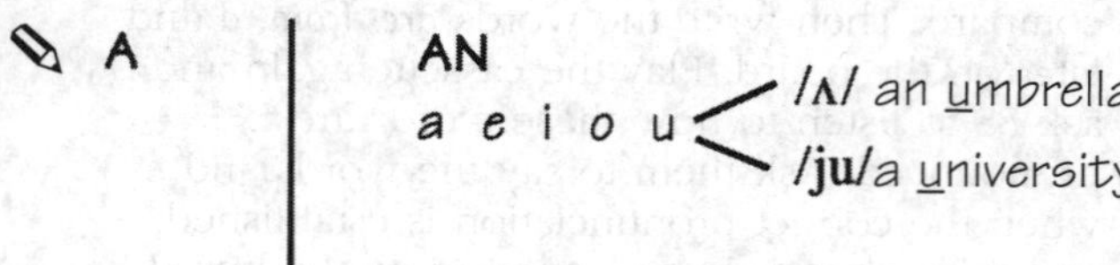

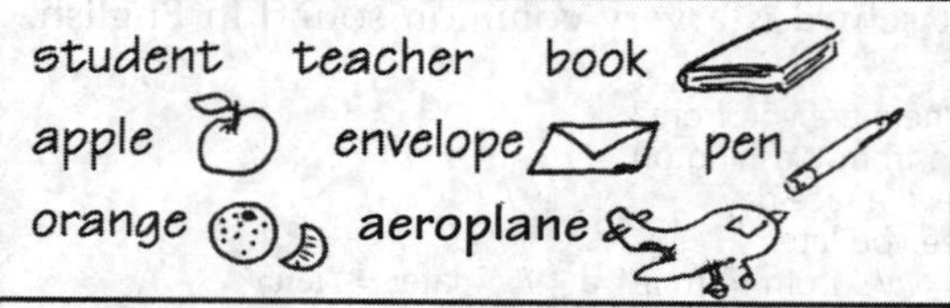

When this has been copied introduce the words *vowel sounds* and *consonant sounds.* Ask SS to give you examples of consonant sounds. Highlight the relationship between *AN + word beginning with a vowel sound* and *A + word beginning with a consonant.* Then using the examples point out that the letter *U* can be pronounced like a consonant or a vowel. To check whether they have assimilated this, ask them to put the words in the correct column. Then focus on the photographs and ask them to find different examples for each part of the exercise. In the feedback, focus on the plural nouns, highlighting irregular plurals.

1 bag, coat, cassette, clock, cupboard, door dictionary
2 apple
3 books, envelopes

Exercise 4 You could use SS' names to reinforce what *word syllables* are and what a *stressed syllable* means, before you play the cassette. It would be useful if SS did recognise the words *syllables* and *stress.* In the many exercises which ask SS to identify these features, you would then simply have to cue *How many syllables? Where's the stress in this word/sentence?*

[0.11]
newspaper
apple
cassette
student
telephone
guitar

Exercise 4a)
apple = 2 syllables cassette = 2 syllables student = 2 syllables
telephone = 3 syllables guitar = 2 syllables

Exercise 4b)
See 4a) above.

Exercise 4c)

A	B	C
guitar	apple	newspaper
cassette	student	telephone

Exercise 5 Feed back by asking general questions as well as getting SS to tell you the items they could remember e.g. *How many did you remember? Was it difficult or easy to remember?* etc.

Extra material and ideas

1 WB page 4, Exercises 1–2, page 5, Exercise 4, page 6, Exercise 7.
2 REVISION AND EXTENSION page 14, Exercise 1, *a/an;* Exercise 3, irregular plurals; page 15, Exercise 4, the verb *to be;* page 19, Exercise 14, subject and object pronouns.

TALKING ABOUT PEOPLE

- *Has got* used for possessions; positive and negative sentences.
- *Whose,* possessive adjectives and *'s.*
- Revision and extension of numbers from 20 to a hundred or hundreds and focus on stress contrast between, e.g. 14 and 40.

L

- Only the third person positive and negative, *has* and *hasn't got,* is introduced in this unit. Other persons and questions are introduced in Unit 1 FOCUS ON GRAMMAR, page 22. The concept is limited to possession in this unit and in Unit 1 this is extended into *have got* used for requests.
- Initially SS are confused by *'s* which as a verb can be either *is* or *has.* Highlight that *got* **cannot** follow *is* (apart from the passive *'s got*), and this is how they can check which verb it is. Point out that *not* is attached to the verb *has* in the negative *hasn't.* SS often try to say **He's got not a car.*

Pronunciation Encourage the use of the short forms *He's / She's / It's got* and *He / She / It hasn't got.* SS may try to pronounce the *s* as /s/ instead of /z/ in /hæznt/. Make sure SS don't omit the /h/ in *hasn't* /hæznt/.

- **Possessive adjectives** *my, your, her, his, its, our, their.* These can present a memory problem for many SS. They need constant correction and review. Highlight that there is **no** *'s* with the possessive adjective *its.* *'s* after *it* is always either *has* or *is.* Note that possessive pronouns are focused on in REVISION AND EXTENSION, page 16, Exercise 7.

Pronunciation Look out for consonant vowel links leading from *his* and *its,* e.g. *his eyes‿are blue* /hɪz aɪs/. All the other possessive pronouns will have either a linking *r* or an intrusive sound when the following word begins with a vowel sound, e.g. *Your‿eyes* /jəraɪz/ linking r.

Your pen /jəpen/ *r* isn't pronounced.

My mother /maɪˈmʌðə/ no intrusive sound after *my.*

My other son /maɪjʌðəsʌn/ intrusive /j/ between *y* and *o.*

- **'s to signal possession** *John's hat, the teacher's coat.* The important thing is to clarify when this is not a short form for either *has* or *is* and it does the same job as the possessive adjectives.

Pronunciation Again look out for consonant vowel links after *'s*.

• **Telephone numbers** Can cause difficulty. With double numbers, e.g. 226 7884 we would say *double two six, seven double eight four* and **not** *twenty-two six* etc. For the number 0 we say /əʊ/ as in the letter *o* (not *zero*). Encourage SS to say phone numbers in blocks, rising at the end of the first block to signal that the number hasn't finished and falling on the final number to signal the end of the phone number, e.g. *double two six, seven double eight four.*

Pronunciation Word stress problems frequently occur with numbers, e.g. *sixteen, sixty* but *sixteen people*. It's worth noting even native speakers often have to clarify numbers: *Was that 'fifteen' or 'fifty'?*

Students' Book (page 10)

Exercise 1a) Check that SS know *'surname, age, a'ddress*. They probably don't know *registering*. Draw attention to the visuals and explain it's the first day and Pablo is starting a new class and the school wants to know his name. If you use a register in class you could make the link with that. You could begin by writing the application form headings on the board, e.g. Surname and ask SS if they know or can guess the answers for you. Rub your information out but leave the headings. Play the cassette and write the SS' answers on the board. If they disagree about information, play the cassette again to establish the correct answer. Highlight *'s = is; 's =* possessive; *his* = possessive adjective (see L).

[0.12]
PABLO: Good morning.
RECEPTIONIST: Good morning. What's your name?
PABLO: My surname's Gomez - that's G-O-M-E-Z and my first name's Pablo – P-A-B-L-O.
RECEPTIONIST: And how old are you?
PABLO: I'm eighteen.
RECEPTIONIST: Where are you from, Pablo?
PABLO: I'm from Mexico City in Mexico.
RECEPTIONIST: And what's your address in Manchester?
PABLO: 14 Park Street.
RECEPTIONIST: And your phone number?
PABLO: Oh one six one – five double two six one three.
RECEPTIONIST: And have you got a car, Pablo?
PABLO: Yes, it's a Fiat.

SURNAME: **Gomez**
FIRST NAME: **Pablo** AGE: **18**
CITY: **Mexico City** COUNTRY: **Mexico**
ADDRESS IN MANCHESTER: **14 Park Street**
PHONE NUMBER: **0161 522 613** CAR: **Yes** MAKE: **Fiat**

Exercise 1b)
This is Pablo Gomez from Mexico City in Mexico. He**'s** 18. Pablo**'s** address in Manchester **is** 14 Park Street and **his** phone number is 0161 522613. He**'s got** a car. It**'s** a Fiat.

Exercise 1c) Highlight the stress differences on the numbers (see L). You could get SS to say these numbers on their own for a partner who writes down what they hear.

[0.13]
twenty-two
thirty-one
fifty
seventy-seven
eighty-five
a hundred
a hundred and five
two hundred and sixty-eight
three hundred and eighty-seven

Exercise 1d) See L above for information.

Exercise 2a) and b) Clear instructions are very important if your SS aren't used to this kind of information exchange activity. Be prepared to interrupt the activity in order to clarify instructions. Monitor SS and correct mistakes as they occur. If SS are making the same mistakes, stop the activity and focus on the problem before letting SS continue.

Exercise 3a)
Possessive adjectives
I **my**
he **his**
she **her**
it **its**
you **your**
we **our**
they **their**

Exercise 3b) Focus SS' attention on the two ways of forming sentences with *whose*. Note that in REVISION AND EXTENSION, page 16, Exercise 9 only one form is practised: *Whose is this . . .*

1 Whose is this computer / OR Whose computer is this?
2 Whose is this pen? OR Whose pen is this?
3 Whose is this cassette? OR Whose cassette is this?
4 Whose is this house? OR Whose house is this?

Extra material and ideas

1 WB page 5, Exercise 5; page 6, Exercises 6 and 8.
2 REVISION AND EXTENSION, page 15, Exercise 5, numbers; page 16, Exercise 6, possessive adjectives; Exercise 7, possessive pronouns; Exercise 8, *'s*; Exercise 9, *whose*; page 17, Exercise 10 *has(n't)* and *have(n't) got*.

PEOPLE DOING THINGS

A

• *There is a* and *There are some* + singular and plural countable nouns.
• Present Continuous: all persons, positive, negative, inverted questions and short answers.
• Demonstrative adjectives *this* and *these*.

L

• *There is a* + singular noun and *There are some* + plural nouns. This does **not** include uncountable nouns. Illustrate that we use *some* when the exact number isn't required. Compare *There are five books on the table. There are some books on the table.* Make sure that you don't use large numbers to illustrate this because that would probably be expressed by: *There are a lot of books on the table.*

Pronunciation Encourage SS to use the short form *There's* and then highlight the possible reduction which often occurs on *There‿are* /ðerə/. Linking *r* occurs in the uncontracted form of *There‿is* and in *There‿are.* If SS use this, their rhythm and sentence stress should improve.

• **Present Continuous** The concept is limited to happening around time now, temporary and unfinished. Even this limited conceptual explanation will be too complex for this level. Therefore, we recommend that you restrict your concept checking to happening at the time of speaking, i.e. now.

• **Form** SS have to know the verb *to be* (all persons) to form the correct auxiliary. The auxiliary is used to form negatives and it's inverted with the subject to form the inverted question form. Short forms cannot occur in positive short answers: **Yes, she's.* (*Yes, she is.*) However, short forms can be used in negative short answers apart from the first person: **No, I am'nt.* (*No, you aren't.*) There is an alternative negative form, e.g. *No, he's not.* You could point this out as an alternative but agree to practise the form presented in the SB.

• **Spelling** Can be problematic, *write* → *writing, swim* → *swimming.* Point out that final *e* is dropped before adding *-ing.* If there is a short vowel + consonant in the syllable before *-ing* the consonant is doubled. Compare *be'ginning* and *'benefiting.*

Pronunciation Highlight and encourage the use of short forms, *I'm* etc. Pay particular attention to the pronunciation of *they're* /ðeə/ vs. *Yes, they are* /ðeɪjɑː/ which often causes problems for SS.

• ***This/these*** SS need to recognise the singular and plural forms. Note *that* and *those* are included in REVISION AND EXTENSION page 19, Exercise 13. It's important that SS understand *this/these* are used when the object(s) or person is physically close. *That/those* are used when the object(s) or person is viewed as being distant in either space or time, e.g. *This is Alan and that's Howard* (Alan is near and Howard is perceived as being more distant in space). The concept of something happening at the moment is expressed by using *this/these* e.g. *This is a lovely party.* When the situation has finished we use *that/those* e.g. *That was a lovely party* (distant in time). However, it's unlikely that you will need to include these uses at this level. It does, however, explain a common S mistake: *This is a good idea* when someone has just finished giving the idea, instead of *That's a good idea.* We would use *This is a good idea,* when the idea hasn't yet been discussed (nearer to time now).

Pronunciation Encourage the consonant vowel link which occurs, *this‿is* and *these‿are.*

Students' Book (page 12)

Exercise 1a) As a warmer you could write the following on the board *You're jogging, You're reading, You're talking* and *You're listening to.* Mime the various actions but not in the order that you have written them up on the board. SS say what you're doing. Repeat, *What am I doing now?* each time you change the mime. This will help you to ascertain which verbs are familiar and it also allows you to illustrate and highlight the concept of the time around now. You could then ask SS to mime actions and you and others try to guess what that SS is doing. Then focus on the photographs in the SB. Allow SS to work in pairs, listing as many items of vocabulary as they can. Feed back and correct mistakes as they come up. Remind SS that they can ask you to spell or write the words and they can ask for meaning. Perhaps elicit the appropriate questions to access this information and write them on the board *How do spell that? Can you write it, please? What does ____ mean?*

Exercise 1b) Read the sentences aloud before playing the cassette. Highlight the difference between *There is a* and *There are some* (see L). Deal with any vocabulary they don't understand. Feed back with the class. If there is disagreement, ask prompting questions to help SS arrive at the correct answers.

[0.14]
1 A man's jogging.
2 There are some postcards on the table.
3 Sam's eating a pizza.
4 There are some apples on the table.
5 Tim's reading a magazine.
6 There's a computer on the table.
7 Sue's talking to Rita.
8 There's a cup of coffee on the table.
9 A man's listening to a walkman.
10 Marco's writing a letter.

1T 2T 3F She's eating a hamburger. 4F 5F He's reading a newspaper. 6F There's a mobile phone on the table. 7F She's talking to a waiter. 8T 9T 10F He's writing a postcard.

Exercise 1c) Demonstrate the activity by initially saying correct or incorrect sentences. But then change your role. Close your book and invite SS to make true or false sentences for you to respond to. Then go to the pair work.

Exercise 2a) This allows a natural change of pace and quiet time for SS to assimilate information about the verb form. Always offer SS the opportunity to ask you questions if they don't understand. Again a healthy attitude to any behaviour which aids learning should be encouraged at all times. Write on the board: *Two people ____ ____. Marco ____ ____ a postcard. Tim ____ ____ a newspaper. Sue ____ ____ to a waiter. Sam ____ ____ a hamburger. Rita ____ ____ a cup of tea.* Invite SS to write their answers on the board as they do the exercise. This can then become the focus for the feedback and spelling can be checked quickly and effectively.

Two women **are smoking**. Marco **is writing** a postcard. She **is talking** to a waiter, Sam **is eating** a hamburger and Rita **is drinking** a cup of tea.

Exercise 2b) If you think SS need more time for individual work, ask them to write more sentences about the photographs. If you think a change of pace and interaction is appropriate, this activity could be done in pairs or as a whole class activity.

A man is jogging. A woman is wearing a cap. A man is listening to a walkman. A taxi is waiting.

Exercise 2c) Again if your SS are not familiar with this kind of information exchange activity, be prepared to interrupt the activity and repeat instructions. Demonstration is an effective way to get instructions across at this level.

Student A

1 On table B, **a boy** is listening to a walkman.
2 On table C, a man is reading **a newspaper**.
3 On table D, a woman is writing **a postcard**.
4 On table E, a man is eating **a sandwich**.
5 A **policeman** is talking to a girl.

Student B

1 On table B, **a girl** is listening to a walkman.
2 On table C, a man is reading **a book**.
3 On table D, a woman is writing **a letter**.
4 On table E, a man is eating **a hamburger**.
5 A **policewoman** is talking to a girl.

Exercise 3a) Draw the following on the board.

THIS/THESE

______ .

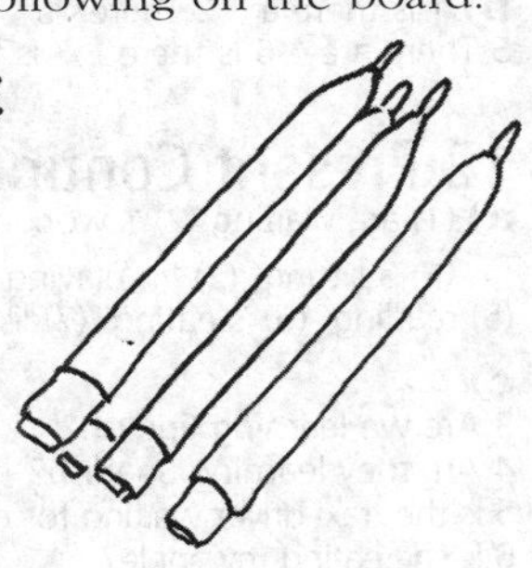

______ .

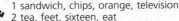

Then walk around the room pointing to different objects, singular and plural nouns repeating *This is a* ____ *These are* ______. After a few examples ask SS to look at the board, think and finish the sentences under each picture. Before doing the activity practise the questions *What's this? What are these?* Encourage SS to use a falling intonation on the questions. If it's possible, allow SS to then walk around the room with a partner asking and answering questions about things in the room. Supply vocabulary where necessary.

What are these? They're oranges.
What are these? They're chips.
What are these? They're feet.
What's this? It's a photograph.

Exercise 3b)

Write the phonemic symbols on the board. Play the cassette and point to the appropriate sound for an example. If you think more examples are required, model the sounds again yourself. You could help SS to produce these sounds by illustrating the position of the tongue in each sound. The lower hand represents the tongue and the upper hand represents the palate.

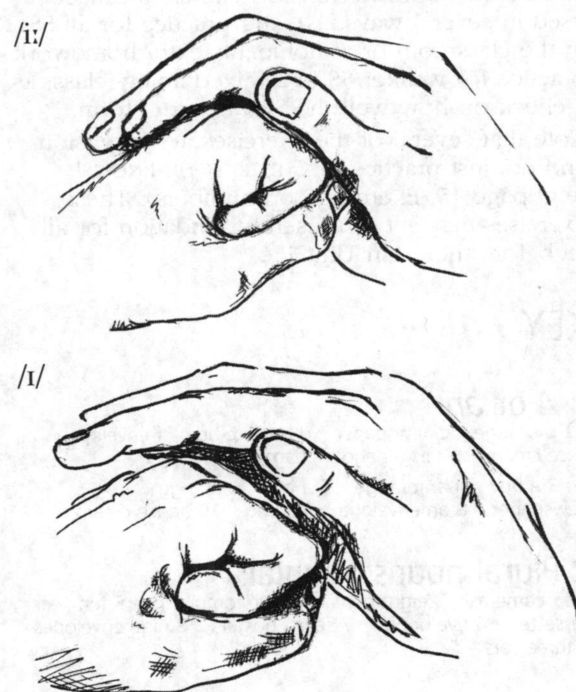

Basically, the tongue begins high and tense with /iː/ is relaxed a little to produce /ɪ/ and relaxed more and lower with /ə/. Get SS to practise the sounds in isolation. As you check SS answers to the exercise, write the words under the appropriate column on the board. Then get SS to practise the words.

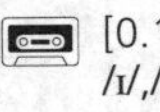

[0.15]
/ɪ/,/iː/,/ə/
tea
sandwich
feet
photograph
chips
orange
sixteen
television
envelope
eat
camera

1 sandwich, chips, orange, television
2 tea, feet, sixteen, eat
3 photograph, envelope, camera

Extra material and ideas

1 WB page 5, Exercise 3; page 6, Exercises 9 and 10; page 7, Exercise 11; page 8, Exercises 13 and 14.

2 REVISION AND EXTENSION page 17, Exercise 11, *there is a/there are some*; page 18, Exercise 12, Present Continuous; page 19, Exercise 13, *this/that/these/those*.

Revision and extension

The REVISION AND EXTENSION exercises can be used in several ways: as extra practice for all SS in the classroom or at home.; as extra homework practice for weaker SS in a mixed ability class; as a check on how well the SS can use a form. Note that several of the exercises are extension and not just practice of CHECK YOUR ENGLISH (e.g. page 15, Exercise 5 on numbers). These exercises may act as a useful foundation for all SS before they start Unit 1.

KEY

1 *A* or *an*

a) b orange c newspaper d bus e boy f envelope g ice cream h taxi i egg j bag

b) 3 a boy 4 an orange 5 a bus 6 an egg 7 a newspaper 8 an envelope 9 a bag 10 an ice cream

2 Plural nouns: regular

2 six cameras 3 eight pens 4 four computers 5 ten cassettes 6 five books 7 seven posters 8 nine envelopes 9 three cars

3 Plural nouns: irregular

2 classes 3 women 4 lunches 5 countries 6 people 7 kisses 8 churches 9 families 10 children

4 The verb *to be*

a) 2 You're 3 They aren't/They're not 4 She's 5 He's 6 It isn't/It's not

b) 3 's 4 're 5 aren't 6 isn't, 's 7 's 8 's 9 isn't, 's 10 'm not, 'm

5 Numbers

a) 2 17 3 15 4 50 5 66 6 42 7 90 8 45 9 64 10 44

b) 4 eighty-six 5 sixty-one 6 sixty

d) 2 three thousand, one hundred and fifty-nine 3 two thousand, three hundred and seventy-eight 4 fourteen thousand, five hundred and eighty-two 5 fourteen thousand, seven hundred and ninety-nine 6 one thousand, four hundred and forty-five 7 two thousand, one hundred and thirty-eight 8 seventeen thousand and two 9 ten thousand, six hundred and twenty-three 10 fifteen thousand, one hundred and sixty-eight 11 sixteen thousand, three hundred and thirty-three

6 Possessive adjectives

2 their 3 its 4 his 5 her 6 your 7 My 8 our 9 his 10 their

7 Possessive pronouns

mine, his, hers, yours, ours, theirs

8 The possessive with *'s*

3 Is it **the teacher's** coat?
4 These are **Jim's** apples.
5 I've got **Jim and Sally's** pizza.
6 Those are **Julie's** postcards.
7 Where are **the policemen's** books?
8 **Sally's** bag is in the classroom.
9 **The man's** radio is in the hotel.

9 *Whose*

a) 3 Whose is this coat? OR Whose coat is this? 4 Whose are these apples? OR Whose apples are these? 5 Whose is this pizza? OR Whose pizza is this? 6 Whose are these postcards? OR Whose postcards are these? 7 Whose are these books? OR Whose books are these? 8 Whose is this bag? OR Whose bag is this? 9 Whose is this radio? OR Whose radio is this?

b) 3 It's the teacher's. 4 They're Jim's. 5 It's Jim and Sally's. 6 They're Julie's. 7 They're the policemen's. 8 It's Sally's. 9 It's the man's.

10 *Has(n't)* and *have(n't) got*

a) 2 She's got a car. 3 They've got two computers. 4 I've got four cassettes.

b) 1 has got, hasn't got 2 has got, hasn't got 3 hasn't got, has got 4 has got, hasn't got 5 have got, haven't got

11 *There is a*... or *there are some*...

a) There are some Are there Is there a is there there are there are some

b) 1 Is there a 2 There's a 3 There are 4 Are there 5 There are 6 Is there 7 Is there 8 There's a

12 Present Continuous

a) (1) are waiting (2) 's working (3) 's doing (4) are talking
(1) 's sitting (2) 'm playing (3) 's watching (4) 's drinking (5) reading (6) 's eating (7) listening (8) 's talking

c)
3 Are we learning English?
4 Are they learning Spanish?
5 Is the taxi driver waiting for me?
6 Is she eating my apple?
7 Are you writing to John?
8 Am I speaking too fast?

d)
3 We aren't learning English.
4 They aren't learning Spanish.
5 The taxi driver isn't waiting for me.
6 She isn't eating my apple.
7 You aren't writing to John.
8 I'm not speaking too fast.

13 *This, that, these* or *those*?

a) These this those that this this

b) 1 This 2 That 3 these 4 that 5 those 6 This

14 Subject and object pronouns

b) me, him, her, it, us, you, them

Unit 1

People and places

> ### Students' Book
>
> **General themes:** families, places and possessions.
>
> **FOCUS ON VOCABULARY:** families, countries and nationalities; revision of *to be*, *has* and *have got* and possessives.
> **FOCUS ON GRAMMAR:** questions and answers: *to be* and *has* and *have got*.
> **SKILLS:** reading and listening (Liverpool and Dublin); vocabulary (using dictionaries); writing (punctuation).
> **SOCIAL ENGLISH:** dates and times.
>
> ### Workbook
>
> **GRAMMAR:** *to be*; *has* and *have got*.
> **VOCABULARY:** the family; numbers and dates; telling the time; countries and nationalities.
> **WRITING:** sound and spelling: *o*; punctuation; a letter to a pen friend.
> **PRONUNCIATION:** word stress (the months of the year, countries and nationalities).

FOCUS ON VOCABULARY

A Families and nationalities

- Families, countries and nationalities.
- Revision of CHECK YOUR ENGLISH (e.g. question words, possessives, *has got*, *to be*,)
- Word stress.

L • **Families** There shouldn't be any conceptual problems in this section but vocabulary will need reviewing consistently to help SS to remember new words. The vocabulary load probably causes the greatest frustration for low level learners of any language. They realise the importance of vocabulary in communication but as almost every word is either fairly new or completely unknown this places enormous demands on the memory.

Pronunciation There may be sound and spelling difficulties. Highlight the following points but avoid technical terminology: the final *e* is silent in wif*e*, niec*e* and uncl*e*; *ph* is pronounced /f/ in ne*ph*ew; the first syllable of *aunt*, *cou*sin and *un*cle all contain the letter *u*; in *uncle* and *cousin* the vowel sound is /ʌ/ but in *aunt* the sound is /ɑː/; *ie* in words is pronounced /iː/ as in *niece*; the *d* in *grandmother* is elided and there is assimilation of the sound *n* which is often (but not always) pronounced as /m/ (/græmʌðə/) and the *er* at the end of a word is pronounced as schwa /ə/ as in *mother*.

Note that the stress on words with two or more syllables in this section is consistent and occurs on the first syllable, e.g. *'grandmother* and *'cousin*.

• **Countries and nationalities** You'll need to review this lexical area frequently until it's clear that SS can identify which word is the noun referring to the country and which is the adjective referring to the nationality. Initially this often causes confusion.

Pronunciation: word stress With this level you will need to consistently highlight word stress patterns, to emphasise to SS that this is an area of English which needs constant attention. Whenever a new word is introduced some kind of visual representation is always helpful. This could be marked on the board in a variety of ways, e.g. a square above the primary stressed syllable (*happy*), which is the SB convention, big and small squares to represent the stress patterns of words (*beautiful*), or the stress mark in the dictionaries you use. Longman dictionaries use the following mark: *examin'ation*.

Choose one system of marking stress and use it consistently. Encourage your SS to note the stress in their notebooks.

With countries and nationalities the pronunciation difficulties centre on word stress and any subsequent sound changes this may create, e.g. *'Italy* /ɪtəlɪ/, *I'talian* /ɪtælɪən/, *Ja'pan* /dʒəpæn/, *Japan'ese* /dʒæpəniːz/, *'Canada* /kænədə/, *Can'adian* /kəneɪdɪən/.

Sometimes there is a sound change even when the stress remains on the same syllable, e.g. *Argen'tina* /ɑːdʒəntiːnə/, *Argen'tinian* /ɑːdʒəntɪnɪən/.

Mobility of word stress is another area of possible confusion. Consider *It's Japan'ese.* and *It's a 'Japanese car.* As a predicative adjective the stress will be on the third syllable. As an attributive adjective the stress will shift to the first syllable unless it is contradicting a previous statement, in which case it will remain on the third syllable. This explanation would be too complex for this level and we recommend that you only model the correct form when SS make mistakes.

Expect considerable L1 interference with pronunciation of countries and nationalities and highlight the difference between L1 and English where appropriate.

• **Question words** *What*, *How* and *Where* from CHECK YOUR ENGLISH are reviewed, and *Who* and *How old* are introduced in this unit.

Students' Book (page 20)

This unit is based on the assumption that SS are familiar with, but not necessarily accurate users of the language covered in CHECK YOUR ENGLISH. If you have a mixed ability class which includes beginners, you could use the exercises in CHECK YOUR ENGLISH, REVISION AND EXTENSION and the Workbook as homework to help weaker SS to catch up.

Exercise 1a) As a possible lead-in to this section you could take in a photo of a film star and ask SS to name any British actors they know and tell them they're going to read about a family of British actors. Alternatively, you could take in photos of you and your family and pass them around. This may have the effect of eliciting or previewing some of the relevant vocabulary as SS try to ascertain who they are. The exercise only asks SS to recognise the names of members of a family.

Your SS might be interested in some of the films in which the Redgraves have appeared.

Sir Michael Redgrave (1908–1985), the father of Vanessa, Corin and Lynn), was in a number of films including Alfred Hitchcock's *The Lady Vanishes* (1938) and *The Go-Between* (1971).

Vanessa is the more famous daughter and has appeared in more than fifty films including *Camelot* (1967), *Isadora* (1968), *Julia* (1977), *Howards End* (1992) and *Mission Impossible* (1996).

Lynn is known for her 'Weightwatchers' advertisements on American TV and films such as *Tom Jones* (1963), *Georgie Girl* (1966) and *The Deadly Affair* (1967).

Corin has appeared in *Excalibur* (1981), *In the Name of the Father* (1993), *Four Weddings and a Funeral* (1994) and *Persuasion* (1995).

Natasha Richardson has appeared in a number of films including *The Handmaid's Tale* (1990); **Joely** has starred in *Drowing by Numbers* (1988) and *A hundred and one Dalmatians* (1996). Natasha's husband, **Liam Neeson** has achieved great success through his roles in *Schindler's List* (1993), *Rob Roy* (1995) and *Michael Collins* (1996). Joely's husband **Tim Bevan** is a film producer, he produced *Four Weddings and a Funeral* (1994).

Pronunciation of names: Vanessa /vənesə/, Joely /dʒəʊlɪ/, Corin /kɒrɪn/, Liam /lɪəm/, Arden /ɑːdən/, Ben /ben/, Annabel /ænəbel/, Natasha /nətæʃə/.

The confusion caused by the *'s* will need highlighting before you begin the exercise. Point out *'s* stands for both *is* and the genitive (possessive) case of the noun. Involve SS in working out which *'s* is the first in the question, e.g. What's Natasha and Joely's mother called?, and write this on the board to act as a reminder. Point out the past forms *married* (*m.*) and *died* (*d.*) in the family tree.

1 Vanessa 2 Tim 3 Corin and Lynn 4 Kika Markham 5 32 (in 1997)

Exercise 1b) Focus on pronunciation, particularly word stress. You could reinforce this by writing words from the text on the board, e.g. *daughter, husband, sister,* and asking SS to mark the stress. It's beneficial to pay a lot of attention to word stress at this level to encourage good learning habits. For further pronunciation practice, ask SS to say what they have written before checking their answers against the cassette. Note that in this exercise the verb *to be* is written *is* but in Recording 1.1 it is pronounced *'s*.

Lynn is Natasha's **aunt**.
Corin is Joely's **uncle**.
Daisy is Natasha's **niece**.
Michael is Daisy's **cousin**.
Michael is Joely's **nephew**.

Exercise 1c)

[1.1]

1 Lynn's Natasha's aunt.
2 Corin's Joely's uncle.
3 Daisy's Natasha's niece.
4 Michael's Daisy's cousin.
5 Michael's Joely's nephew.

Exercise 1d) Before SS draw their family trees ask general questions about their families, e.g. *How many aunts/ uncles/ cousins etc., have you got?* Try to find out who has the biggest family. This will act as a preview for numbers coming up in the SOCIAL ENGLISH section later in the unit, and *Have you got ... ?* in FOCUS ON GRAMMAR.

Exercise 1e) An alternative to group work is to display the family trees around the room. Some SS stand next to their family trees and the others walk around asking questions. Ensure that all SS have a chance to answer questions.

Exercise 2a) You could do rough sketches of the outlines of some countries (including some of the less well-known ones like Switzerland, Mexico, New Zealand etc.) on the board for a quick quiz before focusing on the table (preview) or as a practice activity after SS look at the table (review). You could use the sketches overleaf to help you. See if any SS can name the country from the outline. If not, give the first letter and keep adding more letters as clues. If you have a world map on the wall, allow a few SS to refer to it to get the answers.

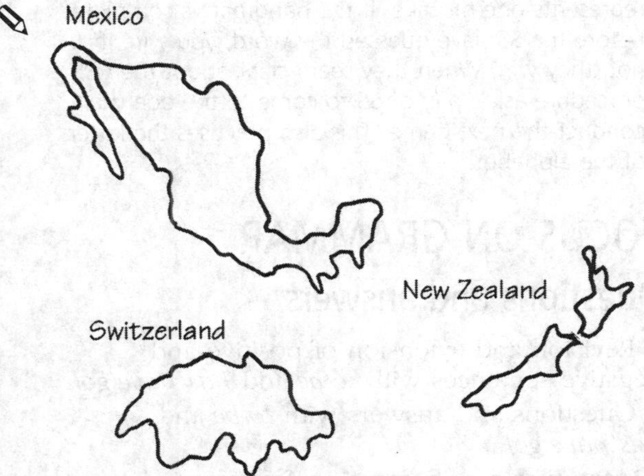

Exercise 2b) Highlight the word stress, particularly where there is a stress change between the country and the nationality.

'Portugal Portu'guese Ja'pan Japa'nese

Exercise 2c)

[1.2]

Poland	Polish
England	English
Italy	Italian
Russia	Russian
Germany	German
Portugal	Portuguese
Japan	Japanese
France	French
Switzerland	Swiss

Exercise 2d) You could get your SS to use dictionaries to help with this. If they aren't very efficient at using dictionaries, assign one or two of the gaps in the table to individuals or pairs. Then SS can teach each other, which offers more speaking practice. Remind them that the word stress is often the same for the country and nationality, but not always.

COUNTRY	NATIONALITY	COUNTRY	NATIONALITY
Spain	'Spanish	Argen'tina	Argen'tinian
'Turkey	'Turkish	Bra'zil	Bra'zilian
'Hungary	Hun'garian	A'merica	A'merican

Exercise 2e)

[1.3]

Spain	Spanish
Turkey	Turkish
Hungary	Hungarian
Argentina	Argentinian
Brazil	Brazilian
America	American

Exercise 3a) Draw SS' attention to the illustrations and ask questions to elicit the information, e.g. *How old is he? Where's he from? Where's his flat?* etc. Note that the cassette gives Liam Neeson's age in 1997 (year of publication of *Elementary Matters*). You may prefer to read the answers yourself giving his age at the time you are teaching. If you think your SS need further help, you could write the necessary words on the board but mixed up, so they have to find the appropriate word for each gap. Link this exercise back to the text about the Richardsons on page 20.

Exercise 3b)

Note that Liam Nelson is forty-five years old in 1997.

[1.4]

Liam Neeson's **forty-five** (years old). **He's from** Balleymena in Northern Ireland and he's got a flat in **New York**. He's an **actor**. He's **married** to Natasha Richardson and he's got **a** son called Michael.

Exercise 3c) You could ask SS to pass their paragraphs around for others to read.

Extra material and ideas

1 WB page 12, Exercise 10, page 13, Exercise 13 and page 14, Exercise 15.

2 Family trees SS draw their family tree but they don't put their name on their tree. In groups SS try to guess whose family tree each one is. If the guess is correct, the group can ask that S as many questions as they want to, about various members of his/her family. The information should be added to the family tree, e.g. the person's age, are they at school, have they got a job, does the S like that family member, the city/town they live in? etc. Note that SS will obviously not be accurate in use of language but this kind of exercise can illustrate that communication strategies are not limited to full accurate sentences. Single words, facial expressions, pointing etc. are all essential skills involved in communicating. The more you practise these skills with SS, the more confident they should become.

3 Display the SS' family trees around the room on walls or desks. The objective is for SS to find the family tree which most closely resembles their own family tree in terms of number of aunts, sisters etc. When they have found the closest, they work as a pair, finding out if there are other similarities, e.g. are their siblings the same age? are their aunts /uncles married or single? etc. If you're teaching in the L1 country, SS could find out whether relatives live locally. You will probably need to write up or cue the questions on the board. You could involve the SS in forming the questions before the activity begins or you could write the questions yourself while the SS are finding a partner. If you choose to do the latter, check that the SS understand the questions you have written.

4 If the class is fairly small, hand out photographs or make an OHT of photographs of your family members. SS could ask you about your family or you could describe a family member and then they try to guess which photo you're referring to.

5 In groups, SS are invited to ask you questions about your family. The members of their group take it in turns to come to you to whisper a question and report back to the group with the answer. Remind the groups to keep a note of the questions and answers. Allow about six minutes for the questions. The objective is for each group to declare a piece of information they have found out about your family. If it's correct, they get one point. In addition, if the other groups do not have that information, the original team gain an extra point.

6 Chinese whispers Line the SS up facing the board in teams and stand at the back of the teams. Have cards with either countries or nationalities written on them. The person at the back of each line comes to you and reads the card with either the country or the nationality. If the card states a country, the S has to whisper the *nationality* to the next S in the line who whispers it to the next S and so on down the line. If the nationality is written on the card, the S whispers the *country* to their team and so on. The S at the front of the line writes the nationality or country (whichever they heard) on the board. The S from the front then comes to the back to read the next card until each SS has written a word on the board. The first team to write the word correctly on the board each time gets a point. If you have a large class, the SS can remain in their chairs and still whisper down or along a row of SS. In this case it would be less disruptive if the S writing on the board remained the same for each team.

7 Word stress snap page 115, 1.1 GW. Photocopy the cards and cut them up. In groups of three or four the SS divide the cards equally between them. The cards should be face down. In turn each member of the group turns over his/her top card and places it in the centre. The next S does the same, placing his/her card on top of the previous card. If the word stress is the same, any S in the group can shout SNAP! If that S is correct, he/she claims all the cards that have been played up to that point in the game. The objective is to win all the cards. If a member loses all his/her cards, they can still shout SNAP! and so have a chance to re-enter the game.

8 Student to student dictation page 116, 1.2 PW. Copy material for SS A and B. SS should have their chairs back to back if possible. They take it in turns to dictate their sentences to their partner. The following questions should be on the board for SS to refer to:

How do you spell that?
Can you repeat that, please?
What does it mean?
(If a monolingual group)
How do you say that in...?

The dictation is designed to encourage SS to ask these questions by including some unfamiliar words and words with difficult spellings.

9 Hangman for countries and nationalities

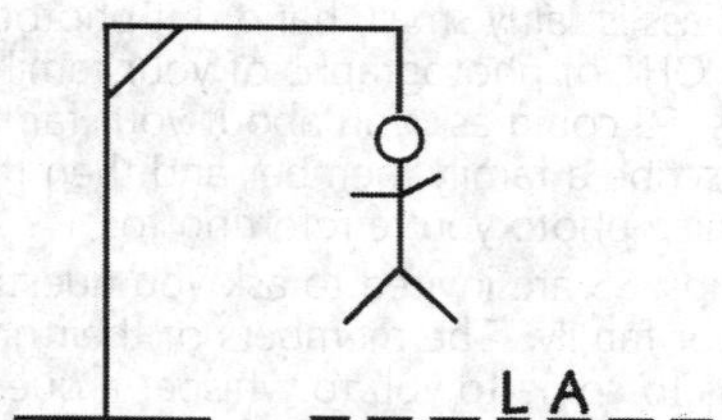

Think of a country or nationality and write the appropriate number of dashes on the board. SS call out letters of the alphabet. When they say a letter from the word, add it to the board. If their letter is not in the word, begin to draw the hangman. (See the complete hangman above.) Each line or shape represents one mistake. If the hangman is complete before the SS have guessed the word, you win. If not, they win. When they seem clear about the procedure ask a pair of SS to come to the board and conduct the next game. This also practises the letters of the alphabet.

FOCUS ON GRAMMAR

Questions and answers

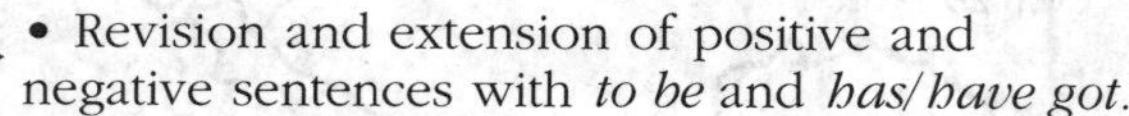

- Revision and extension of positive and negative sentences with *to be* and *has/have got.*
- Questions and answers with *to be* and *has/have got.*
- **Introduction of question forms**

To be should be familiar to elementary students from CHECK YOUR ENGLISH, but it will need reinforcement and correction. The word order of questions, inversion of the subject and verb will need highlighting.

Pronunciation Contracted forms should be highlighted and practised as they more closely represent natural use of the language in positive and negative statements, e.g. *She's/She isn't in class.* Point out that the negative can also be expressed as *She's not/They're not/You're not in class,* etc. Short forms can be used in negative short answers, e.g. *No, they aren't/they're not.* Short forms of *to be,* however, cannot be used in positive short answers. **Yes, she's. (Yes, she is.)*

Have/has got may also be familiar to the students but will need revision and correction. The word order of question forms is complicated by the two verbs. Highlight that it is the *have/has* which inverts with the subject while *got* follows the subject. In Exercise 5 *have got* is used to express possession while in Exercise 6 it is used as a functional exponent to request something.

Some SS may have come across *Do you have ... ?* as an alternative to *Have you got ... ?* Acknowledge it as a correct alternative and point out that it's more commonly used in American English.

Pronunciation The verb *has/have got* also uses contracted forms in natural speech and this should be highlighted and practised. Students may find it confusing that *has* has the same contracted form as the verb *to be* in the third person. Point out that *got* **cannot** follow the verb *to be* (apart from the passive *'s got*), therefore *'s got* is likely to be a contracted form of *has.* In questions the weak form of *have/has* is used /həv//həz/. The *h* is sometimes elided: /əv/ and /əz/. In positive short answers the strong form is used, e.g. *Yes, we have.* /hæv/ and contracted forms cannot be used.

Intonation For both *to be* and *has/have got* a rising intonation is common with inverted questions. A fall or a fall rise pattern is common with questions which begin with question words, e.g. *When/How/Why* etc.

Students' Book (page 22)

To be

Exercise 1a) Model the question and answer for SS and highlight that the inverted question commonly has a rising tone on the main stress but with alternative inverted questions the voice will usually rise on the first tonic and fall on the second. Write the question and answer on the board and add the intonation lines as in the SB.

[1.5]
A: Is Brad Pitt English or American?
B: I think he's American.
C: Is Brad Pitt English or American?
D: I don't know.

Exercise 1b) Ask a few more confident SS to model for the whole class before getting the class to work in pairs. Monitor for mistakes and if you hear consistent mistakes with the verb form, stop the activity and highlight the correct forms. Aim for accuracy.

Is Brad Pitt English or American? American.
Is Campari a drink or a singer? A drink.
Is a nephew a boy or a girl? A boy.
Is a tomato a fruit or a vegetable? A fruit.
Is Big Ben a person or a thing? A thing (a clock in London).
Is an Apple Mac a fruit or a computer? A computer.
Is the Hard Rock a pop group or a café? A café.
Are the Canaries islands or mountains? Islands.
Are penguins bird or animals? Birds.

Exercise 2a) Focus attention on the short answers. Ask SS which answer is more sure, *Yes, he is.* or *Yes, I think so.* Point out that we can't use the contracted form *He's* in affirmative short answers but we can in negative short answers, *No, he isn't./No, they aren't.* Illustrate with examples on the board. To avoid sounding abrupt encourage SS to rise a little before *isn't.* If they do a step fall where each word is at a lower pitch than the preceding one, they may sound dismissive and abrupt.

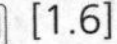
[1.6]
A: Is Brad Pitt English or American?
B: I think he's American.
C: Is Brad Pitt English or American?
D: I don't know.
A: Is Brad Pitt an actor?
B: Yes, I think so.
C: Is Brad Pitt an actor?
D: No, I don't think so.
A: Are the Pyramids in India?
B: Yes, they are.
C: Are the Pyramids in India?
D: No, they aren't. They're in Egypt.

Exercise 2b) Monitor SS for mistakes. If mistakes are frequent, stop the activity and focus on form again. The general knowledge answers to the questions are on page 130 of the SB. This is to allow SS who don't know the answers to do the practice. Let SS try the exercise before they check their answers.

1 Is Disneyland in London? No, it isn't. It's in America.
2 Are the Alps mountains? Yes, they are.
3 Is Pete Sampras a tennis player? Yes, he is.
4 Is Piccadilly Circus a film? No, it isn't. It's a place in London.
5 Are Michael and Janet Jackson married to each other? No, they aren't. They're brother and sister.
6 Is New York the capital of the USA? No, it isn't. Washington's the capital.
7 Are the Andes in South America? Yes, they are.
8 Is Reebok the name of trainers? Yes, it is.

Exercise 3 To reinforce sound/symbol association you might choose to read the text to the SS while they follow in their books. You could also do a question and answer activity before asking them to fill in the gaps.

A: They're English.
B: No, **they aren't**. They're **Russian**.
A: Their house is in Manchester.
B: No, it **isn't**. **It's in London**.
A: Igor's a writer.
B: No, **he isn't**. He's a businessman.
A: Irina and Igor are writers.
B: No, **they aren't/they're not**. **Irina's a writer** but **Igor's a businessman**.

Exercise 4a) If you want to check SS' command of the question form at this point, you could invite them to ask you the questions first before working with each other. Note that only the verb *to be* is practised. Note also that we use *How old are you?* not *What's your age?* in this context.

What's your first name? What's your surname? How old are you? Are you married or single? What's your address? What's your phone number? What's your job?

Exercise 4b) If you correct form during SS' feedback, it may put them off. In which case, make a note of errors, write them on the board after the feedback and ask SS in pairs to correct them. However, if your SS can accept immediate correction, it might promote accuracy.

Exercise 4c) To allow a change of focus and pace you could do this in class time rather than giving it as homework. Allow SS to work together and check each other's work.

Have you got ...?

Exercise 5a) Check that the SS understand the vocabulary items before you begin and can say the words with the correct stress and pronunciation.

Exercise 5b) Practise the pronunciation of the question and short answer in the yellow grammar box. Encourage SS to use a rising intonation and the weak form /həv/ in the question and /hæv/ in the short answer. To make the practice more meaningful you could invite them to ask you questions about your bedroom.

Exercise 5c) If you have a large class, try to include as many SS as possible in the feedback but limit them to one piece of information each. Again, aim for accuracy at this stage by correcting when you think it appropriate.

Exercise 6a) Check the pronunciation of the items, particularly the word stress. You could write the words on the board with the stress marked to remind SS.

Exercise 6b) Find out who remembered the most items.

Exercise 6c) Highlight that *Have you got a..?* is being used as a request and compare it with *have got* to express possession in Exercise 5. Practise the question form and highlight the use of a rising intonation on the tonic and on *please* which sounds very polite.

Extra material and ideas

1 WB pages 10–12 Exercises 1–9.

2 PRACTISE AND CHECK, page 44, for more work on *to be* and *have got*.

3 Profiles page 118, 1.3. Divide the class into groups of 4. Give each S one of the profiles of Simone, Saeed, Kathleen and Reginaldo. Under each profile there are questions about the other 3 people. Together the groups work out the questions from the cues, e.g. *How old is he/she?* When these have been checked for accuracy they ask each other for information about the 3 people whose information they haven't got and fill in the worksheet.

4 Map page 117, 1.4. Hand each S a copy of a map of the world with the borders of some countries outlined and the first two letters of those countries given. As a class, get the SS to complete the names of the countries. Then divide the class into groups of up to six. Supply each group with a set of four people's names. The names should be different for each group and two of the people should be husband and wife (this is to practise *Are they...?*). Together the group decides which countries to put their people in. SS then work with a partner from another group. They exchange their four names, then take it in turns to ask questions to help them find which countries the four people are in. If the question Student A asks is answered with a *No*, Student B asks questions until he/she gets a *No* answer. This sequence is repeated. The winner is the first one to guess where all their partner's people are. Before the activity begins do a demonstration and elicit possible questions, e.g. *Is it a big/small country? Is it a hot/cold country? Is the first letter of the country ...?* Write a selection of these questions on the board to help students.

5 Find the person who has got ... page 120, 1.5. This is a class mingle activity to practise *Have you got a ...?* Give each student one of the five sheets. The objective is for SS to walk around asking the above question about the items on their list which are in shadow until they find someone who has that item. When a S finds someone with that item he/she writes that person's name under the item. The activity is over when a S has found people for all the items that are in shadow. In the feedback you can use the third person form *Who has got a .....?*

SKILLS

- Reading: scanning a text for information.
- Listening for detail.
- Vocabulary development: using dictionaries, identifying word stress through listening and using a dictionary, identifying adjectives and position of adjectives.
- Writing: punctuation (capital letters, recognition of apostrophes, full stops and commas).

Reading and listening

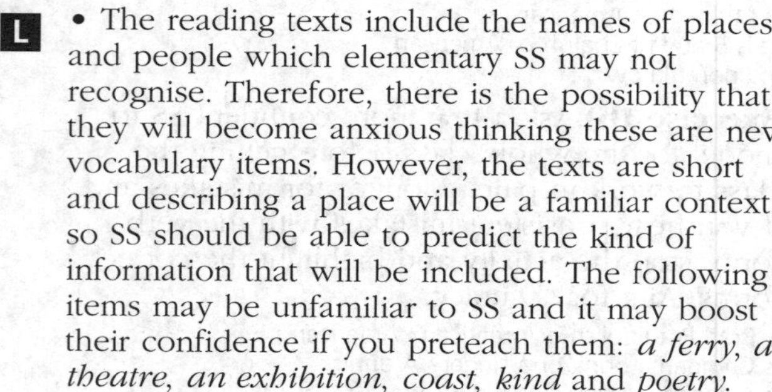

- The reading texts include the names of places and people which elementary SS may not recognise. Therefore, there is the possibility that they will become anxious thinking these are new vocabulary items. However, the texts are short and describing a place will be a familiar context, so SS should be able to predict the kind of information that will be included. The following items may be unfamiliar to SS and it may boost their confidence if you preteach them: *a ferry, a theatre, an exhibition, coast, kind* and *poetry.*

Students' Book (page 24)

Exercise 1a)

Note that all the major reading texts in *Elementary Matters* have been recorded on the class cassette and are marked with a white as opposed to a black cassette symbol. They can be used for simultaneous reading/listening exercises or as follow up work after the SB exercises have been done to reinforce sound/spelling association in SS' minds and allow further time for assimilation of the information. The readers' phrasing will also reinforce chunking which acts as an aid to understanding.

To initiate work on prediction ask SS to name a town or city that they like and one they don't like and to think of why they feel that way. If they are able to express why they have these opinions, allow time for a quick feedback. Establish that Dublin is in Ireland and Liverpool is in England after the reading. The matching activity, which is a type of scanning exercise, can be done individually, in pairs or small groups or as a whole class.

Background information:

The **Albert Dock** is the name of the waterfront in the city of Liverpool in the north west of England.

The **Grand National** is a famous horse race held each year at the Aintree course near Liverpool.

The Beatles were a British popular music group from Liverpool who made their first record in 1962 and became probably the most famous and successful group ever. When they separated in

1970, each member of the group continued to work in popular music. The Beatles were John Lennon, Paul McCartney, George Harrison and Ringo Starr.

Bob Geldof (1954–) is an Irish singer who sang with his band *The Boomtown Rats*, before becoming involved in raising money for people dying from hunger in Ethiopia with the charity Band Aid and the Live Aid concerts which were successful in the 1980s.

Sinéad O'Connor (1967–) (Sinéad pronounced /ʃəneɪd/) is an Irish singer, famous for her shaved head. She is best known for her single *Nothing compares to you*.

U2 are an Irish popular music group from Dublin, known especially for their political songs.

Oscar Wilde (1854–1900) was an Irish writer best known for his play *The Importance of Being Earnest* and his story *The Picture of Dorian Gray*. He is also famous for the many witty and clever things he said in conversation.

George Bernard Shaw (1856–1950) was an Irish writer and critic famous for his clever plays which point out faults in moral attitudes and society. His best-known play is *Pygmalion*.

James Joyce (1882–1941) an Irish writer who greatly influenced the way English novels are written, with his unusual and invented words and different style of writing. His novels include *Ulysses* and *Finnegans Wake*.

Big Ben is the large bell in the clock tower of the Houses of Parliament in Westminster, London. The sound of Big Ben striking is well known to all British people and the tower of Big Ben is often used as a symbol of London or Britain.

Liverpool: a (the Albert Dock), f (the Aintree racecourse), g (The Beatles).
Dublin: b (the River Liffey), d (Guinness beer), e (Sinéad O'Connor).
c is a photograph of Big Ben in London.

Exercise 1b)

They are both near the sea/on the coast. They are both on rivers (the Mersey and the Liffey).

Exercise 1c)

1 Yes, there is.
2 Two.
3 In the spring.
4 No, (it isn't) it's on the east coast.
5 Black coffee, brown sugar, Irish whiskey and cream.
6 No, (they aren't) they're from Dublin.

Exercise 2a)

[1.7]

MAN: I'm from the United States and I'm here for a week. I'm having a great time – I'm going to the theatre and seeing all the famous places. Today my wife and I are going on a sightseeing tour by bus.

WOMAN: I live in London so I don't visit all the tourist places. I like walking and there are a lot of beautiful parks and gardens to walk in. I also like going on a boat down the river – I go with friends and we have a drink or a meal. I love the shops and markets, too, but I haven't got any money to shop – I'm a student.

The man is the tourist.

Exercise 2b) Intensive listening practice. Most of the vocabulary should be familiar as it's taken from the unit. However, you may need to play the cassette more than once. After the first listening, checking SS' answers will give you some idea of how well they have managed to pick out the discrete items from the listening.

1 the woman 2 neither 3 neither 4 the woman 5 the man 6 the man

Vocabulary: using dictionaries

L The positions of adjectives in the articles on Dublin and Liverpool show both attributive position (before the noun) and predicative position (in complement position after the verb *to be*), e.g. *A beautiful day* (attributive position) and *She's beautiful* (predicative position).

Students' Book (page 24)

Exercise 3 Establish that there are two syllables in *famous*. You could refer back to Exercise 2a) and ask where the stress was on the two syllable words in that exercise. Get SS to predict where the stress might be on *famous* and then check it in the extract from a dictionary. This might help reinforce the fact that many two-syllable nouns in English have their stress on the first syllable.

If your SS aren't familiar with the phonemic script, you will need to help them, particularly with the vowel sounds, before you can expect them to be able to use the script effectively. Isolate the sounds /e/ and /i/ then say them in quick succession so they become the diphthong /ei/. Then isolate and model the schwa sound /ə/. Ask SS to practise saying these sounds in isolation and then check back with the dictionary extract to work out the pronunciation of the word. If this word isn't new to SS, you could use another of the adjectives from the text and write it in phonemic script on the board and follow the same procedure working with the vowels first. Note that this is to develop SS' self access skills. They should realise that they're **not** expected to memorise the whole phonemic script nor produce it. Refer SS to the Pronunciation table on page 144.

You could write up examples such as big house, small room etc. Label *big* and *small* as adjectives and *house* and *room* as nouns to give visual backup, then establish that an adjective gives more information about a noun. Don't use the example *famous city* as this is the basis for Exercise 6. Then write up She's big. They're small. From the four examples on the board SS should be able to answer the question about position of adjectives (see L). Without giving terminology, highlight that adjectives frequently precede the noun but can follow the verb *to be*. (See *Extra material and ideas* 2 below.)

1 The first syllable (fa).
2 /feɪməs/
3 Adjectives usually come before nouns. They come after the verb *to be*.

Exercise 4a) You could divide the task up, asking half of the class to look for the answers in the Liverpool text and the others to look for the answers in the Dublin text. You could write their answers on the board ready for the word stress exercise which follows.

Liverpool	Dublin
1 'famous	1 'beautiful
2 'busy, in'dustrial, ex'citing	2 'elegant, grey
3 'popular	4 kind, 'friendly
5 de'licious	

Exercise 4b) Elicit the answers and add the stress marks to the words on the board which have more than one syllable.

[1.8]

Liverpool	Dublin
1 famous	1 beautiful
2 busy, industrial, exciting	2 elegant, grey
3 popular	3 small, old
	4 kind, friendly
	5 delicious

See 4a) above.

Writing: punctuation

SS will need to understand the metalanguage for capital and small letters, comma, full stop and apostrophe. Remind SS of question marks.

Students' Book (page 25)

Exercise 5a) Note that the *Language reference* section has more examples of capital letter use but the exercise focuses on the ones in the text. Establish the meaning of *capital letter* and *small letter* by giving examples on the board, e.g. use a S's name to illustrate the difference. See if SS are aware of other examples of when a capital letter would be used. Then allow them time to study the information in the box and add to and/or correct their suggestions on the uses of the capital letter. It might be advisable to check their understanding by doing the first sentence from the exercise with the whole class, writing it up on the board according to where they think capital letters would occur.

I'm a student at the University of Glasgow in Scotland. Glasgow is on the River Clyde. It's an industrial city but it's also famous for its museums, the Glasgow School of Art and the Scottish Opera. There are two popular football clubs in Glasgow called Rangers and Celtic.

Exercise 5b) Establish the meaning of comma, full stop and apostrophe. You could then ask SS to write different sentences from the text on the board and ask other SS if they agree. Work on it until there is a completely correct version for SS to check from.

Exercise 6 Encourage the SS to swap their written work and check for mistakes before handing it to you. Alternatively you could collect their paragraphs, underline any mistakes and redistribute them in the following lesson. Ask different SS to correct the underlined mistakes. The corrected versions could be displayed around the room and SS could walk around reading each other's paragraphs. Allow sufficient time for SS to complete the writing in class time if possible. This makes it more of a joint effort and not such a daunting prospect as writing it alone for homework.

Extra material and ideas

1 WB pages 14–15, Exercises 17–18.

2 The teacher's cat To reinforce attributive position of adjectives and increase SS' vocabulary you could play this game. Although this is usually played by using the entire alphabet, it's probably wiser to limit the number of letters and write these on the board. The idea of the game is to think of an adjective beginning with the letter of the alphabet indicated, e.g. *The teacher's cat is an ANGRY cat, the teacher's cat is a BEAUTIFUL cat* etc. Normally this would be done with individual SS taking turns. However, for this level it might be less threatening to put SS in pairs and allow them time to think of or look up adjectives before you do the activity as a whole class.

SOCIAL ENGLISH

Dates and times

- **Ordinal numbers**, months, dates, times and prepositions *in* and *on*.

- **Ordinal numbers** Although SS may be familiar with basic numbers from CHECK YOUR ENGLISH don't expect them to be accurate and they probably won't know the ordinal numbers (*first*, *second* etc.).

Pronunciation Ordinal numbers will cause difficulty for many learners because of the consonant cluster caused by the *th* sound /θ/ at the end of the words.

- **Days of the week**

Pronunciation The following spellings may interfere with SS' pronunciation: *Tuesday*, elision of *e* /tʃuːzdeɪ/; *Wednesday*, elision of *d* /wenzdeɪ/; *Saturday*, schwa in the middle /sætədeɪ/. Note that some speakers say /ɪ/ in days like *Tues**day*** and others use /eɪ/. Point out where the stress falls on the days of the week and ask SS to practise saying them, e.g. *Monday*.

- **Months of the year** Highlight the possible written forms for dates, 15 February, 15th February, 15.2. year (UK), 2.15. year (USA). Also point out the possible abbreviated forms: *Jan, Feb, Mar, Apr, Aug, Sept, Oct, Nov, Dec, May. June* and *July* do not have abbreviated forms.

Pronunciation Expect sound/spelling problems with the following months of the year: *February* elision of the first *r* /febjuərɪ/; *August* pronunciation of the first vowel sound. Many SS pronounce this as a diphthong rather than /ɔː/.

Prepositions Highlight the use of *in* for months but *on* for days and dates. Although years aren't practised in the unit, you could highlight that *in* is also used for years. Point out the word stresss to SS, e.g. *January.*

• **Telling the time** Note that in this unit, the time is expressed thus: *It's half past two.* The stress is normally at the end. There is another option available: *It's two thirty* which is not practised in Unit 1 but comes up in Unit 2 in Recording 2.5.

Students' Book (page 26)

Exercise 1 Use the opportunity to practise the sounds and word stress of the days of the week.

Exercise 1a) It would be useful to write this exercise on the board or an OHT for an efficient means of checking their answers.

2h) 3f) 4i) 5b) 6g) 7c) 8a) 9d)

Exercise 1b) It might be useful to differentiate between a calendar and a diary.

[1.9]
the sixth of July
the third of July
the ninth of July
the fourteenth of July
the twenty-second of July
the eighth of July

6th July, 13th July, 9th of July, 14th July, 22nd July, 8thJuly

Exercise 1c) Highlight sound/spelling features (see L). Write the months up on the board and elicit where the stress is on the ones with two or three syllables. Highlight possible ways of writing the date and abbreviated forms for months (see L).

[1.10]
January, February, March, April, May, June, July, August, September, October, November, December

Exercises 1d) and e) Read the caption to the photograph of Bob with the class and then do the first item with the class as an example and write it on the board.

[1.11]
1 Alan's thirty-three. His birthday's in April. It's on Saturday, the fifth of April.
2 Suzie's thirteen. Her birthday's in September. It's on the seventh of September.
3 Jack and Ann are twenty. Their birthdays are in January and May. Jack's birthday is on the third of January and Ann's is on the tenth of May.
4 Vera and Carlos are nineteen. Their birthdays are in February and July. Vera's is on Friday, the twenty-eighth of February and Carlos's is on Thursday, the thirty-first of July.

Exercise 1f) SS may need access to a diary to establish what day of the week their birthday is on.

Exercise 1g) When SS have given feedback on the birthdays they have collected, the class could form a line according to when their birthday comes in the year. Establish January 1st as being on the left of the classroom and December 31st on the right. SS will have to ask each other to repeat their birthday so that they can line up in the correct order. If it's appropriate or of interest to SS, you could establish which SS have the same star signs.

Exercise 2a) and b)
Highlight the alternative ways of saying the time, e.g. three forty-five, quarter to four etc. (see L).

[1.12]
1 It's three o'clock.
2 It's half past two.
3 It's ten to twelve.
4 It's five past three.
5 It's (a) quarter to nine.
6 It's twenty to one.
7 It's (a) quarter past six.
8 It's twenty-five past eight.
Highlight the alternative ways of saying the time, e.g. three forty-five, quarter to four etc. (see L).

2 b 3 g 4 f 5 h 6 d 7 a 8 e

Exercise 2c) Ask a few confident SS to do an example of the question and answer practice for the whole class before closed pair work.

Extra material and ideas

1 WB page 13, Exercises 11, 12 and 14..

2 Number and date bingo page 121, 1.6. PW. Photocopy the bingo sheets for your SS. You read out numbers and dates from the list below. The first pair to have a complete card wins the game.

Numbers used. NOTE: some appear on more than one card.
12 13 17 18 23 25 28 32 33 36 42 45 47 49 54 56 68 72 79 83 85 87 90 101 107 109 110 123 126 128 129 164 167 175 178 189 193 210 213 216 217 222 234 235 246 253 257 268 285 293 296 318 319 333 347 367 423 428 451 452 478 484 497 543 562 564 568 593 607 614 634 666 678 725 781 832 856 867 874 901 905 910 912 926 954 980 984 987 999 1000

Dates used. NOTE: some appear on more than one card.
1 January 6 January 7 January 12 January 13 January 27 January 5 February 13 February 16 February 9 March 15 March 18 March 26 March 27 March 10 April 15 April 22 April 23 April 1 May 3 May 9 May 18 May 20 May 21 May 23 May 11 June 12 June 15 June 19 June 20 June 22 June 27 June 4 July 18 July 31 July 1 August 12 August 22 August 27 August 31 August 6 September 10 September 12 September 4 October 9 October 17 October 21 October 28 October 1 November 12 November 14 November 25 November 27 November 3 December 25 December 29 December 31 December

3 Sailing page 122, 1.7. [Recording 1.13] You might want to use the gapped song *Sailing* to practise the Present Continuous, nouns and pronouns. There is a gapped and a complete version.

Where, when, why and how?

Students' Book

General themes: the office; the weather; general knowledge.

FOCUS ON VOCABULARY: in the office; prepositions of place (1); revision of *there's a..../there are some.../ Is there a ...? Are there any...? How many .... are there?*
FOCUS ON GRAMMAR: Present Simple (1); third person singular verbs with regular and irregular verbs; negatives and *yes/no* questions; question words (*where, when, why, how, what* and *who*).
SKILLS: reading and listening (quiz); vocabulary (keeping records); writing (combining sentences – pronouns, *and* and *but*).
REVIEW: vocabulary (crossword); using your grammar (asking for travel information).

Workbook

GRAMMAR: Present Simple (1).
VOCABULARY: things in the office; prepositions; time expressions (*in, on* and *at*).
WRITING: linking words (*and* and *but*); rewriting a paragraph.
PRONUNCIATION: Present Simple verbs (third person singular endings).

FOCUS ON VOCABULARY

In the office

A • Objects found in offices.
• Prepositions of place.
• Revision of *there is/are*. Extension to *Are there any...?, There aren't any..., How many are there?*, requests and offers.

• **Compound nouns** The vocabulary includes compound nouns *handbag* and *briefcase*. Although these compound nouns are written as one word, this is by no means consistent, e.g. *paper clips, hole-punch*. There is no simple rule. Indeed, this seems to be an area of language which is undergoing change and many native speakers have problems remembering the written form of certain compound nouns. As new compound nouns occur and the problem of the written form comes up, we suggest you highlight the three possibilities. Tell SS to check in a dictionary when they are unsure and then commit the written form to memory.

Pronunciation The stress pattern of the compound nouns is on the first noun *'handbag, 'briefcase*. This should be highlighted for the SS. They may not recognise *handbag* /hæmbæg/ because of the frequent elision of /d/ and the assimilated sound /m/. Note, however, that on the cassette the speaker says /hændbæg/ for clarity instead of /hæmbæg/.

• **Plural forms** Remind SS of *shelf/shelves* and *diary/diaries*.

• **Prepositions of place** can be one word, e.g. *under*, or a two or three word phrase, e.g. *in front of*. SS often leave words out of phrases, particularly the last preposition in the phrase, e.g., **X is front Y* or **X is next Y*. It's important to highlight that the two or three words actually belong together and should be learnt as one unit.

Pronunciation In the prepositional phrases *in front of* and *next to* the weak forms /əv/ and /tə/ are commonly used in spoken English. The fact that SS frequently omit these final prepositions is perhaps because they don't hear them. Therefore, even if you do not insist that your SS produce the weak forms when speaking, they should be made aware of them to help avoid mistakes of omission.

• ***There is/are*** Some of the exercises practise the recognition and use of *there is a/are some....* and *is there a... ?/are there any... ?* Although *a* vs. *some* is revision, you may need to go over the singular/plural aspect of this grammar point again. *Any* is new and we recommend you limit its grammatical description to: We can use *any* in questions and negatives. The fact that we can also use it in positive sentences, e.g. *I'll eat any fruit.* will only complicate matters for this level. SS often avoid *some* and *any*, e.g. **There are bags in the picture. *There aren't bags in the picture* which sound unnatural. The unit avoids uncountable nouns so it is possible to tell SS to use *a* for singular nouns and *some/any* with plural nouns in these exercises. *Some* and *any* are focused on in Unit 8, so this acts as a preview.

• **The functional exponents *Could I...* and *I'll ...* for requests and offers** are flagged but there is no grammatical explanation given. It is sufficient at this level that SS recognise the function and learn these as lexical phrases as one might in a phrase book. Note that *will* and *shall* come up regularly throughout the book as functional items (see Contents Chart).

Pronunciation Encourage SS to use the weak form of *can* /kən/ in requests and to use the contracted form *I'll* /aɪl/ in offers.

This/that are reviewed in this section (see L CHECK YOUR ENGLISH).

Students' Book (page 28)

Exercise 1a) As a quick warmer you could ask

SS in pairs to make a list of as many things in the classroom they can name within one minute.

a tissues b diary c photocopier d handbag e drawer f keys g mug h shelf i briefcase

Exercise 1b)

[2.1]
mugs handbag photocopier drawer diary keys tissues briefcase shelf shelves

Exercise 2a) Allow SS time to study the diagram which illustrates prepositions of place. You may wish to illustrate some of the prepositions in class, e.g. *in front of* and *behind, on, under* and *next to,* to consolidate their presentation in the diagram. After the first listening get feedback and write it on the board. Where SS agree and it's correct, tick the answer. Where there is disagreement, put a question mark. Play the cassette again but this time SS should only concentrate on ascertaining the correct answer. If there is still disagreement, play the cassette again. SS will tolerate listening to the cassette several times if the reason for doing so is clear.

[2.2]
1 There's a diary on the desk.
2 The tissues are next to the diary.
3 There are some keys on the floor.
4 There are some mugs on the shelf.
5 The briefcase is behind the lamp.
6 There's a handbag on the desk.

1T 2F 3F 4T 5F 6T

Exercise 2b) If SS are unfamiliar with these prepositions, it may take some time for them to reach a level of fluency and mistakes will be frequent. Try to encourage weak forms and linkage once they are using the prepositions more confidently.

Exercise 2c) Model the sentences in the grammar box so the SS can hear the effect of the consonant vowel links. You could ask them to draw similar links in the conversation before they begin, to heighten their awareness.

Exercise 2d) You may need to demonstrate the activity with one of the more confident students.

Exercise 2e) Demonstrate by being the one with closed eyes. SS ask you one or two questions.

Exercise 3

If SS are having difficulty remembering prepositions of place and the names of the objects, you could elicit these words and write them on the board before SS begin this exercise. Alternatively, you could allow SS to practise describing their photograph with a S from the other group. Either suggestion should enable SS to focus on meaning and communication rather than struggling to remember vocabulary.

Student A
The pens are next to the diary.
The keys are on the file.
The envelopes are under the mug/next to the diary.
The phone is behind the mug/next to the handbag.
The file is in front of the diary.
The handbag is next to the phone.
The mug is on the envelopes/in front of the phone.
The diary is in front of the woman/next to the pens/behind the file.
The phonecard is on the diary.

Student B
The pens are next to the file.
The keys are on the diary.
The envelopes are in front of the diary.
The phone is next to the diary/behind the file.
The file is in front of the phone.
The handbag is behind the mug/next to the diary.
The mug is in front of the handbag.
The diary is in front of the woman/behind the envelopes.
The phonecard is on the file.

Exercise 4

Preteach the word *borrow*. The other vocabulary is revision.

[2.3]
1
FEMALE: Is this your mug, Pete?
MALE: Yes, it is. Why?
FEMALE: Can I borrow it for my coffee?
MALE: I'm afraid it's dirty. There's a clean one here.
2
WOMAN 1: Whose are those tissues?
WOMAN 2: Mine. Why?
WOMAN 1: Could I have one, please? I've got an awful cold.
WOMAN 2: Of course you can. Help yourself.

1a, 2b

Exercise 3b) After each line pause the tape to allow SS time to write. Get feedback after the first listening and decide if a second listening is necessary.

1
A: Is **this** your mug, Pete?
B: Yes, it is. Why?
A: **Can I** borrow it for my coffee?
B: **I'm afraid** it's dirty. **There's** a clean one here.
2
A: **Whose are** those tissues?
B: Mine. Why?
A: **Could I have** one, please? I've got an awful cold.
B: **Of course you can.** Help yourself.

Exercise 3c) Get SS to practise the weak forms in isolation before going on to the conversation.

Exercise 3d) Note that the gaps contain the core language of each dialogue. After SS have practised, finish the section by asking the more confident SS to say one of their conversations for the whole class.

Extra material and ideas

1 WB page 19, Exercises 9–10.

2 Picture search page 122, 2.1. Make copies of the picture for SS. Tell them they are looking for 12 things you can usually find in an office and 6 things you can't usually find in an office.

mug pen keys computer photocopier briefcase book shelves envelopes desk lamp stamps taxi TV bed boat football child/girl

3 Picture dictation to practise prepositions of place This can be done either as a whole class activity or as a S to S dictation. Using vocabulary you are sure SS know, draw a picture for yourself, keeping it secret from the class, placing things in various places. You then dictate where the things are in the picture and SS draw the picture, e.g., *in the centre there's a desk, under the desk there's a coffee mug* etc. This will practise recognition of the prepositions. If you want SS to practise using the prepositions, they could draw simple pictures and dictate in the same way to a partner. If you have a language laboratory available, SS could record their dictations and then draw several pictures by moving to different machines and listening to other SS' descriptions. Don't forget to allow time for feedback where SS check their picture against the original drawing.

4 Where are the mugs? page 123, 2.2. Give SS copies of the picture. They should write as many sentences as they can, i.e. *There's a mug ... / There are some mugs ...* They should use the words in the box to help 'position' the mugs, i.e. *There's a mug on the shelf.*

FOCUS ON GRAMMAR

Present Simple (1)

• Present Simple positive and negative sentences and *yes/no* questions with the third person singular.
• Question words.
• Time expressions introduced by the prepositions *at, in* and *on*.

• **Present Simple** The concept presented in this unit is restricted to routines/habits and general states. It focuses on the third person singular in statements, negatives and questions. Even if SS have met this tense before they are unlikely to be clear about either its form, meaning or use. (Note that the unit does **not** include subject questions, e.g. *Who lives here?*)
You will need to highlight the following aspects of form repeatedly before any degree of accuracy is achieved.
Remembering the third person *s* in positive sentences.
The use of auxiliary verb *does* in negatives and questions. The main verb reverting to the infinitive in questions.
Word order in questions and negatives, e.g. *Does he play...?*
Spelling difficulties arising with the third person *-s*:
play – plays (vowel before *-y*, add *-s*)
carry – carries (consonant before *-y*, change the *y* to *i* and add *-es*)
catch – catches (verbs ending in *-tch, -sh, -ss, -x,* add *-es*)
do – does (*do* and *go* add *-es*)
Pronunciation The pronunciation of *-s* is influenced by the preceding sound, a vowel or a voiced consonant encourages final /z/: *cleans* /kliːnz/, a voiceless sound encourages a final /s/: *paints* /peɪnts/, verbs ending in *-tch* and *-sh* encourage /ɪz/: *washes* /wɒʃɪz/. Because the /s/ and /z/ endings are less marked in connected speech they're not focused on in the SB. However, SS tend to overuse the /ɪz/ ending which is the focus in the SB. If SS can differentiate when to use /ɪz/ and not use it, this will immediately make for a marked improvement in their pronunciation. In questions and negatives the weak form of *does* is commonly used (/dəz/ and /dəznt/). In short answers the strong form is used /dʌz/.
• **Time expressions** *at + time /the weekend/ night*; *in + the morning/afternoon/evening*; *on + day*. These expressions generally come at the beginning or end of a sentence. SS also meet *on Mondays, in the evenings* to emphasise habit.

Students' Book (page 30)

Exercise 1a) Note that there is a recording of this text on the cassette. Use the photograph to elicit information, preteach vocabulary and help SS predict the content of the passage. You may want to tell SS that the *Underground* is commonly referred to as *the tube*. Use the visuals to preteach *jacket, mask* and *track*. You could read the text to the SS or play the cassette while they follow in their books. This will ensure that they finish at the same time and you can move on to the gap fill exercise. SS could do this individually and then check with another S who has finished at the same time. Note that *because* is introduced in the text and might need explaining or translating. You could use the following example: 1 *She gets up after two hours.* 2 *She wants to sleep on Saturday night.* The reason for 1 is *because* of 2.

1 loves 2 arrives 3 puts 4 stops 5 goes

Exercise 1b) You may need to illustrate or explain the meaning of *often*. If you can't use translation, you could draw the following cline on the board:

never — often — always
0 — 80 — 100%

Don't labour this point as it is only to enable concept checking and is not meant to introduce the concept of frequency adverbs which comes in Unit 3.

1 is correct

Exercise 1c)

is loves lives travels puts cleans works gets gets up wants

Exercise 1d) It is important to highlight the third person *-s* as this is often omitted. You could draw a large S on the board, underline it, add an exclamation mark, anything which might create an impression on SS' memories.

s

Exercise 2a) Focus on the example and then ask SS to make a sentence for the second picture cue. You could assign certain sentences to SS and ask them to write these on the board. This provides a quick reference for checking and correcting. When SS have finished the exercise, you only need to ask if they agree with the sentences on the board. If there is some disagreement, put a question mark next to the number and then let them listen to the cassette.

Exercise 2b)

[2.4]

1 He lives in London.
2 He works in a school.
3 He teaches Spanish.
4 He smokes.
5 He drinks wine.
6 He speaks French.
7 He rides a bike/(bi)cycle.
8 He plays football.
9 He watches TV.
10 He goes to the cinema.

Exercise 2c) You could offer more recognition practice by telling SS about someone you know. After they have worked in pairs you could ask more confident SS to tell the class about someone they know.

Exercise 3a)

Write the questions on the board so you can focus attention on the use of the auxiliary *does* and the fact that the main verb reverts to the infinitive. Highlight the weak and strong form of *does* in questions and short answers and the contracted form of the negative short answer. Note that the alternative form for 11.30 (*eleven thirty*) is given on the cassette. In Unit 1 the *half past* form is presented.

[2.5]

1
A: Does Sylvie arrive at eleven thirty?
B: Yes, she does.
2
A: Does she work by herself?
B: No, she doesn't. She works in a group.

Write the questions on the board so you can focus attention on the use of the auxiliary does and the fact that the main verb reverts to the infinitive. Highlight the weak and strong form of does in questions and short answers and the contracted form of the negative short answer.

Exercise 3b) Do the first question/answer with the whole class to check they have understood what is required to form questions. Point out the time expressions and draw the following chart on the board for SS to copy:

Time expressions

AT	IN	ON
(time)	the morning	
8pm	the afternoon	
	the evening	

1 Does she go to work by bus? No, she doesn't.
2 Does she arrive at work at 10.30 in the evening? No, she doesn't.
3 Does she work at weekends? No, she doesn't.
4 Does she get home at 5.30 in the morning? Yes, she does.

Exercise 4 Note that the question words, *When* and *Why* are new. Highlight that *When* = *What time* and *Why* = *asking for the reason*. You might want to link to *because* in the Sylvie text. Check SS' answers then allow them time to practise saying the questions and answers in pairs. Focus attention back to the Time expressions box on the board and ask SS to look at the questions and answers and find another example for AT (night) and find an example of ON. Then add to the box ON + days, e.g. *Monday, Tuesday.*

2a) 3e) 4c) 5b)

Exercise 5 Before SS start, you might want to check some of the following vocabulary: *cycling, cooking, fishing, actor, TV presenter, fashion model.* However, make sure that by doing this you don't answer the questions in the exercise thereby preempting the information exchange activity.

Point out that the exercise requires SS to use the question words *What, Where* etc. and draw their attention to the questions grammar box on page 31. If your SS aren't used to doing this kind of information exchange, be prepared to take it step by step. Initially divide the SS into two groups, A and B, and ask SS to read the texts as quickly as possible. Wait until at least the majority, if not all, have finished reading before going onto the next set of instructions. If you think they need assistance with forming the questions, you could allow all of Group A to work together on forming the questions before working with a partner from Group B and vice versa. Alternatively, you can pair A and B SS and monitor them closely. If they are experiencing difficulty in forming the questions, stop the activity, do a couple of examples from A and B's questions and then let them continue.

Student A Questions and answers about Antoine de Caunes
1 Where does he live? (He lives) in Paris.
2 Who does he work for? (He works for) British TV.
3 When does he get up? (He gets up) early.
4 What does he drink for breakfast? (He drinks) tea.
5 What does he do? He's a TV presenter.
6 How does he go to work? (He goes to work) by train.
7 What languages does he speak? (He speaks) very good English.
8 Who does he live with? (He lives with) his son and his daughter.
9 What does he do in his free time? (He likes) cycling and cooking.

Student B Questions and answers about Nikki Campbell
1 What (job) does she do? She's a model.
2 Who does she work for? (She works for) a fashion photographer.
3 Where does she live? (She lives) in London.
4 Who does she live with? (She lives with) her mother, brother and her cat.
5 When does she get up? (She gets up) at 7 am.
6 What does she eat for breakfast? (She eats) fruit.
7 How does she go to school? (She goes) on foot.

8 What languages does she speak? (She speaks) French, German and English.
9 What does she do in her free time? She listens to music and watches football on TV.

Exercise 6a) Ask SS which sentence in the Nikki caption is positive and which is negative. Highlight the use of the contracted form of the auxiliary *does* + *not* and that the verb reverts to the infinitive. Use visual highlighting, colour, boxes, underlining etc.

Exercise 6b) Make sure SS understand they have to make a negative and positive sentence when they find an information error in the journalist's notes.

Nikki
She doesn't eat a sandwich. She eats fruit.
She doesn't go to school by bus. She goes on foot.
She doesn't speak two languages. She speaks three (languages).
She doesn't like fishing. She listens to music and watches football.
Antoine
He doesn't work for a French newspaper. He works for British TV.
He doesn't live in London. He lives in Paris.
He doesn't drink beer for breakfast. He drinks tea.
He doesn't live with his mother. He lives with his son and (his) daughter.

Exercise 6c) This practises questions beginning with *Why* and the conjunction *because.*

1 Why does Antoine get the 7 am train from Paris to London?
2 Why does Nikki eat fruit for breakfast?
3 Why does Nikki speak German?

Extra material and ideas

1 WB pages 16–19, Exercises 1–8; page 20, Exercise 11.
2 PRACTISE AND CHECK, page 44 for more work on the Present Simple (1).
3 Jumbled sentences To reinforce word order of questions and negatives divide the SS into groups of 8 or 9 and give each one a number from 1 to 8 or 9. Dictate the words for **A** below, and each S writes down the word for her/his number. If there's a S without a word or question mark, they should be responsible for rearranging the SS in their group so that they line up to form a correct sentence. Otherwise the group arranges itself into the correct order. The group to form the correct sentence first wins. Continue with the words for **B** and so on. SS should write their words big enough to be seen from a distance by the other groups. If your class is too small to have groups of 9, dictate 2 or 3 words to each S in smaller groups and they can stick the words on the wall in the correct order or write the sentence on the board.

A 1=does 2=7.30 pm 3=go 4=at 5=she 6=where 7=pm 8=? (question mark)
Answer: *Where does she go at 7.30 pm?*
B 1=leave 2=? 3=in 4=Alan 5=when 6=the 7=does 8=home 9 =morning
Answer: *When does Alan leave home in the morning?*
C 1=in 2=not 3=afternoon 4=Janet 5=work 6=does 7= the 8=. (full stop)
Answer: *Janet does not work in the afternoon.*
D 1=go 2=on 3=morning 4=? 5=does 6=to 7=Pam 8=Saturday 9=school
Answer: *Does Pam go to school on Saturday morning?*

4 Information exchange page 124, 2.3. PW To practise Present Simple questions and review telling the time. Copy worksheets A and B for each pair. SS have to write questions then interview their partner and complete the sentences on the worksheet. Demonstrate from each worksheet so that SS understand that they must ask each other questions.

SKILLS

• Reading: predicting the content of a text, reading for detail.
• Vocabulary: study skills, ways of recording new vocabulary, further work on phonemics.
• Writing: subject, object and possessive pronouns to link sentences.

Reading

• Revision of numbers.
• Some of the key vocabulary will be new for SS, e.g. *nail, skin, bone, rats, none, times* and *per cent.* However, most are concrete and there is plenty of visual support. Other items which may need clarification are *active volcanoes,* and *centre of the earth.*

Students' Book (page 32)

Exercise 1a) If all the vocabulary items are unfamiliar and you want SS to use dictionaries, it would be an efficient use of time to split the task among the SS, who first check in a dictionary and then teach each other the words.

a nail b ice c bones d the earth e heart f the moon g eye h rain i volcano j rat k rubbish

Exercise 1b) You could introduce a competitive element and get SS to work in teams. Before listening you could chart the teams' answers on the board so that scores can be added up once the answers have been checked.

Exercise 1c)

[2.6]
1 There are two hundred and seventy-three stations on the London Underground.
2 There are two hundred and six bones in your body.
3 The Latin word *septem* is seven.
4 Seventy-five per cent of the water on earth is ice.
5 Your skin changes every six weeks.
6 It is six thousand three hundred kilometres to the centre of the earth.
7 Your heart beats seventy to eighty times a minute.
8 There are eighty active volcanoes under the sea.

Exercise 1d) Tell SS they don't need to read all the text to do this activity. However, as a scanning activity it will help them to locate the required information for the next part of the exercise.

1 273 2 206 3 7 4 75 5 weeks 6 6,300 7 70–80 8 80

Exercise 1e) SS will need to read the text in Exercise 1d) in detail to answer the T/F exercise but they should now be able to locate the appropriate text fairly quickly. You could set a time limit to encourage them to read more quickly, unless you think this will cause SS to become anxious.

1T 2T 3F 4T 5F

Vocabulary: keeping records

• The vocabulary in this section should be familiar and some is drawn from the texts so SS can concentrate on possible ways of recording vocabulary effectively. The exercise includes recognition of the phonemic script.

Students' Book (page 33)

Exercise 2 Tell SS to refer to the texts and find words for the two 'spidergrams'. There may be disagreement about what could reasonably be added to each spidergram, e.g. *rain* might be suggested as a word for the THE EARTH spidergram, but others might think this would be better on a WEATHER spidergram somewhere else in their vocabulary book. The point is that vocabulary records are personal. As long as the SS can see an association it's valid. Ask SS their opinion about this way of recording vocabulary.

Suggested answers:
The body: bones, eye, nail, feet, skin
The earth: ice, volcano, the moon, rain, water

Exercise 3a) Ask SS what extra information is in the second example (i.e. a stress mark and a sentence). This way of recording vocabulary gives SS the pronunciation, part of speech, word stress, translation and an example of its use. Whereas some items can have visual representation, point out it would be difficult to illustrate *beautiful* in a student's vocabulary book. This will raise awareness that different items can be recorded differently.

1 No, it's an adjective.
2 /braʊn/
3 The first syllable.

Exercise 3b) Encourage SS always to mark the stress when recording new vocabulary.

Exercise 3c) If SS aren't particularly good at recognising phonemic script, a useful guideline is to practise a little and often. You could begin each lesson by writing simple words in phonemics on the board, e.g. /bed/. Gradually work up to simple sentences which require a response, e.g. draw an egg on the board and in phonemics write, Is this a bed? /ɪzðɪsəbed/. Another way to encourage recognition is to write comments on S's homework in phonemics, e.g. *very good* /verɪgʊd/. Remember that recognition is usually all that's required so that SS can access pronunciation in a dictionary and copy it into their notebooks. Therefore we do **not** recommend that you spend time getting SS to produce phonemic script.

Extra material and ideas

Keeping vocabulary books Ask SS to buy or supply them with a small notebook to record new vocabulary. In pairs give SS a word they don't know and ask them to look it up in a dictionary. They should then make a record of it in their notebooks according to the guidelines in the SB. When they have finished they teach their word to another pair. This word is then added to that pair's vocabulary books. The new words you give them could be taken from later units, e.g. *lamb, bacon, crisps, roll, sweater, trousers, cardigan*. This will then act as a preview for future vocabulary. To help SS become more proficient at using dictionaries you could allow time at the end of lessons to look up one or two new words.

Writing: combining sentences

Review of possessive pronouns (see CHECK YOUR ENGLISH), object pronouns and review of subject pronouns and possessive adjectives. SS usually take quite a lot of time to use these accurately. We recommend that you correct pronoun mistakes as they happen to reinforce accuracy and aid memory.

Linkers: *and* and *but.*

Students' Book (page 33)

Exercise 4a) Draw the table on the board and do the first one with the class. Monitor SS' work and ask some SS who have the correct answers to write them on the board. This allows you to have the attention of the class whilst you highlight features such as *her* → *hers.*

SUBJECT PRONOUN	OBJECT PRONOUN	POSSESSIVE PRONOUN
	me	mine
he	him	his
she	her	hers
it	it	
we	us	ours
you	you	yours
they	them	theirs

Exercise 4b)

1 This is Lucy's car. It's **hers**.
2 This is my mother. I phone **her** in the evenings.
3 Are these **yours**?
4 These are your CDs and my CDs. They are **ours**.
5 This is my new handbag. Do you like **it**?

Exercise 5

1 but 2 and 3 and 4 but

Exercise 6a) and b) Before checking with the whole class you could ask SS to read their paragraphs to a partner to see if they agree. This will offer more speaking and listening practice.

Mica is a singer. She lives in north London with her daughter, Monet. She is married **but** (she) is separated from her husband. Mica's got a BMW **and** she drives **it** to the recording studio. She likes clothes **and** (she) spends a lot of money on **them**. Mica admires Nelson Mandela **and** (she) thinks **he** is a great man.

Extra material and ideas

1 WB page 20, Exercises 12–13.

2 Reinforce the pronouns by doing simple transformation drills.

Possessive adjective to possessive pronoun. You give a prompt, e.g. *It's my coat.* and the S transforms the possessive adjective to the possessive pronoun, *It's mine.* etc.

Possessive adjective to object pronoun. You give a prompt, e.g. *I like my sisters.* S responds with *I like them.* etc.

If these are done quickly and fairly frequently in the early stages of learning, they can help SS gain greater accuracy. It's advisable quickly to prepare the prompts in advance to ensure you have enough and that you include all the pronouns.

An alternative is to have the prompts written, give these to SS and they conduct the transformation by prompting each other in a class mingle activity.

Dictate a short, incorrect paragraph with only subject pronouns, e.g.

*I like **I** sister but she doesn't like **I**. When she has chocolates, I know they are **she**, but I eat **they**. When **she** friends come to **we** house I eat **they** chocolates, too. I love chocolate and I can eat it all day. When I have some I don't give any to **they**, it's all for **I**.*

Ask the SS to write down what you say but tell them there are X number of mistakes. There are 9 mistakes in the above paragraph. When they have finished writing, let them work with a partner to find and correct the mistakes. Ask different SS to dictate a sentence from their corrected version back to you. Write these on the board and ask the other SS if they agree. Continue until the corrected paragraph is written on the board.

my me hers them her our their them me

REVIEW

Revision of vocabulary from CHECK YOUR ENGLISH and Units 1 and 2.

Revision of verbs *to be* and Present Simple third person singular, positive, negative, questions and short answers.

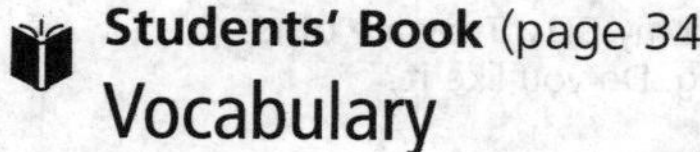

Students' Book (page 34)

Vocabulary

Exercise 1

This activity can be done individually (at home) or in pairs or groups.

Across	Down
3 born	2 aunt
7 waiter	4 drawer
9 Turkey	5 tea
11 one	6 cousin
12 surname	8 Polish
	10 shelf

Exercise 2 a) and b)

Note that this activity is deliberately freer. Help SS with the pronunciation of the place names and link the activity back to the texts on Liverpool and Dublin in Unit 1 SKILLS. Divide the class into two groups, A and B, and allow them time to prepare for the activity. While Group B are digesting the tourist guide's information, let Group A work together on the questions they will need to ask. Monitor Group A's questions and try to catch as many mistakes as you can before they do the roleplay. Do the same for B. This activity is likely to take quite a long time if you allow sufficient preparation time.

Exercise 2c) Make sure SS realise this is a note not a letter. When they have finished they could mingle and try to find someone with a similar plan for the day's outing.

Extra material and ideas

Incomplete sentences page 123, 2.4. PW. Give each S a copy of the incomplete sentences. They should begin by crossing out all the inappropriate pronouns according to whether their partner is female or male. Then each S should complete the sentences according to what they think their partner will say. When they have finished, they swap papers and add up how many correct guesses they made.

Have a break

Students' Book

General themes: food and drink.

FOCUS ON VOCABULARY: food and drink; *would you like a/some, I'd like ..., I'll have ..; one and ones.*
FOCUS ON GRAMMAR: Present Simple (2); *do you ever...?*; positive and negative sentences, all persons; questions and short answers; frequency adverbs (*never, sometimes, usually* and *always*).
SKILLS: listening (the weather forecast and the song *Singin' in the rain*; reading (holiday questionnaire); vocabulary (opposites of adjectives); writing (a postcard).
SOCIAL ENGLISH: money and shopping for food.

Workbook

GRAMMAR: Present Simple (2); Present Continuous or Present Simple?
VOCABULARY: food.
WRITING: an immigration form; punctuation.
PRONUNCIATION: silent letters.

FOCUS ON VOCABULARY

Food and drink

- Snack food and drinks.
- Countable and uncountable nouns, *a* and *some*.
- *One/s* used as a substitute for countable nouns.
- *'ll* introduced as the functional exponent for making decisions.
- Requests and offers.

- **Countable and uncountable nouns** This whole area can be difficult for SS to grasp. Although it is possible to make certain uncountable nouns plural, e.g. *two teas/coffees/ yogurts*, it is less confusing at this level if you tell SS not to use the plural form with uncountable nouns and highlight that they can make plural forms by stating the quantity e.g. *two cups of tea/coffee.*

Pronunciation Point out the word stress on the following compounds *'orange juice, 'mineral water* (noun + noun) but *hot 'chocolate* (adjective and noun) and *Apple 'Macintosh* (brand name).

SS often pronounce the *u* in *biscuits* and the *a* in *toasted.*

The consonant cluster /sps/ in *crisps* is difficult for many SS.

Highlight features of linkage such as *cup‿of* /kʌpəv/, *glass‿of‿orange* /glæsəvɒrɪndʒ/.

Consonant vowel links certainly help SS to achieve a better sense of rhythm and it's worth pointing them out whenever they occur.

- ***one/s*** is used to avoid repetition of the noun. It can't be used with uncountable nouns.
- ***some*** The SS have already met *some* in CHECK YOUR ENGLISH and Unit 1, but it was restricted to plural nouns. In this section it is used with uncountable nouns. Remind them that it is used with both plural and uncountable nouns.

Pronunciation Encourage them to use the weak form of *some* /səm/.

- **Language style** is highlighted. Styles of language can be manipulated to convey many moods and messages, e.g. very polite forms can be used to show sarcasm, and it isn't as simple as polite/impolite, formal/informal. However, it's still useful to indicate which forms can be used in different situations. The conversation includes more formal and less formal ways of offering. *Would you like...? Do you want...?* Whereas either form could be used with a friend, the more polite form, *Would you like...?* is used when the assistant addresses the customer. This can be seen as being more respectful.
- ***'ll*** is introduced as a lexical phrase used for making decisions. We recommend that you only illustrate its functional use and avoid grammatical explanation (see SB Unit 7 page 78 for other uses of *'ll*).

 **Students' Book** (page 36)

Exercise 1a) As a lead-in, establish the meaning of *count.* If possible, take in two cups, one filled with water. Pour the water from one cup to the other. While you're doing this ask them to count the water. They can't. Establish this is *uncountable.* Hold up three fingers and ask SS to count them. They can. Establish this is *countable.* Other examples could be *air* and *door.* Then ask SS to read the grammar box page 36. Allow SS a few minutes to work on their own. They could then join three or four other SS to see if between them they can identify most of the items.

Note that the main photograph and the small photographs contain words that are not on the menu. However all the items provide vocabulary support for this section and the next and some are just useful to SS, e.g. *salt and pepper*. It must be stressed that the items in the photographs provide vocabulary *support* and are not meant to match exactly the items on the menu, e.g. *ham* is shown but not *ham salad/roll/sandwich*. You might want to begin with a quick vocabulary check on the small lettered photographs a–m before doing any work on the menu. Alternatively, you could ask SS to brainstorm as many food items as they know the words for in English. Which are the same in their language? Pay attention to pronunciation, e.g. the silent *u* in *biscuit*, the stress in *'sandwich*. Note that *coffee* and *tea* came up in CHECK YOUR ENGLISH and that there are chocolate biscuits and cakes to help with *hot chocolate*. Show in the photographs the words for *packet*, *pot*, *cup*, *glass* and *bottle*.

Items on the menu: a (soup), c (lemon), e (chicken), g (ham), h (yogurt), i (tea), j (chocolate cakes), k (salad), l (cheese), m biscuits.
Items not on the menu: b (onion), d (salt and pepper), f (eggs).
n (crisps), o (cola), p (mineral water), q (orange juice).

Exercise 1b) Encourage SS to use the consonant vowel links and weak forms (see L). Focus attention on how prices are said. We needn't say *pence* if the price involves pounds: *three pounds twenty-five*, but without pounds we say *pence*: *twenty-five pence* or *p*. This will be a preview for the SOCIAL ENGLISH section at the end of this unit.

[3.1]
Food
A ham sandwich is two pounds ten.
A ham roll is two pounds.
A ham salad is three pounds fifteen.
A cheese sandwich is two pounds twenty-five.
A cheese roll is two pounds five p.
A cheese salad is three pounds forty.
A chicken sandwich is two pounds fifty.
A chicken roll is two pounds thirty.
A chicken salad is three pounds fifty.
Tomato soup is two pounds fifteen.
A packet of biscuits is ninety-five p.
A chocolate cake is eighty p.
A lemon cake is eighty p.
A fruit cake is eighty p.
Natural yogurt is eighty-five p.
Fruit yogurt is eighty-five p.
A packet of crisps is seventy-five p.

Drinks
A pot of tea is one pound forty.
A cup of tea is sixty-five p.
A pot of coffee is one pound seventy.
A cup of coffee is eighty p.
Hot chocolate is one pound thirty.
A glass of orange juice is one pound fifty.
A large glass of cola is one pound twenty.
A small glass of cola is ninety p.
A bottle of mineral water is seventy-five p.

Exercise 1c) Continue to focus on features of sound linking.

Exercise 2

[3.2]
ASSISTANT: Hello. Can I help you?
LUKE: Yes, I'd like a glass of cola, please.
ASSISTANT: A large one?
LUKE: No, small, please. And a chicken roll and some crisps.
ASSISTANT: Cheese and onion crisps?
LUKE: No, plain ones, please. Oh, and a cup of coffee.
ASSISTANT: Do you take sugar?
LUKE: Yes, two, please.
ASSISTANT: OK. Here you are. Is that it? So – that comes to four pounds seventy-five altogether, please.
LUKE: Thank you.

A chicken roll, a packet of plain crisps, a glass of cola and a cup of coffee.

Exercise 2a)
1h 2e 3g 4a 5f 6j 7d 8i 9b 10c

Exercise 2b) You may need to pause after each sentence to allow SS time to check. However, when the order has been established, play the cassette through again without stopping.

Exercise 2c) You could work with SS to identify consonant vowel linking in the conversation before they practise it, e.g. *a glass‿of*, *a cup‿of*.

Exercise 3a) and b)
Ask SS to read the grammar box illustrating the use of *one* and *ones*. Meanwhile write on the board.

1 *These are Belgian chocolates. Would you like a Belgian chocolate?*

2 *I'd like some oranges. Big oranges, please.*

Ask SS to think about what they have read and to improve these sentences with *one* and *ones*. Then play the cassette.

[3.3]
JEFF: What do you want?
JILL: A roll, I think.
JEFF: Chicken?
JILL: No, a cheese one, please. What about you?
JEFF: I think I'll have a ham sandwich, and a strawberry yoghurt.
ASSISTANT: Would you like something to drink?
JEFF: Yes, hot chocolate for me. But, what about you, Jill?
JILL: Nothing, thanks. Or have they got any mineral water?
ASSISTANT: Of course. Here you are. Would you like to pay altogether?
JEFF: Yes, that's fine. How much is it?
ASSISTANT: Seven pounds, five p.
JEFF: Thanks. Here you are.
ASSISTANT: Ninety-five p change. Thank you very much.

Jill has a cheese roll and some mineral water. Jeff has a ham sandwich, a strawberry yogurt and some hot chocolate.

Exercise 3c) Focus on style (see L). You could also point out that *I'd like a ...* is considered to be more polite than *I want a ...*

Would you like something to drink? is more polite.

Exercise 3d) Again, ask SS to think about sound linking when they practise. To encourage them to do the best they can, and practise more than once in order to improve, you could ask each group to perform for another group who then reciprocate.

Exercise 4a and b) These speaking activities allow SS to make language choices rather than working from a set dialogue and they will probably make more mistakes. Note the ones you hear and use them as the basis for a review activity in the following lesson, e.g. an exercise which includes correct and incorrect sentences where SS have to identify the incorrect ones and correct them.

Extra material and ideas

1 WB pages 24–25, Exercises 11, 12 and 14.

P **2 Crossword** pages 126, 3.1. Food and Drink.

Across	Down
2 soup 5 mineral water	1 sandwich 3 orange
8 chicken 9 bacon	4 cheese 5 milk 6 apple
11 strawberries 12 sugar	7 onion 8 crisps 10 bread

P **3 An Action Chain** page 126, 3.2. Photocopy the material and cut it up. (If you can enlarge the pictures on the photocopier then this is recommended.) This action chain is to practise: *Would you like a drink? Would you like something to eat? Yes, I'll have a /some ______, please.* Reviewing food and drink vocabulary. If possible, stand SS in a circle and demonstrate the activity with one of the cards. Turn to the S on your right, show them the picture of food or drink and ask: *Would you like a drink? Would you like something to eat?* Elicit from the S or supply, *Yes, I'll have some /a _____ please.* Let this card be passed around and make sure the question and answer are being practised. Then feed pictures in at various points in the circle so that SS don't have to wait so long to get a card. When the card has gone round all the SS, remove it from the circle. If you hear a lot of mistakes, stop the activity and focus on the problem before continuing. Other questions and answers can be practised later, e.g. *Have you got any/ a _______? Yes, here you are.*, or *No, I'm afraid we haven't.*

FOCUS ON GRAMMAR

Present Simple (2): *Do you ever ...?*

A • Present Simple: *I/ you/ we/ they* positive, negative, questions, short answers.
• Adverbs of frequency: *always/ usually/ sometimes/ never* with the verb *to be* and Present Simple.
• Review Present Continuous (time now) and contrast with Present Simple.

L • **Present Simple** Reinforce the concept of habit/routine/general truth which was introduced in Unit 2 with the third person singular. In this unit SS focus on *I/ you/ we/ they* and the use of *do* in negatives/questions and short answers.

Pronunciation *Do you _____ ?* is often pronounced /dʒə/ and *do* is often reduced to /də/ in *Do they ____ ? Do we _____?*

• **Adverbs of frequency** follow the verb *to be* and generally precede the main verb in the Present Simple. Certain adverbs can be placed in initial, mid and end position, e.g. *Suddenly he left. He suddenly left. He left suddenly.* Most adverbs can be placed in the mid and end position e.g. *I often go there. I go there often.* However, for this level it's wiser to play safe and tell SS to place the adverb in the mid position. Point out that although *never* is negative the verb retains the third person *-s* . Compare these for SS: *He doesn't eat ham. He never eats ham.*

• **Present Simple and Present Continuous** Having two verb forms referring to the present is often confusing for SS. Only contrast the concepts of *now* vs. routine (see CHECK YOUR ENGLISH for Present Continuous). Present Continuous and Present Simple used for future plans is in Unit 7 SOCIAL ENGLISH page 78.

Students' Book (page 38)

Exercise 1a) Begin by reviewing any of the grammar sections from Unit 2, e.g. ask questions about Antoine de Caunes, *Does he like tea? Tell me something else about him* etc. Write the question, answers and a positive sentence on the board to one side. This will act as a reminder and a comparison when you focus on the form for *I, you, we, they.* Using the picture in the SB, establish the situation: a Russian journalist interviewing English people about what they eat every day. Ask SS to look at the first question and write it on the board. Compare it with the third person question on the board. Ask SS to identify the difference and the similarity, *do* vs. *does*, the main verb is in the infinitive and the word order is the same in both cases. Use colour, boxes, underlining etc. to give visual support.

Model the questions for SS using sound linking and weak forms /dʒə/ for *Do you... ?* so the SS recognise it when they hear the cassette.

Exercise 1b) PW. Check that SS understand *Thai* as in *Thai* food (*Thailand* = country, *Thai* = language/people/adjective).

2D 3E 4B 5A

Exercise 1c) Before playing the cassette, ask a stronger pair of SS to tell you their answers. Write these on the board and ask if the others agree. Then play the cassette and check. You shouldn't need to play it more than once as it only requires SS to recognise sentences.

[3.4]
SERGEY: Do you drink tea or coffee?
PETER: Both. I drink coffee in the mornings to wake me up and I have a cup of tea in the afternoons.
SERGEY: Do you like foreign food?
PETER: Yes, I do. I love it. I cook Italian and Thai food at home.
SERGEY: When do you have your main meal?
PETER: In the evenings, at seven. I don't eat a lot at lunchtime – just a sandwich and some soup.
SERGEY: Do you drink beer with your meals?
PETER: No, I don't. I like wine or water with meals. But I drink beer when I go to the pub.
SERGEY: Do you ever eat bacon and eggs for breakfast?
PETER: I don't have breakfast – there isn't time. But we have bacon and eggs on Sundays.

Exercise 1d) Before you begin, ask SS to tell you something we know about Peter. Check that SS use the third person singular *-s*. Refer back to the examples on the board.

1 Does he ever eat foreign food? Yes, he does.
2 Does he ever drink wine? Yes, he does.
3 Where does he drink beer? At the pub.
4 What does he eat at lunchtime? A sandwich and some soup.
5 When does he drink coffee? In the mornings.

Exercise 1e) This is an awareness-raising and not a practice exercise, comparing the Present Continuous used for **happening now** and the Present Simple used for **habits and routines**. Before beginning, guide SS to the concepts, e.g. on the board write the cues *you/wear/jeans?* SS ask you the question. Then write *s(he)/wear/jeans/now?* Ask one S to ask another this question about you. Write both the questions and answers on the board. Correct any mistakes and ask SS what the difference is in meaning. When you have established the idea of now vs. routine, focus on the questions in the SB.

1 Is he drinking coffee now? No he isn't.
2 Is he speaking to Sergey now? Yes, he is.

Exercise 1f) Focus on the example and ask SS why Sergey uses the Present Simple question and not the Present Continuous. After SS have finished, you could invite them to ask you the questions to see if anyone has similar routines/habits to you.

Exercise 2 Possibly, draw the cline from the SB on the board to focus attention. Point to the percentage and repeat the words *always* and *never*. If you can think of an example which is relevant to the class to illustrate these it would help clarify meaning, e.g. a S who always comes early, does her homework, always wears glasses, never wears X, never comes late, never forgets her homework etc. Draw a line to represent the 50% mark on the cline and ask SS if *sometimes* and *usually* are more or less than 50%. Again if you can use personalised examples it may be more meaningful and memorable. Try to ensure all the personalised examples are of a positive or humorous nature. For example, we don't recommend, *Juan never does a stroke of work*, no matter how tempting it might be! Then allow SS a moment to read the gapped sentences before you play the cassette. You could ask them to predict the gapped word.

[3.5]

1 I **always** drink coffee in the mornings and I **sometimes** have a cup of tea in the afternoons.
2 I **sometimes** cook Italian and Thai food at home.
3 I **never** eat a lot at lunchtime.
4 I **usually** drink beer when I go to the pub.
5 I don't **usually** have breakfast. But we **always** have bacon and eggs on Sundays.

Exercise 2b) Focus on word order of adverbs (see L).

1 The adverbs *(always, usually, sometimes, never)* come **before** the main verb.
2 The adverbs *usually* and *always* come **after** *don't*.

Exercise 2c) The *Language reference* includes examples of initial and end position of adverbs. However, tell SS that they won't make a mistake if they put adverbs after the verb *to be* and before the main verb.

After.

Exercise 2d) Let SS choose whether they want to work alone or in pairs.

2 don't have 3 think 4 usually have 5 cook 6 eat 7 usually drink 8 sometimes have

Exercise 3a) Note that the pictures are there to stimulate ideas and you might want to check the vocabulary first, e.g. *have a shower, have a bath.* Monitor SS and if mistakes are frequent, stop the activity, focus on accuracy and then let them continue.

1 What time do you get up?
2 Do you have a shower or a bath?
3 What do you have for breakfast?
4 Do you read the newspaper or listen to the radio?
5 How do you get to work?
6 When do you have your main meal?
7 When do you finish work?
8 What do you do in the evenings?

Exercise 3b) Encourage SS to take notes from the listening. Stop after each question and answer to allow them time to note the answer down. You may need to play the cassette twice.

[3.6]

In the week I always wake up early because my alarm clock goes off at five o'clock. I usually go back to sleep and get up at about six. Then I have a shower, get dressed and have a big breakfast – soup and meat. I also listen to the radio for about half an hour. I get a bus to town. I start work at eight and then I have lunch at twelve. Lunch is the main meal of the day in Russia and we have three courses. I finish work at five and go home. I'm very tired so I usually stay in and watch television. I sometimes visit friends but I never go to restaurants because they're too expensive. I go to bed early, about ten o'clock.

Exercise 3c)
Note that this exercise revises the third person *-s* as a contrast to the *I* form in Exercise 3b).

Suggested answers:
He gets up at about six.
He has a shower and gets dressed.
He has a big breakfast.
He listens to the radio for about half an hour.
He gets a bus to town.
He starts work at eight.
He has lunch at twelve.
He finishes work at five and goes home.
He stays in and watches television or visits friends.
He never goes to restaurants.
He goes to bed early about ten o'clock.

Exercise 3d) Again, this is an awareness exercise. It isn't meant to offer extensive practise. Focus on the concept of time around the present not the exact time represented by *now*.

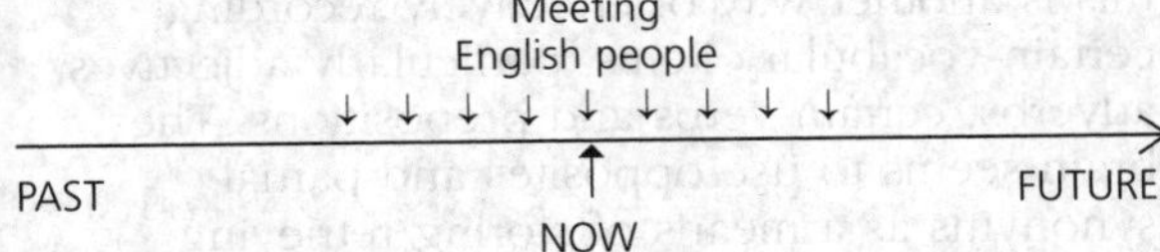

He's meeting English people. He's interviewing/talking to English people. He's drinking English beer. He's eating English food.

Exercise 4a) and b) SS could interview each other before or after doing the exercise but only if you haven't already used the idea in this grammar section.

Exercise 5a and b) Get a few suggestions about the routines of the people in the photographs (Michelle Pfeiffer, Eric Cantona, Prince Charles and Tina Turner) to help less imaginative SS. You could give guide questions if you feel your SS need them: *What time do you get up? What do you have for breakfast? Who do you have lunch with? What do you do in the afternoons? Who do you have dinner with? What do you do in the evenings? When do you go to bed?* Alternatively, substitute the photographs with people they know or are interested in.

Exercise 5c) Encourage SS to exchange letters with another S to check for mistakes. The letters could be displayed round the room and SS could write on the letter the name of the person that they think it is.

Extra material and ideas

1 WB pages 21–25, Exercises 1–4, 6–10 and 15.
2 True or False? Write the following on the board:
WHAT? WHEN? DO YOU EVER?
eat for breakfast go to bed read a newspaper
watch on TV get up have a shower
favourite drink your birthday write a letter
sport/play study go to the cinema music/like
have your evening meal have a holiday
wash your hair go out in the evening

Divide the SS into groups of four or five. They take it in turn to be interviewed by the other members in the group. Each member asks one question using the prompts on the board. The SS being interviewed should tell two lies and give two correct answers. The interviewers have to decide which are the lies. Do a demonstration by getting SS to ask you questions. Check that they know when it's a Present Simple question, when it's a question with the verb *to be* and the meaning of *How often ...?*
4 Write the following question cues on the board and ask SS to form the questions about the **weekends** (or the equivalent days off if religious days occur on days other than Sunday).
1 Sleep/late? (What time/get up?) Example: *Did you sleep late?*
2 Go/shopping? (Where? What/buy?)
3 What/wear at weekends?
4 Go out/Saturday evening? (Where?)
5 When/go bed?
When you have checked these they should ask at least three SS the questions.

SKILLS

- Listening for gist and detail.
- Vocabulary: related to the weather and holidays, adjectives and their opposites.
- Reading and writing postcards.

Listening

- Highlight that *It's raining/snowing* is the Present Continuous whilst *sunny, cloudy* etc. are adjectives. Note we can use *rainy* as an attributive adjective, *a rainy day*.
- Although the song includes unfamiliar vocabulary there is a pre-listening activity to check meaning. In addition you might want to preteach the words *smile* and *face*.

Students' Book (page 40)
Exercise 1a) As well as asking about today's weather you could give the following cues *yesterday?* and *tomorrow?*
You may need to pause the cassette to allow SS time to write their answers in the table.

[3.7]

ANNOUNCER: This is the world's weather at one o'clock today. Here in Britain it's cloudy everywhere, with some rain, particularly in the Manchester area. Temperatures are low – ten degrees Celsius . But on the other side of the world in Argentina it's a warm twenty-four degrees Celsius and very sunny. In Hong Kong it's a mild eighteen degrees Celsius and quite windy. However, parts of North America are having their first snow of the year. On the east coast, people in New York are waking up to snow showers and a cold three degrees Celsius. But if you think that's cold, in Moscow the temperature is a freezing minus ten degrees Celsius with fog, making driving very difficult.

Exercise 1b) Cue SS to ask you the question. Just in case *would* causes problems emphasise that you and they are in class but the question is asking where you would like to be. Use the short form *I'd* when you answer the cued question and encourage SS to do the same when they answer.

Buenos Aires Sun 24
Hong Kong Wind 18
New York Snow 3
Moscow Fog -10

Exercise 1c) Make sure SS know how to say *de'grees* and *'Centigrade* or *'Celsius*.

This is a self-checking exercise.

Exercise 2a) The film of *Singin' in the rain* was made in 1952. Gene Kelly, the actor in the photograph, died in 1996. It is considered a classic and was directed by Stanley Donan and Gene Kelly.

[3.8] (See SB, page 140, for all the words to *Singin' in the rain and not just those printed in the unit.*)

Ask SS why they think he looks so happy when the weather is so bad.

He's happy.

Exercise 2b) If you think this will take too much time, divide the task between SS and ask them to teach each other. Check the meanings of the words.

glorious: very beautiful; *feeling*: something you feel; *laugh*: the sound you make when you think something is funny; *heart*: the part of your body which sends the blood round your body; *stormy*: when the weather is very bad, with wind and rain; *chase*: to follow someone/something quickly to catch them; *smile*: what your face does when you are happy; *ready*: to be prepared for what you're going to do.

Exercise 2c) Allow SS time to read through the lyrics before you play the cassette. You can pause after each line to allow SS to note the number down, or play the cassette several times.

(See SB, page 140 for the words to *Singin' in the rain*.)

Exercise 2d) Write the phonemic symbols for the vowel /eɪ/ on the board above the words, and the phonemics for each word next to the words, *chase* /tʃeɪs/, *place* /pleɪs/. Likewise, write /ʌ/ above *love* and /lʌv/ next to it. Then add the rhyming words.

Face rhymes with *chase* and *place*. *Above* rhymes with *love*.

Exercise 2e) Check SS know the words and concepts of the seasons.

Reading, writing and vocabulary

- Check the following : *'campsite, 'sunbathe, 'seaside, 'countryside* for Exercise 3. For Exercise 5 check, *fast 'food, 'art galleries.*
- Highlight the use of the preposition *by*, ***by** plane, car* etc.
- Opposites: adjectives, e.g. *ex'citing* and *'boring.*

Students' Book (page 41)

Exercise 3a) and b) Make sure SS don't add the cue to the head question, e.g. *Where do you go to the seaside?* They need the inverted question *Do you ...?* for the questionnaire. You may need to give help with the cues e.g. *Other? Other places? Do you go to other places? Do you travel by coach or bike?*

Exercise 3c) Get feedback on how many SS like the same kind of holiday.

Exercise 4a) Get SS to read silently.

1 A 2 B 3 A 4 A

Exercise 4b) Again, the time for this activity can be shortened by dividing the class into Groups A and B and assigning words to each group to check. SS then teach each other. However, if they are becoming more proficient at using a dictionary or you think they know some of the vocabulary, let them work individually. Check with the whole class, writing the pair of opposites on the board. You could mention that this is another way of effectively recording certain vocabulary items, particularly adjectives, adverbs, certain verbs and prepositions. The brain seems to use opposites and partial synonyms as a means of storing/retrieving vocabulary based on association.

cheap/expensive awful/lovely boring/exciting hot/cold dirty/clean old/new quiet/noisy slow/fast bad/good

Exercise 4c) It would be a bonus if real postcards could be used to write on! Let SS read each other's 'postcards'.

Extra material and ideas

1 Crossword page 127, 3.3.

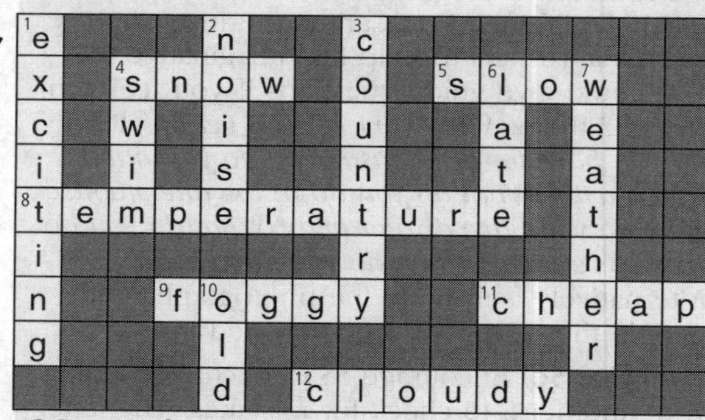

2 Postcards page 128, 3.4. Divide the class into Groups, A and B, and hand out the appropriate postcard. SS have to change the underlined adjectives on each postcard to their opposites. When they have finished, they find a partner from the other group and check their answers.

3 Opposites page 127, 3.5. Divide the class into groups of four. Copy and cut up the material for each group. The words should be spread out faced down on a desk. SS take it in turns to turn over two words. If the words are opposites, the S can keep them and has another turn. If they aren't antonyms, the words are put face down again and the next S has a turn. The winner is the one who has collected the most word pairs.

SOCIAL ENGLISH

- Money.
- Collocation of quantity and food.

- Preteach the following items: *notes, coins pounds, pence* and *p* /p/.
- The word *money* is uncountable which is often difficult for SS to accept. Highlight that we say *some* with *money*, but *a/4* etc. (*pound/s*) with *I need some money. I need a pound.*
- SS may know some of the more basic collocations in this section, e.g. *a cup of, a bottle of, a glass of,* but the majority will probably be unknown items. Uncountable nouns: *cheese, juice, shampoo, chewing gum, soap.* Countable nouns: *potatoes, sweets* and *matches.*

Pronunciation Soundlinking from the preceding consonant to *of* /əv/occurs in all the examples, e.g. bottle of /bɒtləv/. *Kilo_of* uses an intrusive /w/ sound to link the two vowels at the word boundary /kiːləʊwəv/.

Students' Book (page 42)

Exercise 1a) If you have access to real British money, take it in. Note that the word *specimen* has been included in the photograph for legal reasons. SS should ignore it but if they are curious you could say it means *example*.

[3.9]
1 five pounds
2 a pound
3 (a) fifty p
4 two ten ps
5 twenty p

Exercise 1b) You may want to point out that if you only have five pound notes and you need coins, you ask, *Have you got any change?*

1 the five pound note 2 the fifty p, two ten ps and twenty p

Exercise 2a) If you have access to real American money, take it in.

[3.10]
1 twenty dollars
2 five dollars
3 two dollars
4 twenty-five cents
5 ten cents
6 three cents

Point out the collocation for an American dollar is *dollar bill* not *note.*

Exercise 2b)
$27.38

Exercise 3a) Allow time for SS to read through the phrases, and pause the cassette to let SS match the picture with the phrase. Highlight the linkage in the phrases (see L).

[3.11]
1 a packet of chewing gum
2 a bottle of shampoo
3 a piece of cheese
4 a bar of soap
5 a kilo of potatoes
6 a box of matches
7 a can of cola
8 a carton of milk

1 n 2 e 3 c 4 b 5 a 6 f 7 d 8 g

Exercise 3b) You could take the opportunity to remind SS which nouns are countable and which are uncountable. Ask SS to practise saying these in preparation for Exercise 3c).

Exercise 3c)
a bar/piece of chocolate, a packet of cigarettes, a can/kilo of tomatoes, a packet of crisps, a bottle of mineral water, a box/packet of tissues, a piece of cake, a bottle/can of beer, a kilo of onions, a packet/kilo of sugar, a bottle/can/carton of orange juice

Exercise 4 Tell SS to make a note of the price next to the item. Find out who spent the most and who spent the least.

Extra material and ideas.

Money quiz page 128, 3.6. Divide the class into pairs. Read out the names of the following currencies and ask SS to write either the country of origin or the nationality to revise vocabulary from Unit 1 FOCUS ON VOCABULARY. Then hand out the worksheet and SS continue the exercise. Note that sometimes there is more than one possible answer, e.g. dollar for the USA, Australia, Canada.

Currency	Country	Nationality
dollars	the USA	American
	Australia	Australian
	Canada	Canadian
pounds sterling	Britain	British
yen	Japan	Japanese
drachma	Greece	Greek
peseta	Spain	Spanish
franc	France	French
	Belgium	Belgian
	Switzerland	Swiss
rouble	Russia	Russian
ringgit	Malaysia	Malaysian
schilling	Austria	Austrian
peso	Argentina	Argentinian/Argentine
	Mexico	Mexican
forint	Hungary	Hungarian
zloty	Poland	Polish
lire	Italy	Italian

Practise and check key (Units 1-3)

PRACTISE

1 *To be:* questions and answers

1
2 am 3 'm
2
1 is 2 's 3 Is 4 is 5 Are 6 aren't, 're not 7 's
8 's
3
1 Am 2 aren't, 're not 3 are

2 *Have* and *has got*

2 Has Sue got a sandwich ? No, she hasn't.
3 Has Jim got a watch? Yes, he has.
4 Has Sue got a dictionary? Yes, she has.
5 Has Jim got a stamp? No, he hasn't.
6 Has Sue got a pen? Yes, she has.
7 Have Sue and Jim got drinks? Yes, they have.
8 Have they got (any) pizzas? No, they haven't.

3 The Present Simple (1)

a)
1 lives 2 travels 3 doesn't work 4 doesn't like 5 arrives 6 opens 7 makes 8 has 9 reads 10 loves 11 meets 12 finishes 13 gets 14 watches 15 does

b)
3 Does Alice like the journey to London? 4 What does Alice do at lunchtime? 5 Why does Alice like her job? 6 When does she finish work? 7 What does she do in the evenings?

c)
3 No, she doesn't. 4 She has a sandwich in the office and reads the newspaper. 5 She meets a lot of different people. 6 She finishes work at five o'clock. 7 She watches television or does some housework.

4 Present Simple (2)

a)
2 Do you 3 do 4 What do you like/eat

b)
6 Do you have 7 do 8 Do you speak 9 don't

CHECK

1 The Present

2 's 3 's 4 've got 5 are 6 watch 7 don't understand 8 speak 9 are 10 're working 11 don't usually work 12 start 13 finish 14 is 15 speaks 16 go 17 are

2 Correct the mistakes

2 fifth of March 3 Greece 4 to 5 some 6 usually have 7 's raining 8 a 9 her 10 theirs, mine

3 Prepositions

a)
2 from 3 to 4 at 5 on 6 by 7 on 8 with 9 to 10 on 11 by 12 in 13 at 14 At 15 to 16 to

b)
2 in 3 next to 4 under 5 in front of

4 Vocabulary

1 The weather: rain, snow, clouds, windy
2 The office: briefcase, diary, drawer, shelf
3 Food: cheese, biscuit, onion, soup
4 The family: daughter, wife, niece, cousin

TEST

There is a progress test, for Units 1–3 on pages 150 and 151 of this book for you to photocopy for your students. See page 158 for the Key.

Fashion and films

Students' Book

General themes: clothes and films.

FOCUS ON VOCABULARY: clothes; colours; revision of Present Continuous.
FOCUS ON GRAMMAR: *can* and *can't* for ability; adjectives and adverbs of manner.
SKILLS: reading (Stephen Spielberg's films); vocabulary (meaning from context); listening (people talking about films); writing (a film review).
REVIEW: vocabulary (wordsearch); using your grammar (bingo and a letter to a pen friend).

Workbook

GRAMMAR: *can* and *can't*; adjectives or adverbs; revision.
VOCABULARY: clothes; opposites (verbs); verb/noun collocation.
WRITING: spelling; replying to an invitation.
PRONUNCIATION: *can* and *can't*.

FOCUS ON VOCABULARY

People and clothes

- Describing people: adjectives, clothes, colours, simple physical descriptions, personality, accessories e.g., *a watch*.
- Review position of adjectives introduced in Unit 1 SKILLS Vocabulary (page 24).
- Review of frequency adverbs and Present Simple.
- Review of Present Continuous.

- **New adjectives:** *kind, a'ttractive, sad, in'telligent.*
- **Adjective order** to describe hair, length before colour. There is more on adjective order in SB Unit 12 (page 114).
- **Pronunciation** word stress: with most of the items in this section the stress is on the first syllable so pay particular attention to words which don't follow this pattern, e.g. *in'telligent, a'ttractive*.

When a noun is preceded by an adjective the primary stress is typically on the noun. However, there is usually a strong secondary stress on the adjective e.g. *green coat*.

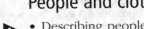

Students' Book (page 46)

Exercise 1a) To find out what colours and clothes SS know, you could begin with a variation of the game I Spy. You think of something in the room and say, *I spy* or *I see something beginning with the letter XXX and it's (colour).* If your SS don't know the word, let them point to the item they think it is. If they're correct, they choose the next item, and so on. Alternatively, you could ask SS to name clothes for cold weather and clothes for hot weather. Then do the exercise. Make sure SS understand when the item of clothing extends over the parts of the body represented by the letters A and B.

1a) cap = A, socks = B, coat = A and B, jacket = A, jeans = B, sweater = A, trousers = B, skirt = B, hat = A, cardigan = A, trainers = B, dress = A and B, T-shirt = A, shoes = B

Exercise 1b)

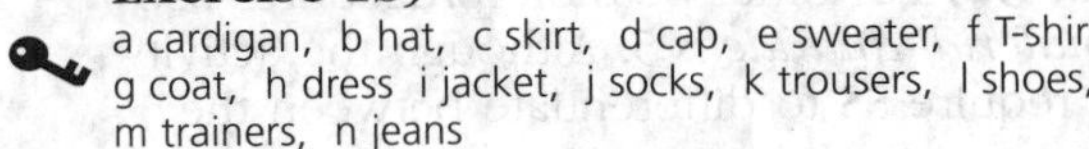

a cardigan, b hat, c skirt, d cap, e sweater, f T-shirt, g coat, h dress i jacket, j socks, k trousers, l shoes, m trainers, n jeans

Exercise 1c)

Pauline's wearing a red hat and a red cardigan. Steve's T-shirt is yellow. Alex's jacket is black. Pauline's wearing a blue sweater and a blue skirt. Steve's cap, socks and jeans are blue. Alex's dress is green. Jim's trousers and socks are grey.

Exercise 1d) You could read this aloud. Tell SS to stop you when they hear a mistake. They correct you and then you carry on. This could extend into a PW activity. The pair agree on a S to describe. One of the pair describes the person and the other stops them when they hear a mistake.

1 Steve's wearing blue jeans, a yellow T-shirt and a blue sweater. He's got blue socks and white trainers. He's wearing a blue cap.

2 Pauline's wearing a long blue skirt, a red cardigan and a red hat.

Exercise 1e) If you have used any of the suggested games, leave this exercise out. You may have reached overkill!

Alex is wearing a green dress, a short black jacket and black shoes. Jim is wearing grey trousers, grey socks, brown shoes and a brown coat.

Exercise 2 If you think SS have practised this vocabulary enough, leave this activity out or use it as a revision activity in a future lesson.

Exercise 3a)
To revise letters of the alphabet and spelling, ask the SS to spell the words from the gap fill and write them on the board as they suggest them. Correct where necessary.

[4.1]

PAULINE: I'm **wearing** a **red cardigan** in this photo. I love **red**. It's my favourite **colour**. I've **got** about **ten sweaters** at home and **five** of them are **red**. I also love **blue**. All my **skirts, dresses** and **trousers** are **blue**.

Exercise 3b) Ask SS to guess what colours you like and don't like based on the colours they have seen you wearing. Ask them to interview other SS about colours and clothes. See if they can find someone who has similar taste.

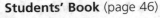

Exercise 3c) To highlight the difference, ask SS to tell you why the Present Simple is used in Exercise 3b) and the Present Continuous in this exercise. You could ask SS to stand facing a partner. They should note what their partner is wearing. They then turn away from their partner and face a new partner. Without looking back they tell the new partner what the original partner is wearing. The new partner checks and corrects the description.

Exercise 4 Highlight the order of adjectives describing hair – length before colour. Let SS work individually if there has been a lot of group or pair work.

1 a) Pauline b) Jim c) Pauline d) Jim
2 a) Jim b) Alex c) Steve d) Pauline

Exercise 5a) For other possible procedures see *Extra material and ideas* 5. Although the activity doesn't require SS to differentiate between the following questions, you might choose to highlight the difference.

What's she like?

What does she look like?

Associate an appropriate answer with each question to show that the second question is only asking for a physical description.

Compare the statements: *She/He is friendly.* and *She/He looks friendly.* Ask SS which one we use when we **know** about the person to highlight the aspect of certainty vs. impression. Check the concepts of the adjectives: *sad* (opposite of *happy*), *kind* (set up a situation where you can help someone e.g. pile books onto a student then offer to help carry them), *attractive* (associate with *beautiful*), *intelligent* (associate with a famous person they will know, e.g. Einstein). Practise pronunciation and highlight the stress patterns.

Exercise 5b) Make sure SS realise they only need to write notes at this point. They could write single words next to the questions.

Exercise 5c) and d) The group's sentences could be displayed and SS could walk around and read each other's description.

Exercise 5e) SS could exchange their sentences with a partner and then could ask questions to get more information about the person their partner has described. Feedback could be telling the class about anything interesting they have found out about the person their partner described.

Extra material and ideas

1 WB page 29, Exercise 8.

2 Questionnaire: How much do you care about clothes and fashion? page 129, 4.1. Hand out the questionnaires to SS. Each S interviews two other SS. Limit the time to 5 minutes. SS form groups of four

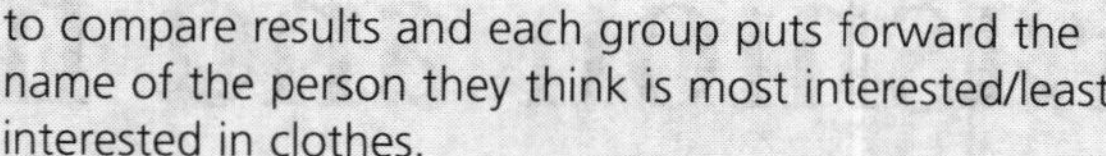

to compare results and each group puts forward the name of the person they think is most interested/least interested in clothes.

3 If possible, take in some magazines, clothes catalogues or pictures of people wearing different types of clothes. Divide the class into male and female (if appropriate). In groups of three, they try to find 4 items of clothing they would all be happy to wear and 4 items they would all like their girlfriend/boyfriend or husband/wife to wear. Two groups could then join and compare choices.

4 Place pictures of people round the room. They should share some similar physical characteristics and be wearing similar types of clothing. On the board write the following:

HAIR EYES HEIGHT CLOTHES OTHER *e.g. glasses, watch*
– She/He looks ... (*e.g. friendly*).

In pairs SS secretly choose two of the characters to describe. They discuss and write a simple description of each character. They exchange descriptions with another pair who then try to guess which pictures the original pair were looking at.

Alternatively, give each pair a picture. They write a description which includes 6 mistakes. They exchange the description and the picture with another pair who find and correct the 6 pieces of incorrect information.

5 A guessing game Describe a S in the class but use negatives e.g. *This person isn't wearing a white shirt.* Continue until someone guesses who you're thinking of. It's a process of elimination. Try not to look at the person you're describing. SS could continue the game in smaller groups once they understand the process. Alternatively, divide the class into groups of five or six. One of the group leaves the room. The others choose a member of the group. The first S returns and tries to find out who the group has chosen by asking questions, *Is this person wearing a ______?* The winner is the one who guesses correctly with the least number of questions. SS are only allowed to ask 1 direct question: *Is it X?* If they're wrong they are out of that round of the game.

FOCUS ON GRAMMAR

- *Can/can't* for ability.
- Adverbs of manner.
- Adjectival and adverbial phrases and modifiers: *not good/quite good/good/very good at X.*
- Review of Present Continuous.

- ***Can*** Without using unnecessary terminology, highlight that the modal auxiliary *can* has no third person *-s*, it is its own operator in questions and negatives, it comes before the main verb and it is followed by the base form of the verb. Highlight the spelling of *cannot* and point out it's unusual for the negative to be one word if it isn't a contracted form. Compare *do not, cannot/don't, can't.*

Pronunciation The weak form /kən/ is commonly used in statements and questions but is pronounced /kæn/ in short answers.

The negative is pronounced /kɑːnt/ in both statements and short answers.

• There is visual support to illustrate the vocabulary, e.g. *stand on one leg, spell X backwards* etc.

• **Adverbs** Highlight the common ending *-ly* but point out that there are irregular forms e.g. *good* → *well.* (Note that *friendly,* used in FOCUS ON VOCABULARY, is an adjective not an adverb.) The position of adverbs is a complex area of grammar as many of them can occur in initial, mid and final position. However, when evaluating how well something is done, as is the case in this section, the adverb is normally placed **after** the verb, e.g. *She sings well.* Highlight that the modifiers *quite* and *very* come before an adjective or adverb. The following irregular adverbs are introduced: *well, hard, fast.*

• **Adjectival phrases** *good at, very good at* etc. Highlight the use of the preposition *at,* which is followed by either a noun or gerund, e.g. *good at* ***English****, good at* ***cooking***.

Pronunciation Encourage the use of the weak form of *at* /ət/ and sound linking *good_at*.

Students' Book (page 48)

Can and *can't* for ability

Exercise 1a)

It's quite easy to convey the concept of *can/can't* for ability. The following is a suggestion you might like to use to illustrate the concept. Draw the faces above next to each other at the top of the board. Above the happy face write I can ... , above the sad face write I can't ...
(cannot)

Stand under the happy face and say: *I can speak English.* Move under the sad face and say: *but I can't speak X.* Highlight the use of the weak form (see L).

Then use the visuals in the SB to check the meaning of the vocabulary. Invite SS to ask you the questions and demonstrate any of the things you can do.

A stand on one leg B walk backwards in a straight line
C touch your nose with your tongue D touch your toes
E do the splits F stand on your head

Exercise 1b) Invite SS to ask you the questions and demonstrate any of the things you can do. SS can then quickly put a tick or a cross next the things they can and can't do.

Exercise 1c) and d) Practise pronunciation of the question and short answer. Highlight the use of the weak and strong form of *can* (see L). In the feedback if there are SS who are willing to demonstrate their ability, all the better. However, a S may not be dressed in a way that they can, for example, stand on their head and maintain a sense of modesty! This is a light-hearted activity, and should allow for much humour. Join in with the SS where you can. After the fun, highlight the forms for positive sentences, questions and short answers. Pay particular attention to the weak and strong forms (see L).

Exercise 2

[4.2]

1 I **can** speak French but I **can't** speak Spanish.
2 I **can't** ride a bicycle but I **can** drive a car.
3 I **can** play the piano but I **can't** play the guitar.

Exercise 3 and 4 If your SS are willing, you could ask some to come and mime what they can/can't do under the drawings of the faces – see Exercise 1a). The others guess what it is the S can do and what the S can't, but would like to be able to do.

Adjectives or adverbs?

Exercise 5a)

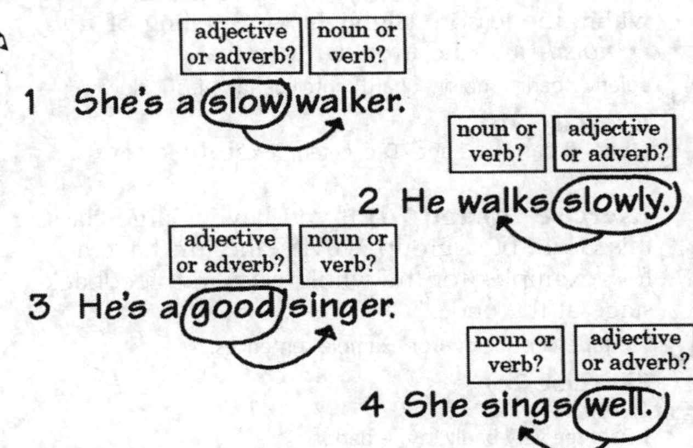

Use the examples above to clarify the different parts of speech. You could write up the following and put lines through to indicate the incorrect use of an adverb and adjective.

She's a ~~slowly~~ walker. He walks ~~slow~~.

Highlight that *-ly* is a common suffix for adverbs but point out that there are irregular adverbs: *good* → *well, fast* → *fast, hard* → *hard.*

Use the exercise in the SB to check that SS have understood.

Fluently is an adverb, it describes the verb *speak*.

Exercise 5b) SS often expect the preposition *in* in the phrase *good at X*. Allow time for SS to note their answers down. You may need to pause the cassette after each piece of information. Alternatively, you could play it through once but tell SS they will hear it again so they know if they miss it the first time they'll have another chance. Note that the gap fill is a description of what the mothers say. It is not the dialogue itself.

[4.3]
A: Ben's a good swimmer. He can swim very fast for a six-year old.
B: Can he?
A: Yes, and he can play football quite well now, too. What about George?
B: He doesn't like football or swimming, but he speaks Spanish fluently and he can sing and dance beautifully.
A: Can he?

Ben is a **good** swimmer. He can swim **very fast** and he can play football **quite well**, too. George speaks Spanish **fluently** and he can **sing** and **dance** beautifully.

Exercise 6 If you used the example sentences and visual support in Exercise 5a), you could repeat the same visual clues of circles and arrows to reinforce the part of speech and the word order.

1 good; well 2 quickly; slow 3 interesting 4 relaxing; quickly 5 easy; easily 6 hard 7 quietly 8 fast

Exercise 7a) Because these exercises may be quite short, remember to vary the pattern of interaction and classroom dynamics; individual, pair or group work or a whole class activity. This allows for a variety of pace and focus within the lesson. Highlight the spelling of *noisy* → *noisily* and the irregular adverbs.

quietly badly noisily hard intelligently fast slowly

Exercise 7b)

A bat, B parrot, C ant, D cheetah, E cat, F tortoise, G mouse

Exercise 7c) and 7d) If you have a large class, this could be a group activity and just have a few examples for the whole class in a feedback stage at the end.

See tapescript below for example sentences.

Exercise 7e)

[4.4]
1 Bats see very badly in the dark.
2 Parrots speak very noisily.
3 Ants work very hard.
4 Cheetahs can run very fast.
5 Cats are very intelligent.
6 Tortoises walk very slowly.
7 Mice are very quiet.

Exercise 7f) You could write some adjectives and adverbs on the board. Point to one e.g. *quite good at*, and everyone then thinks of something they are quite good at. Get feedback, see if people have mentioned similar things. Point to the next word and so on.

Extra material and ideas

1 WB page 26, Exercise 1, page 27, Exercises 2–4, page 28, Exercises 5–6.

2 PRACTISE AND CHECK, page 70 for more work on *can* and *can't* and adjectives and adverbs.

3 Find someone who Bingo Draw a box with nine squares on the board and ask SS to copy it. Write one of the following in each box: *can _____, can't _____, can _____ well, can't _____ very well, is good at _____, is not very good at _____, is quite good at _____, is good at _____, can _____ fast.*

In pairs SS decide what to put in the gaps, but after that they work independently so they should each make a copy of the square. In a class mingle activity they ask each other questions according to what they have put in the gap, e.g. *Can you swim well?* The winner is the S who is the first to get a name for each square.

P **4 Find the mistake** page 129, 4.2. Divide the class into groups A and B, and hand out a copy of the appropriate worksheet. They should work with another member of the same group and decide which sentences are incorrect and then correct them. Explain that not all the sentences are wrong. SS then work with a member of the other group. Together they will have all the correct sentences. Allow time to check that they have worked out which are the correct sentences. The activity focuses on all the grammar in this section and reviews grammar from earlier units.

Student A's sentences
1 He can play the piano.
2 You can't sing very well.
5 He never comes to class.
6 Can you do the splits?
8 You speak English well.
10 He runs fast.

Student B's sentences
3 Are you good at tennis?
4 My brother walks quite slowly.
7 She's a good swimmer.
9 She works hard.
11 They speak English fluently.

SKILLS

- Reading: scanning and reading for detail.
- Vocabulary: parts of speech, guessing meaning from context.
- Listening and writing: listening for detail, writing a short review of a film.

Reading

- There is quite a lot of unfamiliar vocabulary in the texts. However, items such as *toy plane*, *'prison camp, shark* etc. have visual representations. You may have to translate the word *'helicopter* or illustrate it. The following vocabulary will also probably be unfamiliar: *drops, 'crowded, coast, shark, attacks, look for, get away* (as in *escape*) but these form the basis of the vocabulary work in Exercise 3c). If SS seem anxious, reassure them that they will look at the meaning of the words in the exercises.

Students' Book (page 50)

Exercise 1 As a warmer and prediction exercise begin by asking what films are currently showing at local cinemas (if that's appropriate). Ask SS to name their favourite films, actors, type of film etc. To encourage SS to ask questions, invite them to ask you about your favourites. All the photographs relate to Steven Spielberg films. Once you have established the titles check to see if any S has seen any of them. Ask for their opinion.

Background information on Steven Spielberg and his films:

Steven Spielberg (1947–) American film director and producer. His films include: *Duel* (1971), *The Sugarland Express* (1974), *Jaws* (1975), *Close Encounters of the Third Kind* (1977), *Raiders of the Lost Ark* (1981), *ET* (1982), *Indiana Jones and the Temple of Doom* (1984), *Indiana Jones and the Last Crusade* (1989), *Hook* (1991), *Jurassic Park* (1993), *Schindler's List* (1993).

Exercise 2a) Don't focus on unfamiliar vocabulary at this point to see how well SS can look for clues even in texts which have unfamiliar vocabulary. They're only trying to locate which film it is at this point.

1 *Empire of the Sun* 2 *Jaws* 3 *Jurassic Park*

Exercise 2b) Preteach other items you feel are necessary for your SS. However, the vocabulary section asks SS to check words they haven't understood so make sure you don't preteach all unknown words (see L). The reading texts have been recorded on the Class Cassette for you to use if you want to reinforce the sound/spelling relationship.

Empire of the Sun, toy plane: photograph bottom left, prison camp: photograph bottom right
Jaws, shark: photograph top left, boat: photograph top centre
Jurassic Park, dinosaurs: photograph centre right, storm: photograph centre

Exercise 2c) Allow SS to refer to the text to find the answers otherwise this becomes a memory test rather than a comprehension check.

1T 2F 3F 4F 5T 6F

Exercise 2d) Monitor SS' question forms. If you hear a lot of mistakes, you could stop and focus on accuracy then let them continue. If there is a reasonable level of accuracy, just note the mistakes that occur and draw attention to them at some later point. You might want to consider correcting mistakes as they occur if you feel this wouldn't cause SS to lose confidence.

1 What toy does he drop? His toy plane.
2 Why do the three men go out in Brody's boat? To look for the shark.
3 Is Brody a policeman? Yes.
4 What was on the island? A park full of dinosaurs.

Extra material and ideas

1 Film reviews Write the titles of films currently showing at local cinemas and ones which have recently come off. If a S has seen one of these films, write his/her name next to the film. Ideally you want one name next to each film. The other SS choose a film they haven't seen and interview the S who has seen it. To help the interview you could elicit and write questions on the board, e.g.

Is it a good film? Who are the actors? What is the story about? Is it an American / English / Italian etc. film ?

The SS should take notes and this information can be written on the board next to the film title, or on posters placed around the room. You could end the activity by asking SS which films they would like to see, which they wouldn't like to see and why.

2 Film quiz GW. based on fairly recent and current films is a good idea. Write the titles of several films on the board. Each group should write the numbers 1 to X (depending on the number of questions you have) on a sheet of paper. The groups could mark each other's papers when you're checking the answers.

Possible questions:
1 Which film is (name of actor) in?
2 Which film happens in (country)?
3 Which film is about (story line)?
4 Which film won an Oscar?
5 Which film is on at the (name of local cinema)?
6 Which is a (type of film e.g. horror) film?
7 Which is a (nationality) film?

P **3 Gapped dialogue** page 130, 4.3. PW. Divide the class into two groups, A and B. Photocopy the gapped dialogues. SS from the same group could work together to complete the conversation. SS then find a partner from the other group and check their answers. Between them they have the complete correct dialogue. Take this opportunity to focus on good pronunciation and appropriate rhythm and stress. With the class, identify any consonant/vowel sound links, e.g. *Is there‿another film‿on?* SS then practise saying the dialogue. As they are practising, monitor the pairs and work on improving their pronunciation, rhythm and stress. If there is a problem common to many SS, stop the practice and focus on the mistake. Ask for volunteers to say the correct sentence in front of the class. Praise SS who sound natural, interested and have appropriate sentence stress and intonation etc.

Vocabulary: meaning from context

Students' Book (page 51)

Exercise 3a) The names of the parts of speech should now be familiar. Highlight that there are two parts to the phrasal word verbs *go out, look for*. There are more phrasal verbs in Unit 6.

2 adjective 3 noun 4 verb 5 verb

Exercise 3b), 3c) and 3d) These exercises are designed to encourage SS to accept more responsibility for extending their own vocabulary. Feed back with the whole class and comment on the usefulness of the words to give SS some idea of frequency, e.g. in everyday contexts *empire* would be less frequent than *crowded.*

Exercise 3e) This is a good opportunity to check on how well the SS are keeping vocabulary records. If at the end of each lesson you allow them a few minutes to add new words to their records, you may be establishing a good habit. It's important at this level to allow SS the time needed to achieve an objective. This doesn't mean the pace has to be slow but it does mean we have to be realistic in our expectations of what can be done in any given period of time. Elementary SS may be frustrated if they feel they are just collecting a series of unfinished tasks.

Listening and writing

L

• SS should know some of the adjectives from this section, e.g. *sad, 'interesting.* However, they may not know: *'funny, 'frightening, fan'tastic, te'rrific.*

• This section previews the Past Simple of the verb *to be* which comes up in Unit 5.

Students' Book (page 51)

Exercise 4 Check unfamiliar adjectives (see L). Model the pronunciation as they have to recognise it from a cassette. Note that Exercise 4a) only asks SS to identify the film, i.e. global listening. Before doing the second more intensive listening in Exercise 4b), read the questions aloud. Either stop the cassette after each person speaks, or tell SS they can hear it more than once and let them dictate the number of times they need to hear it. However, this sometimes causes problems if you have a particularly wide range of ability in the class. If this is the case, you can ask the stronger SS to continue with other work, or go on to the next exercise and allow the weaker SS the opportunity to listen until they feel fairly confident that they have understood most of the texts. You won't be able to do this every time, but it seems only fair that the lessons are paced to favour different abilities at different times, so that we don't only cater to the needs of one ability level. Check the answers when all SS have answered the questions.

After the exercise you could let SS read the tapescript while you play the cassette again to reinforce sound symbol association. It can also help SS to recognise how language is chunked, thereby encouraging better reading skills.

[4.5]

SALLY: Yes, I really enjoyed it. It was quite exciting – very fast. And it was also very funny. And of course I like Harrison Ford – he's great. But the big thing about the film is that it's also got Sean Connery in it – he's Indiana's father. I know he's old but I think he's incredibly sexy. He was the best James Bond ... definitely!

WAYNE: No, I didn't really like it. It was too frightening – I don't really like scary films. I know a lot of people didn't go swimming in the sea afterwards – even in England. But it was well-acted and the music was terrific.

LOUISE: Spielberg took the story from a book. I thought it was a very moving film – very sad – and very intelligent. But it's quite long and it's all in black and white. Liam Neeson played the man who saved the lives of all these people. I think he's a fantastic actor.

Exercise 4a)

1 *Indiana Jones and the Last Crusade* 2 *Jaws* 3 *Schindler's List*

Exercise 4b)

1c) 2c) 3a)

Exercise 5a) Don't do this if you used the suggested warmer at the beginning of the SKILLS section.

Exercise 5b) and c) If reading aloud is difficult for your SS, the reviews can be displayed round the room and SS can walk around and read each other's.

Extra material and ideas

Film and book reviews

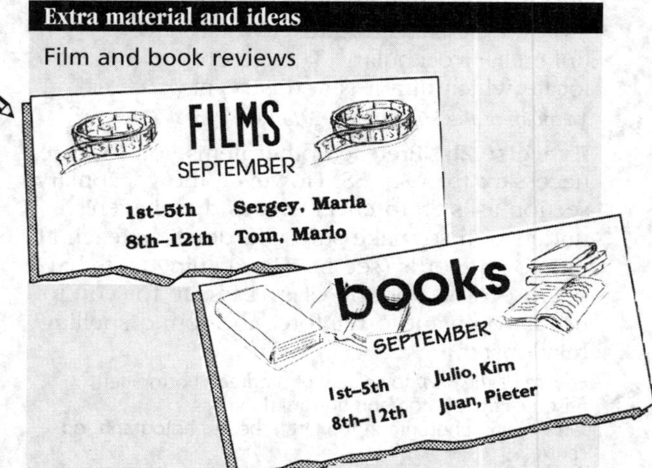

Make two posters for the classroom wall. One headed FILMS the other BOOKS. Write the dates of each week of your course on the posters and next to each week write the names of two or three SS. The SS are allowed to choose whether they want to review a book or a film. They should be prepared either to tell the class about the book they have read or the film they have seen in their designated week. Remember to allow a few minutes at the end of the lessons for SS to give their review to the group. After the SS have told the group about the film or the book, the title, author, actors, director etc. can be added to the posters with either a happy face or sad face to indicate whether the S is recommending it or not. Note that the book or film doesn't have to be in English.

If you wanted SS to write a review instead of telling the group, you could have two review books in the classroom. SS could take one of these books home when it's their turn and write a review and bring it back to class. You could check it periodically, and encourage SS to read each other's reviews.

REVIEW

- Vocabulary: food and clothes.
- Present Simple: questions and short answers.
- Frequency adverbs.
- Present Continuous.

Students' Book (page 52)

Vocabulary

Exercise 1

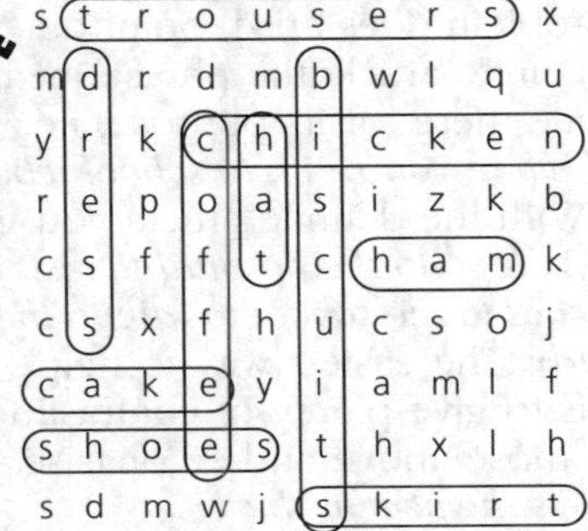

Exercise 2 If you suspect SS' wardrobes are extensive, limit the number of items you ask them to list. For food, you could put categories up on the board and ask SS to list a favourite under each one e.g. fruit, vegetable, fish, meat (unless vegetarian) dessert, drink, other. Invite them to ask you about your favourites thereby offering more question practice.

Using your grammar

Exercise 3a) Highlight that SS will need to use the Present Simple or Continuous in the questions. Also remind them of the word order of frequency adverbs.

Do you sometimes drink tea in the afternoons?
Do you always have toast for breakfast?
Are you enjoying the lesson today?
Do you always have a shower in the evenings?
Do you ever have a bath in the evenings?
Do you eat fish on Fridays?
Do you go on holiday in July?
Do you ever get up before 7 am?
Are you working hard today?
Do you sometimes have a large breakfast?
Do you ever sleep late on Saturdays?
Do you usually buy cheap clothes?
Do you always go to bed after midnight?
Do you take exercise every day?
Do you sometimes watch TV in the morning?
Do you always listen to the radio in the morning?

Exercise 3b) You may need to give a short demonstration and make sure SS understand they have to get a line but it can be in any direction. Allow time for feedback.

Exercise 4 It would be wonderful if you could arrange a real letter exchange. Real pen friends are probably out of the question but they could exchange letters with another English class of a similar or slightly higher level. If you or your SS have access to the Internet, there are often pen pal files available.

Extra material and ideas

1 Word search puzzles (see Exercise 1 above). Ask SS to write these for each other. Write some lexical areas on the board e.g. Countries, Food, Drink, Clothes, Adjectives, Adverbs. SS should only choose one or two lexical areas to make their puzzle. They can do this individually or in pairs. They then exchange with another S or pair of SS. They should tell the other SS what lexical area(s) the words are from. This could be a homework exercise and used as a warmer in the next lesson. Impress upon them that spelling is important and should be checked before they exchange puzzles.

A dangerous woman?

Students' Book

General themes: towns and cities; directions; a detective story.

FOCUS ON VOCABULARY: towns and cities; prepositions of place (2).
FOCUS ON GRAMMAR: Past Simple (1); positive and negative sentences of regular and irregular verbs.
SKILLS: vocabulary (opposites of adjectives and negatives with *un*-), reading and listening (continuation of the story in FOCUS ON GRAMMAR); writing (linkng words); listening and speaking (the end of the story).
SOCIAL ENGLISH: directions.

Workbook

GRAMMAR: Past Simple; Present Simple or Past Simple?
VOCABULARY: prepositions of place; opposites (adjectives).
WRITING: linking words; punctuation.
PRONUNCIATION: Past Simple of regular verbs; word stress in three-syllable words.

FOCUS ON VOCABULARY

Towns and cities

- Describing a town.
- Prepositions of place.

L **• Pronunciation of vocabulary**

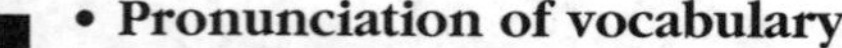

Although the number of syllables varies in the words presented in this unit, the stress usually comes on the first syllable. However, often a common mistake is for SS to stress the first syllable of *hotel* and *police* instead of the second: /həʊ'tel/ and /pə'liːs/. Note that a common pronunciation of *police* is reduced to one syllable /'pliːs/ and that this is even more likely to occur in the compound noun *police station*.

• **Prepositions of place** are a problem for many SS at this level either because of L1 interference or the demands they make on the memory. Again, 'little and often' is the best approach. You could begin each class by asking questions, *Is José sitting next to Maria? Where is Mohammed sitting?* Unlike tenses, prepositions of place may not be used that frequently in the everyday language of the classroom so you need consciously to review them and treat them as vocabulary. If they aren't reviewed fairly frequently, SS tend to forget them quickly.

Pronunciation Encourage the use of the weak form /əv/ *of* in prepositional phrases and linking *r* in *corner‿of* /'kɔːnərev/.

• The examples of the zero article are limited to names of streets and towns. Further examples are introduced in Unit 6.

• **Adjectives** SS should use ones they know but you could add others that are less familiar e.g. *'ugly, 'terrible, 'awful, 'excellent*.

• This section doesn't delve into the difference between ***to*** *church/school/hospital/prison* and ***to the*** *church/hospital/school/prison* and we don't recommend highlighting this to SS at this level. However, if the problem does arise, point out that without the definite article the phrase means the person has gone there for its purpose, i.e., *you go to hospital when you're ill, to school when you're a student*. With the definite article you go there as a visitor: *You go to the hospital to visit a patient, a parent goes to the school to talk to the teachers not to study*. The easiest way to help them understand is to give plenty of contrasting sentences such as those above and emphasise the question: *Why is the person there?*

Students' Book (page 54)
Exercise 1a) As a warmer ask SS to comment on the town where they are living or come from and other cities they have visited. Ask them what they like and/or dislike about them. Tell them about towns and cities you like and dislike. Before asking SS to use dictionaries, check if they know any of the vocabulary. Ask them to pronounce the words before you model them to check whether they are using stress marks and phonemics to help work out the pronunciation of words. If not, remind them they can access the correct pronunciation by using the information in dictionaries.

a church, b supermarket, c police station, d telephone box, e traffic lights, f railway station, g park

Exercise 1b) Remember SS will need time to locate the places and mark them in the boxes. Note that some words are international e.g. *hotel*.

hospital: bottom left, market: bottom right, cinema: centre left, hotel: centre far right, bus stop: top left, pavement: bottom centre, garage: centre far right

Exercise 1c) Again, give SS time to note which pattern each word belongs to. Practise saying all the vocabulary items covered in Exercise 1a) and b) as they need these in the speaking activities which follow. Pay particular attention to the stress on *ho'tel* and *'police station* (see L).

[5.1]
1 hospital 2 market 3 cinema 4 hotel 5 bus stop 6 pavement 7 garage

A	B	C
hospital	market	hotel
cinema	bus stop	
	pavement	
	garage	

Exercise 1d) If you want SS to practise question forms; *Is there a...? Are there any...? Has it got a...? Has it got any...?*, turn this into a question and answer activity in pairs.

Exercise 2a) Some prepositional phrases were introduced in Unit 2, e.g. *next to, near, behind* etc. This exercise should act as a review and can be done quickly as a whole class activity. Write SS' suggestions on the board but don't indicate whether they are right or wrong. The answers are in the listening which follows.

1 post office 2 railway station 3 telephone box and traffic light 4 library 5 park 6 supermarket

Exercise 2b)
Ask whether their answers were right or wrong and correct the answers on the board accordingly.

[5.2]
I like my town. It's small – about 30,000 people – but it's nice to live in.
Look at the map. The town centre is really the High Street. When you come into the town from the south there's a market on the right. On the left, opposite the market is the post office. Near the post office is the hospital and behind the hospital is the railway station. On the corner of Station Street there's a phone box and some traffic lights. There's also a cinema, which has very good films. On the other side of the High Street, between the bank and the pub, there's a library. There's also a new hotel near the library but it's not in the High Street.
At the end of the High Street there's a museum on the right, near a lovely park and on the left there's a supermarket, with a big church next to it.

Exercise 2c) Do one with the class to demonstrate the activity.

The car park is behind the supermarket.
The police station is next to the cinema.
The post office is opposite the market.
The museum is near the park.
The travel agent is between the theatre and the garage.

Exercise 2d) and e) If you think SS have done enough work on describing a town, leave these exercises out or ask them to write sentences for homework beginning: ***This is*** *next to the police station*. etc. You could then use this as a warmer activity in the next class. SS exchange sentences and work out what *This* means in each sentence. Alternatively, SS could write a description of their town.

Exercise 3a)

A library B theatre C post office

Exercise 3b) There's no need to stop the cassette after each conversation. SS are only matching and they should get this quite easily from single word clues in each one e.g. *books*.

1 library 2 theatre 3 post office

Exercise 3c) Stop the cassette after each sentence to allow SS time to fill in the gaps.

[5.3]
1
A: **Could I borrow** these two books?
B: **Have you got** your card?
A: Yes, **here you are**.
2
A: **I'd like** two seats for the evening performance tomorrow, please. **One adult, one child.**
B: Yes, **of course**. Twelve pounds and six pounds. That's eighteen pounds altogether.
3
A: **Can I have** three stamps for Turkey, please.
B: That's one pound fifty, please.
A: And **can I send** this parcel? **How much is it?**
B: That comes to four pounds ninety five, please.

Exercise 3d) You could assign places to different SS to make sure a variety of conversations are practised, or ask SS to choose different ones before you start. Before SS create their own conversations practise the example conversation and ask two confident SS to roleplay it for the class. Monitor the pair work and ask the better ones to model theirs for the class. Ask the others check questions to see if they understood the conversations. Make a note of mistakes. These could be written on the board and in pairs SS try to correct them. Tell SS to come to the board and correct any mistakes they can. If you have limited your correction focus to pronunciation, write the words which were mispronounced on the board. If SS can't give the correct pronunciation, this might be an opportunity to practise using dictionaries to access pronunciation through the phonemic script.

Extra material and ideas

1 WB page 34, Exercise 7, page 35, Exercise 9.
2 Prepositions of place

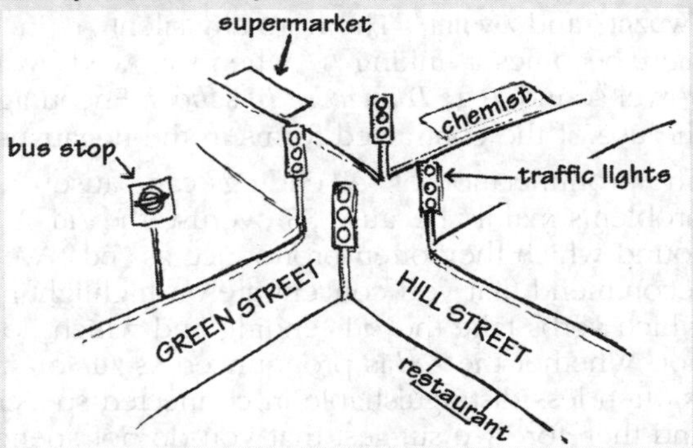

PW. Draw this plan on the board and ask SS to copy it. Write the following on the board: **hospital, hotel, car park, cinema, bank, library**. SS decide for themselves on their own map where these should go. When they have written them on their plan they work with their partner. You specify the first building to look for e.g. the bank. Each S asks an inverted question trying to locate where their partner has put it on his/her map, e.g. *Is it near the supermarket?* They take it in turns to ask the questions. The first to locate where their partner's building is wins that round and is allowed to choose the next building and ask the first question. Ask if anyone had the same buildings in the same place.

3 If you have access to a set of cuisenaire rods, you could share them between groups of SS who take it in turns to arrange the rods and ask the other members of the group questions, e.g. *Where is the blue rod? Is the red rod next to or behind the yellow rod?* This revises colours. If you don't have these rods, SS can arrange their belongings on the desks (books, pens, bag, notebook, keys etc.) and ask similar questions, e.g. *Where are the keys?*

FOCUS ON GRAMMAR

Past Simple (1)

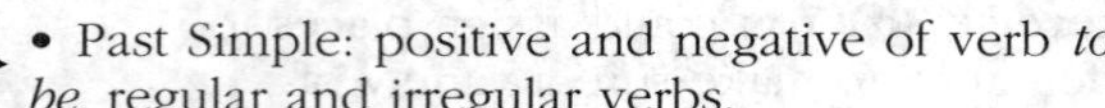

A • Past Simple: positive and negative of verb *to be*, regular and irregular verbs.

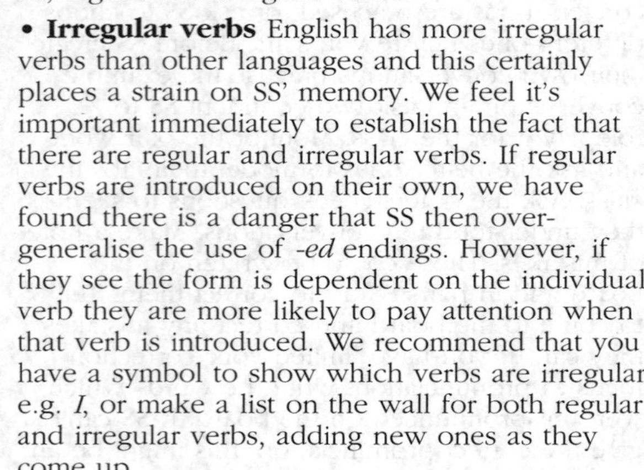

L • **Irregular verbs** English has more irregular verbs than other languages and this certainly places a strain on SS' memory. We feel it's important immediately to establish the fact that there are regular and irregular verbs. If regular verbs are introduced on their own, we have found there is a danger that SS then over-generalise the use of *-ed* endings. However, if they see the form is dependent on the individual verb they are more likely to pay attention when that verb is introduced. We recommend that you have a symbol to show which verbs are irregular e.g. *I*, or make a list on the wall for both regular and irregular verbs, adding new ones as they come up.

• The verb *to be* is its own operator in the negative, e.g. *She wasn't at school yesterday.* Other verbs use *did* + *not*.

Pronunciation Encourage the use of the weak forms of *was* /wəz/and *were* /wə/ in statements. In the negative, the strong form is commonly used /wɒznt/ and /wɜːnt/. The normally silent /r/ in *were* becomes a linking /r/ when followed by a vowel sound, e.g. *They were in school.* Encourage the use of the contracted forms in the negatives.

The pronunciation of *-ed* endings can cause problems mainly because SS overuse the /ɪd/ sound which they often pronounce as /ed/. We recommend that you concentrate on highlighting which verbs take the /ɪd/ ending and which do not. Whether the *-ed* is pronounced as /d/ or /t/ is often less distinguishable in connected speech and therefore we suggest that you do not spend time differentiating between the two.

Students' Book (page 56)

Exercise 1 Write names of famous detectives you think SS may know on the board and ask what they have in common, e.g. Poirot, Sam Spade, Philip Marlowe, Sherlock Holmes and include any local TV characters, too. Establish the word *de'tective.*

Note that rather than going straight into the reading and listening in the SB you could play the cassette and ask SS to see if they can understand any of the story. Assure them they are going to hear it and read it again later. Tell them the story is in the past. Use gesture, dates etc., if they don't know the word *past.* After the listening ask them if they can give you any information or words from the story and write these up on the board. Turn to the book and ask them to read the multiple choice exercise. See if any of the information on the board answers the questions. Now SS' listening is focused, play the cassette again and feedback on the exercise.

[5.4]

It was a very hot day in New York. I opened the window in my office, but it didn't help. It was still hot.

I had a long cold beer. That helped.

It was ten o'clock in the morning and there were no clients. No clients means no money. I was nervous. My bank manager was nervous. I had another beer. I wasn't nervous any more.

At ten fifteen she walked into my office. She was blonde and she was beautiful. I didn't move. I did nothing.

She sat down and took one of my cigarettes. I gave her a light. She smoked in silence. She wanted something. But what?

Then she looked straight into my eyes and spoke. Her eyes were very blue – like the sea. She said "Mr Spencer, my name's Diana White. I want your help and I can pay."

She put ten thousand dollars on my desk. I was interested, very interested. I didn't speak. I waited.

"Yesterday evening I arrived home very late. I was tired. I went into the bedroom. I saw a newspaper on the bed but my husband, Philip, wasn't there." I listened to her story.

Exercise 1a)

1b) 2a) 3b) 4b)

Exercise 1b) Focuses on regular verbs.

opened helped walked smoked wanted looked waited arrived listened

Exercise 1c) Test SS' understanding by asking them to form the Past Simple of *talk, like, play.*

-d

Exercise 1d)

Focuses on /ɪd/ and non /ɪd/ endings (see L).

[5.5]

opened helped walked smoked wanted looked waited arrived listened

waited, wanted. Because they are /ɪd/ endings.

Exercise 1e) The endings /t/ and /d/ may be difficult to hear where there isn't a consonant vowel link as there is in *arrived‿on* /ə'raɪvd‿ɒn/.

[5.6]

1 You looked beautiful.
2 They always arrived on time.
3 We walk to school.
4 We listened to jazz.

1b) 2b) 3a) 4b)

Exercise 1f) Focuses on irregular verbs. Return to Exercise 1b) and identify the verbs there as regular verbs – they have the same ending. Explain that not all verbs are regular. You could ask SS to shout them out as they find them and write the infinitive and the Past Simple form on the board.

was/were had did sat took gave spoke said put went saw

Exercise 1g) If SS discover any mistakes in the verbs written on the board from Exercise 1f) whilst they are checking in the Irregular verbs list, ask SS to correct them on the board. You could then wipe off either the infinitive or Past Simple form of a verb from the board and ask SS to recall what was there. Keep backtracking to help SS to remember the forms.

Exercise 1h) Highlight that the verb *to be* is different from all other verbs in the past. It doesn't have an *-ed* ending so it's irregular and the negative is different from all other past verb forms. You will need to review this quite a few times before you can expect accurate use of the form. It's worth asking SS to copy the full conjugation of the negative of the verbs *to be, talk* and *go* in the past. This then gives an example of *to be* and an irregular and irregular verb. The act of writing it down should aid memory and they will be able to see the pattern that emerges with *talk* and *go*.

1 wasn't 2 did

To help you make a quick assessment of how well all this information has been assimilated, write the following on the board and ask SS to come to the board and correct any mistakes they find. Tell them not all of the sentences have mistakes.

1 He were'nt at home yesterday.
2 He no go to work last week.
3 I didn't watch TV last week.
4 They didn't be hungry at breakfast time.
5 The train wasn't late this morning.
6 Henry didn't went to the cinema with Ginny.
7 I didn't wanted a drink so I go home after work yesterday.
8 Mary sit down but she not speak to me.

1 wasn't 2 didn't go 4 weren't 6 didn't go 7 didn't want, went 8 sat down, didn't speak

Exercise 2a) Before doing the gap fill ask SS to read through the text and ask them the following comprehension questions. Don't expect them to use the Past Simple with any accuracy when answering. The Past Simple question form is introduced in Unit 6 so this will act as a preview for the FOCUS ON GRAMMAR section there.

Where was Manuel from? Did he speak English? Did he go to England for a holiday? Why didn't the beautiful girl understand him? What did Manuel do?

Ask SS to work on their own and then check with a S who finishes at the same time. This allows for SS working at different speeds. The slower ones won't have time to check with another S before you feed back with the whole class. Write the gap numbers 1–20 on the board and write up the SS' answers before checking the answers on the cassette.

1 was 2 wasn't 3 spoke 4 didn't speak 5 decided 6 stayed 7 went 8 saw 9 had 10 was 11 said 12 didn't understand 13 went 14 walked 15 was 16 didn't go 17 went 18 started 19 was 20 went

Exercise 2b) After listening ask SS to correct any mistakes on the board.

[5.7]
Manuel was a twenty-two-year-old barman from Spain. He was tall and slim, with long hair and brown eyes and he wasn't married. He spoke French and German but he didn't speak English. However, he decided to go to England for a holiday. He stayed at a 'Bed and Breakfast' at the seaside in Brighton. On his last day he went to the beach for a swim. Suddenly he saw a beautiful girl. She had long brown hair, green eyes and a nice smile. It was love at first sight! He said something in Spanish but the girl didn't understand and went away. Manuel walked slowly back home. He was heartbroken. The next day he didn't go back to Spain. He went to a language school and started to learn English. Six months later his English was quite good so he went back to the same beach.

(Suggested answer) Manuel met the girl again. He said 'Hello, my name's Manuel.' She said 'Hi, my name's Sarah.' They had a drink in a bar. They drank beer. Then they went to a restaurant and had chicken and chips. At eleven o'clock they went to a disco and they danced. At eleven thirty the girl's boyfriend arrived and saw them. He was very angry. Manuel bought him a drink and they started to talk.

Exercise 2c) Get SS to exchange stories and see if they can find any past verb form mistakes in each other's work. Ask some more confident SS to read out their stories.

Exercise 3a) You could give a short demonstration of the activity by telling them about meeting a special person in your life.

Exercise 3b) Collect the stories and choose some of the more interesting ones and read out the corrected version at the beginning of the next lesson. Alternatively, you could put the stories on the wall for students to read.

Extra material and ideas

1 WB page 32, Exercises 1–3, page 33, Exercises 4–6.

2 PRACTISE AND CHECK, page 70 for more work on the Past Simple (1).

3 Irregular Past Simple Bingo page 131, 5.1. Give each S a photocopy of a Bingo card. Read the infinitive forms out one by one:

arrive be begin come do drink feel find give go have hear help hit kill know leave light listen marry open put say see sit sleep smoke speak take think try wait wake walk want

If a S has the Simple Past form on their card, he/she ticks it. The winner is the first to get a complete card.

4 Crossword page 132, 5.2 GW A and B. A has DOWN words on their crossword and they must supply DOWN clues for B . B has ACROSS words on their crossword and they supply ACROSS clues for A. A and B then tell each other their clues until the crossword is complete. The clues will be expressed in the same way: *It's the Past Simple of X*, so SS only concentrate on working out which verb they need to give in the clue. This is a self-checking activity as together the SS have all the correct answers.

		1 b		2 s	l	e	p	t		3 c	a	m	e		
		e		p											
		g		o		4 h	a	d		5 h		6 p	u	t	
		a		k						i					
7 w	a	n	t	e	d			8 l	i	t					
a						9 f						10 s	a	11 w	
l				12 t	h	o	u	13 g	h	14 t		m		o	
k				o		u		a		r		o		k	
e		15 w		o		n		v		i		16 k	n	e	17 w
18 d	r	a	n	k		d		e		e		e			e
		s								19 d	i	d			n
			20 w	a	i	t	e	d					21 s	a	t

5 PW Half the class (As) should face the board and half (Bs) should have their backs to the board so they can't see it. Write the following words on the board: *Yesterday, shop, money, credit card, shoes.*
A (facing the board) tells B (who can't see the board) a little story which includes those words. A then goes to a different B student and repeats the same story. Bs now have to guess which 5 words are written on the board. They should be able to guess because although the two stories they hear are different, the prescribed 5 words will be included in both stories.
Alternatively, to allow SS time to think up a short story, conduct the activity in the following way as it means Bs aren't kept waiting. Rather than having the words on the board you supply words for As and different words for Bs. As and Bs tell each other stories so both have a chance to guess the words.

SKILLS

- Vocabulary: opposites including prefix *un-*.
- Reading: prediction, reading for detail.
- Writing: linkers *and, but, so, because.*
- Listening and speaking: prediction, listening for detail, inference, telling a story.

Vocabulary and reading

- **The prefix *un-*** is introduced to signal opposite and negative adjectives. Although *un-* is by far the most common prefix, used in this way SS should not think this is the only possibility. Give an example to show another, e.g. ***dis** like, **in** correct.* However, only focus on *un-* for production.

Pronunciation The prefix **un-** is normally a secondary stressed syllable e.g. *unhappy* unless used for contradiction, e.g.

A: *He's very happy these days.*

B: *He's not. He's very unhappy.*

However, SS tend to give the prefix primary stress importance irrespective of the context. This is particularly the case when they are learning about the prefix. Highlight that the primary stress usually stays on the adjective.

- Apart from the vocabulary covered in Exercise 3 the following may be unfamiliar: *kill, a re'lationship, 'footstep, blood, fridge.*

Students' Book (page 58)

Exercise 1 Demonstrate by asking for the opposite of *good* and *sad.* Practise these words as SS often mispronounce them: *'normal, 'awful, 'wonderful, 'enemy.* Make sure SS realise not all adjectives can take a prefix to make them negative. Give an example of where this isn't possible e.g. we can say *unhappy* but not **unsad.* Focus on word stress (see L).

2c) 3 e) 4g) 5b) 6a) 7d)

Exercise 2a) Before beginning this exercise quickly review the detective story from FOCUS ON GRAMMAR. Write the names **Spenser, Diana, Philip** on the board and ask SS to tell you about them.

2B 3A 4E 5D

Exercise 2b) As a S gives suggestions for how the story continues, ask others if they agree.

Exercise 2c) Find out if anyone predicted the next part of the story correctly. If you have a mixed ability class, when the stronger SS finish ask them to underline all the Past Simple verb forms, positive and negative, in the text. Ask them to write the infinitive form above the positive verbs. This should allow time for the others to catch up and will prepare the stronger SS for Exercise 2e) where you can use them to help the weaker SS. (There is a recording of the reading on the cassette if you feel your SS would benefit from a listen and read activity.)

Exercise 2d) Ask SS to justify their answers by referring to the information in the text.

1T 2F 3F 4F 5F 6F 7F 8T 9T 10T

Exercise 2e) If you asked the quicker SS in Exercise 3c) to prepare for this exercise, pair them with SS who didn't have time to do it so they can help. Check the pronunciation of the irregular Past Simple forms.

felt fell slept came thought lit found knew left began heard hit woke up drank

Writing: linking words

Students' Book (page 59)

Exercise 3 Establish the aim of the exercise by writing **and because but so** on the board. Highlight that *because* introduces a reason and *so* introduces a result. Remember it came up in the SB Unit 2 FOCUS ON GRAMMAR, page 30. Avoid terminology by using *Why?, What did she do?* Although SS haven't focused on Past Simple question forms they should be able to understand, e.g.

She didn't have any money ***so*** *she went to the bank.*

She went to the bank **because** *she didn't have any money.*

Ask: Which tells me why she went to the bank? (*because*)

Which tells me what she did? (*so*)

Say the following sentences and ask SS to put them together:

I went to the shop. I bought some milk. (Establish *bought* is the past of the verb *buy* by writing: buy → bought on the board) *I went to the shop and bought some milk.*

Tell SS the exercise practises four ways of joining sentences together and point to the linkers on the board. When SS have had time to study the examples in the book, ask some to read the sentences out to the class. Then highlight the uses of the linkers.

Finally, ask SS to read the sentences in the SB, and tell them to ask if they have any questions. This reflective stage allows weaker SS more time to assimilate the information.

Exercise 3a)

1 so, and 2 because 3 but, and, because 4 so 5 because

Exercise 3b) To help SS gather ideas let them work in small groups.

So that they don't see this as too daunting a task you could set a word or time limit to show them you're not expecting them to write the final chapter! Collect some that have different ideas and read them to the class, correcting as you read them.

Listening and speaking

L • Check SS understand *shot* and *heard.*

Students' Book (page 59)

Exercise 4a) SS could predict on their own and then compare with a partner.

Exercise 4b)

[5.8]

A man answered the door. He was tall and heavy. He was wearing a white jacket with six gold buttons. Well, five, actually because one was missing.

I said "Good evening, Mr Lomax. I'd like to speak to Miss Taylor, please."

We went into a big sitting room. The film star was there. She looked dangerous.

I know that you were blackmailing Philip White.You promised not to tell his wife about your relationship if he gave you money. I know that," I said to Divine. "But why did you and Lomax kill him?"

"He wanted to tell the police that we were blackmailing him," Divine said "So we had to kill him."

"And you put his wife's fingerprints on the gun while she was asleep?" I asked.

"Yes, that was easy – a few sleeping pills in her drink."

I took my phone out of my pocket.

"That's not a good idea," Lomax said and took a gun out of his pocket.

"You did well, Spenser," he said. "But not well enough. I'm sorry, but you know too much."

At that moment I heard a shot. I thought I was dead. But Lomax fell to the floor and Divine screamed, "You!"

I turned round. It was Diana White and she had a gun in her hand. She looked pale – and very beautiful.

"I followed you here," she said. "I wanted to know the truth about my husband."

It was the only time in my life that a woman saved my life – and paid me ten thousand dollars!

Make sure the SS understand '*blackmail* as a concept even though the actual word doesn't occur in the text.

1b) 2a) 3b) 4b) 5c)

Exercise 4c) You could tell each S to choose one picture and tell their group that part of the story.

Extra material and ideas

1 WB page 35, Exercises 8 and 10, page 36, Exercise 11.

2 Intensive listening SS turn to the tapescript in the back of their book, page 140. Read part of the script to them but change a number of the words (include words which might normally cause problems, e.g. *wasn't* instead of *was*). SS should identify which are the incorrect words you used. Don't include too many changes as they will find it difficult to listen and write at the same time. Perhaps pause at the end of each sentence so that if you have changed a word they have time to write it down. If you do pause, you should do so even for sentences in which you haven't changed anything otherwise SS will know when words have been changed. They could then check with another SS to see if they agree.

3 Find the mistakes PW. Using the tapescript as a reference read out an incorrect summary of the story. Decide in advance how many facts you're going to change and tell the SS how many mistakes they're listening out for. Alternatively, you could write the incorrect summary or ask SS to write a short incorrect summary of part of the story (you could allocate certain paragraphs). They could exchange their summaries with another pair of SS who then try to find the mistakes.

Suggested summary with eight mistakes.

Lomax answered the door to Spenser. Lomax was tall and thin and he was wearing jeans and a T-shirt. Spenser wanted to speak to Diana White. Diana and Lomax were blackmailing Philip White. Divine put Lomax's fingerprints on the gun while Diana was asleep. Divine put sugar in the glass of water. Divine shot Lomax and saved Philip's life.

Lomax was tall and **heavy** and wearing a **white jacket with six gold buttons**. Spenser wanted to speak to **Divine Taylor**. **Divine** and Lomax were blackmailing Philip White. Divine put **Diana White**'s fingerprints one the gun while she was asleep. Divine put **sleeping pills** in the glass of water. **Diana** shot Lomax and saved **Spenser's** life.

SOCIAL ENGLISH

A • Getting and giving directions.

L • SS may have difficulty remembering the directions. Allow a reasonable amount of time

for practising recognition of the directions before asking them to produce them.

Students' Book (page 60)

Exercise 1 If some SS finish reading the letter quickly, ask them to study the directions in the grammar box. Ask a few questions to check SS understand the purpose of the letter: *Who's having a lunch party on Saturday?* (Joanna) *Can Lynne come to lunch?* (Yes). *Why did Joanna write this letter to Lynne?* (Lynne doesn't know the way/directions.) *Where does Joanna live?* (25, Queen's Square, Bath.)

Exercise 1a)

Queen's Square

Exercise 1b) Pause the cassette for SS to find the places.

[5.9]

1

JOANNA: Go out of the house and turn right. Go straight on into Gay Street. You'll see the Circus at the end. Turn right round the Circus and take the first turning on the right. You'll see them on your right.

2

JOANNA: Go outside. Turn left. Go straight on along Barton Street. Cross the road at the end and it's on the right.

3

JOANNA: Turn left into Barton Street when you go out of the house. Walk straight on – you'll pass the Theatre Royal on your right, and turn left into Westgate Street. At the crossroads turn right into Stall Street and you'll see them on your left.

1 The Assembly Rooms 2 The Theatre Royal 3 The Roman Baths

Exercise 2) Demonstrate by giving some directions if you feel they need more recognition practice, then point out the layout of an informal letter using Joanna's letter as a model: where the address is, no name above the address, where the date comes, the opening greeting and closing sentence. If you think it's of interest or use to the class you could also show them how an envelope is addressed in Britain.

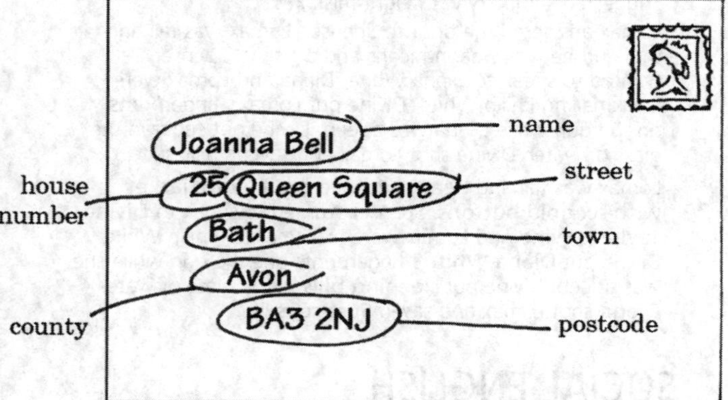

Extra material and ideas

Kim's game with shops page 133, 5.3. PW. Either make an OHT from the P material or make copies for SS. Explain it's a memory game. They can look at the picture for one minute only. They then have to remember what was in each shop. The S who remembers the most items and has the least number of incorrect items is the winner.

A matter of life and death

Students' Book

General themes: leisure activities; biographies of famous people.

FOCUS ON VOCABULARY: leisure activities; *like, enjoy, don't mind, don't like doing*; adjectives to describe leisure activities; the/zero article.
FOCUS ON GRAMMAR: Past Simple (2); questions with *was* and *were*; questions with *did*; time expressions.
SKILLS: reading (Rudolph Valentino); vocabulary (phrasal verbs); writing (biographies of famous people).
REVIEW: vocabulary (word game); using your grammar (a sound and picture story).

Workbook

GRAMMAR: Past Simple (questions and answers); *like doing* and *would like to do*.
VOCABULARY: leisure activities; adjectives with *-ed* or *-ing* endings; phrasal verbs; synonyms.
WRITING: postcards.
PRONUNCIATION: sound and spelling: *e*.

FOCUS ON VOCABULARY

Leisure activities

A
- Leisure activities and their collocations.
- Adjectives: including *-ed* vs. *-ing* endings.
- *like/don't mind/don't like* + noun or gerund.
- *The* or zero article.
- Revision of Present Simple.

L
- The following may be unfamiliar: *'ballroom dancing, 'drawing, 'motocross, 'snowboarding, 'stamp collecting.*

- **Verb and noun collocations** centred around sports invariably causes problems. Highlight which nouns take *do* and which take *play*. Note that *go* + noun, e.g. *to go swimming*, has not been included as at this level this can easily be avoided by using the Present Simple – *I swim, I run, I jog, I ride* etc.
- ***Like/don't like*** can be followed by either an infinitive form or a gerund. The gerund is more commonly used and as *don't mind* must be followed by the gerund we recommend that you only highlight the *-ing* form. Remind SS that a noun can also follow these verbs. The adjective and preposition *interested in* + noun or *-ing* is also introduced.
- Check the following adjectives: *'tiring, fun, re'laxing, safe, 'awful, 'boring.*

Pronunciation SS often use a diphthong in the first syllable, pronouncing *awful* as /aʊfəl/ instead of /ɔːfəl/ and they often stress the third syllable of *interesting* instead of the first.

- ***-ed/-ing* adjectives** are a problem for many learners at this level. It's often helpful to compare the feeling inside me (= *-ed* ending) and my opinion about the thing I'm thinking about/looking at (= *-ing* ending).

However, don't expect SS to assimilate this immediately.

(My feeling)
I'm interested in modern art.
(My opinion)
That's an interesting painting.

- ***The* or zero article** The following aspects are highlighted: *the* is used for specific things (reviewing Unit 5) compared with the zero article when talking about things in general with plural or uncountable nouns, e.g. *I like apples/bread.* However, we strongly advise a drip feed approach to this area of grammar. A 'little and often' will probably be more effective than aiming for immediate and complete understanding. As long as SS have the outline of what is involved in this grammar point, they will be more conscious of it as they meet it and slowly gather more information. As teachers we can reinforce this process by highlighting examples that arise in future texts and activities. (See *Extra material and ideas* 4).

Students' Book (page 62)

Exercise 1a) Use this warmer to establish what leisure vocabulary the SS know. Ask them to write the numbers 1 to 11 on a piece of paper. Mime the activities in the photographs. SS write the name of the activity next to the appropriate number. Remember to note the numbers yourself. Note that when the answers to the exercise have been checked you could reinforce recognition of the pronunciation by asking the SS: *Who likes motocross?* etc. Alternatively, SS could practise saying the activity words by interviewing each other.

1b 2j 3a 4h 5k 6c 7g 8f 9i 10e 11d

Exercise 1b) Focus attention on the grammar box. Highlight the use of the *-ing* form after *like/don't mind/don't like* and check the meaning of *don't mind.* You could use facial gestures, hand gestures etc. to illustrate and compare meaning.

Exercise 1c) and d) You could also invite SS to ask you about your preferences. Correct mistakes as they occur in the feedback to the exercises. This can be done quite unobtrusively if you repeat the correct form as though you were checking to confirm the information.

Exercise 2 Before GW check the meaning of the less familiar adjectives e.g. write *motocross* and *yoga* on the board and ask which is *relaxing*. Write a **+** and a **–** sign on the board and ask SS to list the adjectives according to whether they are positive or negative. Practise pronunciation (see L). Point out that the we don't always need to use the *-ing* form before the noun, e.g. *I don't like (watching) television.* If you think SS will be bothered by the *-ing* and *-ed* endings of *interesting* and *interested in*, you could give an initial explanation (see L). However, because this is such a complex area if SS are using the forms appropriately, then rely on acquisition at this level. In feedback ask SS to tell you about the opinions of another S from their group.

Exercise 3a) Play the cassette through once to match the people and photographs on the left.

[6.1]

MIDDLE-AGED MAN: enjoy drawing. I'm not interested in painting, but I love drawing. It's a very relaxing hobby and it's interesting. It's also quite cheap. I drive into the country and sit and draw trees.

OLDISH WOMAN: I like motorbikes. I go to motorcross. It's exciting and I love it. I know it's dangerous but I don't mind. I also love being with young people.

TEENAGE BOY: I look after birds. I think it's fun. I buy some of my birds but I also find sick birds in the street and take them home. Usually they can't fly and they're hungry and thirsty. I give them food and water – and sometimes milk.

A = d (drawing), B = k (motocross), C = f (keeping birds)

Exercise 3b) When the SS are answering the more detailed questions, stop the cassette after each person and allow SS time to note down their answers.

A
1 He enjoys drawing.
2 He's not/He isn't interested in painting.
3 It's relaxing.
4 He draws trees.

B
1 She likes motorbikes.
2 She goes to motorcross.
3 It's exciting.
4 It's dangerous.

C
1 He looks after birds.
2 He thinks it's fun.
3 He buys some (birds) and he finds some (birds) in the street.
4 He gives them food and water.

Exercise 4a) Ask SS if they have seen any Sharon Stone films and what they know about her e.g. age, nationality. Elicit some examples of questions before the pair work. Encourage appropriate sentence stress and a rising intonation on inverted questions.

Background information on Sharon Stone:
Sharon Stone (1958–) American film actress. Her films include: *Total Recall* (1990), *Basic Instinct* (1991), *Sliver* (1993) and *Casino* (1996).

Exercise 4b) Monitor SS while they're writing and correct mistakes. You could do the guessing feedback as a whole class activity or in groups. If you do it with the whole class, you could slip in a paragraph about yourself and see if anyone spots it.

Extra material and ide

1 WB page 40, Exercises 6 and 8, page 41, Exercises 9–10.

2 Choices Choose a variety of leisure activities and preteach any that are new to SS. SS should be standing for this activity. You offer a choice e.g. You can go swimming or ballroom dancing, and designate one side of the room for each activity. SS go to the side they have chosen and tell the other SS in the same group why they chose that option. The discussion will be basic but should practise *I don't like like* + noun/gerund e.g. *I don't like water* and review *can/can't* for ability, e.g. *I can't dance*.

3 Gap dictation. Write the following on the board:
1 excited/exciting 2 relaxed/relaxing 3 frightened/ frightening 4 bored/boring 5 interested/interesting 6 bored/boring

Dictate the following four sentences signalling when the SS should leave a gap. When you have finished the dictation the SS complete the sentences with the correct option from the board. They then dictate the sentences back to you. SS create sentences for numbers 5 and 6 and dictate the gapped sentences to a partner who completes the sentence with the correct option. You will need to check these sentences.

1 I was very ______ when I went to America for the first time. (excited)
2 I always feel very ________ after a bath. (relaxed)
3 I saw a film last night. It was really ______. (frightening)
4 I'm really ________. I think I'll go to the cinema. (bored)
5 ____________________________________
6 ____________________________________

4 Action chain *I like* ___ *but I don't like* ______ page 134, 6.1. Photocopy and hand out the paired pictures to SS. You will need to demonstrate the activity as it involves shifting sentence stress as well as practising the use of the zero article with countable and uncountable nouns.

Stand SS in a circle and demonstrate with the first card. Give the S on your right the first card and elicit from him/her:

A: *I like apples but I don't like apple juice.*

Then you say:

B: *Oh, I like apple juice but I don't like apples.*

Then give the card to the next person who practises with the next student. Feed in cards at different points of the circle. When SS understand the activity, feed in cards at different points of the circle so SS further round aren't kept waiting.

FOCUS ON GRAMMAR

Past Simple (2)

- Past Simple questions and short answers: with *was/were* and *did*.
- Time expressions: *when I was, last year/month/Sunday* etc., *ago, in + month/year, yesterday + morning/afternoon/evening.*

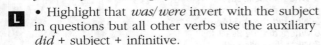

- Highlight that *was/were* invert with the subject in questions but all other verbs use the auxiliary *did* + subject + infinitive.
- There are a great many irregular verbs in English and these will need constant reviewing.
- Note that only object questions are practised in the unit.

Pronunciation

Point out and encourage SS to use the weak forms of *was* /wəz/ and *were* /wə/ in statements and questions. However, highlight that the strong form of these verbs is used in short answers /wɒz/, /wɜː/. Continue to highlight which *-ed* ending verbs are pronounced /ɪd/.

- **Time expressions** Highlight the following: *When* in *When I was* is not a question word; there is no preposition in expressions beginning with *last* or *yesterday*, (compare *in the evening* and *yesterday evening* and *in 1996* and *last year*). We use the preposition *in* with months and years but if the date is mentioned the preposition *on* is used. SS often try to express *ago* by saying *before* e.g. **I went there three years before.* Time expressions usually come either at the beginning or end of a sentence.

Students' Book (page 64)

Questions with *was* and *were*

Exercise 1a) and b) Review, and perhaps even write on the board, the Past Simple of the verb *to be*, positive and negative. Write a question mark on the board to signal that this is the grammar focus of the lesson. The quiz could be a team competition as long as your class can treat it in a light-hearted manner.

[6.2]

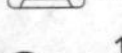

1 Men first went into space in 1957.
2 The French Revolution was about two hundred years ago.
3 The first false teeth were in Italy.
4 Tyrannosaurus Rex was a dinosaur and a pop band.
5 The 1996 Olympic Games were in Atlanta.

Exercise 1c) Practise the weak and strong forms of *was* and *were* (see L). Monitor SS for mistakes of form and correct. Feed back with the class. To offer more practice of the question form, in the feedback get SS to ask questions across the room to other pairs.

Exercise 1d) Ask SS to write out the questions from the cues and check a few of these before they work with a partner. Tell them to note down their partner's answers. They could then work with a different partner and tell them about the person they interviewed. Monitor this activity closely and aim for accuracy.

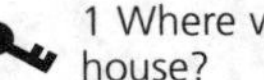

1 Where was your first home? Was it an old house or a new house?
2 What was the first film you saw? Was it frightening or funny?
3 When was your first English lesson? Was it boring or interesting?
4 What were your favourite songs / clothes / games when you were a child?

Questions with *did*

Exercise 2a) Review a regular and an irregular Past Simple verb, positive and negative forms, before beginning the listening. Establish the meaning of *highlight* as *a very happy and important thing in your life that you will always remember.* If you can think of a highlight in your life, tell them.

[6.3]

NORMAN: Three years ago my daughter had a baby girl and I became a grandfather for the first time.
VICKY: When I was twenty-one I travelled round the world with a friend from university. We visited the Far East, Australia and the States.
MARTIN: I passed my driving test last year and bought a very old car for two hundred pounds.
LAURA: In September nineteen ninety six I stayed in New York with a friend. I fell in love with her brother and we're getting married this year.

1 Norman 2 Vicky 3 Martin 4 Laura

Exercise 2b) and c) Do this quickly with the whole class.

2c) 3f) 4g) 5b) 6h) 7a) 8d)

Exercise 2d) Try to elicit the question form before looking at the example in the SB e.g. give the cue *have/baby* and see if the SS can make the question. Ask SS to compare this question with the verb *to be* in the question form. Highlight again that the verb *to be* is its own operator in negatives and questions while other Past Simple verbs use *did* and the main verb reverts to the infinitive form.

1 No, she didn't. She visited the Far East, Australia and the (United) States.
2 No, he didn't. He bought a very old car.
3 No, she didn't. She fell in love.

Exercise 2e) Allow time for SS to read the questions. This will focus their listening. Pause the cassette as you go through to give them time to note down answers.

1 Three years ago. 2 When she was twenty-one. 3 Last year.
4 Two hundred pounds. 5 A friend.

Time expressions

Exercise 3 Highlight main features (see L above). Then write the following sentences with mistakes on the board.

I left school 6 years before. I had a holiday in last month. I was born 1986. When was I young I had a bike. My birthday is at September. John went to the cinema in yesterday evening.

I left school 6 years **ago**. I had a holiday ~~in~~ last month. I was born **in** 1986. When **I was** young I had a bike. My birthday is **in** September. John went to the cinema ~~in~~ yesterday evening.

Ask SS to close their books and see if they can correct the mistakes. If they can't, let them refer back to the SB.

2 In 3 In 4 31 years ago (in 1997)

Exercise 4a) Do one sentence with the class to reinforce word order of question forms.

1 What did you eat yesterday morning?
2 Where did you go last Saturday?
3 Where did you live when you were twelve?
4 How many years ago did you learn to swim?
5 Did you go to the cinema last month?
6 When did you start English classes?
7 Did you have a picnic last year?
8 When were you born?

Exercise 4b) Model and practise the pronunciation of the questions before the PW. Use a fall or fall rise pitch movement on the tonic. According to the pitch movement you have modelled, write one of the following on the board.

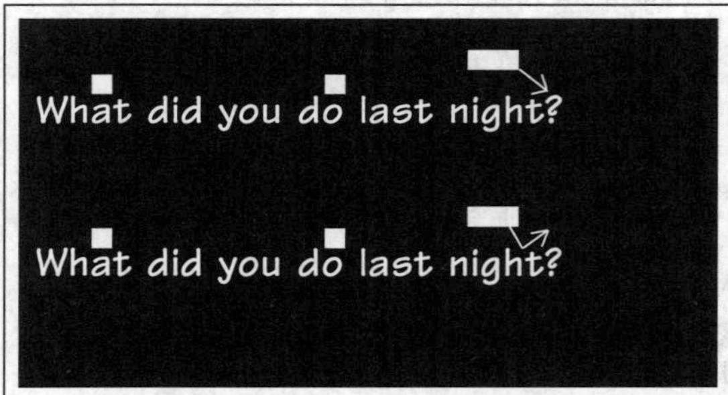

Point out that the large stress mark signals the main/most important stress. Allow time for feedback. Elicit other possible questions e.g., *Where did you go for your holiday? Was it good?/Did you like it? What did you do? When did you go? What did you do on your last birthday?* etc.

Exercise 5a) You could read the first part of the story aloud or listen to it on the cassette while SS follow in their book to help sound/spelling recognition. Ask if they know the story, is it a story they have in their culture, do they know what the moral/message of the story is? etc.

2 What did the old woman ask for?
3 What did the prince say?
4 What did the old woman do?
5 What did she give the prince?

Exercise 5b) Ask two SS to demonstrate the first example to check that the class understands the mechanics of the exercise. Monitor the question forms they use and correct individual SS. If there have been a lot of mistakes and SS were unable to self correct, this will indicate you need to highlight the form again. You could ask some SS to retell parts of the story to the class in their own words. SS can check their answers by looking at the other S's worksheet.

STUDENT B's questions
1 Where was Belle's father lost?
2 Why was the Beast angry?
3 What did he do?
4 Why did Belle go to the castle?
5 What did she find?
6 Where did she run?
7 What did the Beast do?

STUDENT A's questions
1 What did Belle and the Beast do?
2 What did she want?
3 What did Belle say?
4 Where did the men go?
5 Why did they go there?
6 Where did the Beast fall?
7 What did Belle do?
8 What did Belle do?

Extra material and ideas

1 WB page 37, Exercises 1–2, page 38, Exercise 3, page 39, Exercise 4 and page 40, Exercise 5.
2 PRACTICE AND CHECK, page 70 for more work on the Past Simple (2).
3 Dates in a box GW. Divide the class into groups of three or four. Each S writes down three important dates in their lives on separate pieces of paper. These could be birthdays, weddings, when they met their boy/girlfriend, an excellent holiday, passing an exam, driving test etc. Each group is given a container of some kind: a box, hat or envelope. The pieces of paper are put into the container. In turn each SS takes out one of the dates and the person who wrote it claims ownership. The other SS ask questions to get as much information as they can. Then another date is picked. SS could be asked to choose which is the most unusual 'story' in their group and this could form the basis of a feedback session with the whole class.

SKILLS

• Reading: prediction, reading for gist and detail, scanning a text for information.
• Vocabulary: phrasal verbs.
• Writing: a paragraph sequencing events in a person's life.

Reading

• Reading: The following items may be unfamiliar: *to dream of doing something, set 'off, 'handsome, oppor'tunity, pains, appendi'citis, 'fan club.*
• If you think the text will be difficult for your SS, spend more time on the prediction stage so that they're aware of the nature of the content. It is then much easier as they are checking their predictions against the information in the text.

Students' Book (page 66)

Exercise 1a) Ask SS if they know any famous dead actors. Focus on pictures of Valentino. Elicit the questions and write them on the board.

1 What nationality was he?
2 Why was he famous?
3 Was he married?
4 What did he die of?

Exercise 1b) Add SS' questions to the board.

Exercise 1c) As SS find answers they could come and write them next to the questions on the board. The text is recorded on the Class Cassette if you want to use it to reinforce the sound/spelling relationship.

Exercise 1d) Allow SS time to glance over the text again otherwise it's a memory test.

A4 B5 C1 D3 E2

Exercise 1e) Model the numbers if necessary and get SS to practise saying the numbers to help pronunciation.

1 Valentino went to New York when he was 18.
2 He went to California in 1917.
3 In 1919 he got married to Jean Acker. He changed his name to Rudolph Valentino and he played the part of a Latin lover in *The Four Horsemen of the Apolcalypse*.
4 In 1922 he got married to Natasha Rambova.
5 125 million people saw his film *The Sheik*.
6 He got a thousand love letters a week.
7 He died on the 23rd of August, 1926.
8 A hundred thousand people came to see his dead body.

Exercise 1f) SS will need to refer back to the text. If your SS are particularly slow at scanning for information, you could divide the class into two groups. Ask the A group to work on numbers 1 to 5 and the B group on 5 to 9. Feedback could begin with number 5 as both groups will have answered this question.

1 How many brothers and sisters did he have?
2 When did his father die?
3 Why did he want to go to America?
4 What was his first big job?
5 Who were his wives?
6 What part did he play in *The Four Horsemen of the Apocalypse*?
7 How many love letters did he get a week?
8 Why did he go to hospital?
9 When did he die?

Exercise 1g) As SS identify words they don't know, ask them to tell you and write them on the board. If any other S thinks they know a word on the board, put her/his initial next to it. This should help facilitate the second part of this exercise. Allow time for checking that SS have the correct meaning of each word for the context.

Extra material and ideas

1 In a multilingual teaching situation you could ask SS to think of a famous person from their country. In small groups of different nationalities they could tell each other about their famous person. If you wanted them to practise the Past Simple tense, you could insist that they choose a person from their country who is now dead. This could be used as an oral stage preparing SS for the writing activity on SB page 67.
2 After the reading exercise the class could be divided into five groups, each responsible for one paragraph. The group prepare and ask questions to the other groups to see how much they can recall. The 'tension' can be increased by adding rules such as if the question is grammatically incorrect, the team answering the question scores a point for recognising the sentence was incorrect and can gain another point by correcting the grammar. This means that on such occasions the team has the chance of scoring three points.

Vocabulary: phrasal verbs

L • SS have come across all of the phrasal verbs except *look up* in Units 1 to 6. Three of the verbs, *pick up, look up, turn off,* have more than one meaning. Phrasal verbs are complex in terms of form and meaning and it is probably better to treat them only as vocabulary items at this level and avoid any complex explanation such as transitive/intransitive, separable/ inseparable etc.

Pronunciation Point out the use of the weak form of the preposition in *look for* /fə/.

Students' Book (page 67)

Exercise 2a) and b) If you have covered the leisure vocabulary in FOCUS ON VOCABULARY, write look after on the board. Ask SS to say what this can collocate with, e.g. *birds, children, plants*. Highlight that the verb has two parts. Ask SS if they know any other verbs like this. Ask them to give examples in sentences and add them to the board. Identify them as either phrasal verbs or multiword verbs. Ask SS to study the grammar box in the SB. Note that this is an awareness-raising exercise which demonstrates that some uses are literal in meaning, e.g. *to pick up clothes from the floor* and others are not, e.g. *to pick up a language*. Ask check questions to see if SS have understood that some are more literal than others. Although the dictionary extracts identify the particle as either an adverbial or a prepositional particle, don't draw attention to this as it's too complicated for this level.

1 set off 2 look the word up 3 looking for 4 looked after 5 was brought up

Extra material and ideas

1 WB page 41, Exercise 11.
2 Because there are so many phrasal verbs it is advisable to make a special feature of them in class. You could have a box specifically for these verbs, adding new ones as they come up in texts etc. This box could be used at the beginning or end of lessons for review sessions. Examples:
1 SS pick out a verb from the box and explain its meaning to their partner who guesses the verb.
2 S picks out a phrasal verb and writes a sentence to illustrate its meaning etc.
You could also have a poster on the wall specifically for these verbs, putting them in sentences to show their meaning. Then cover up the verbs with pieces of paper for SS to try and remember which verb went with each sentence. Whatever techniques you choose, SS will benefit from the time you spend on

these verbs. There is often no equivalent in the SS' L1, and even if they have phrasal verbs in their L1, the meaning is often different.

3 Recording phrasal verbs can be done according to their stem e.g. *look up/after* etc. or according to their particle *pick up*, *look up* etc. It's difficult to know which is more memory friendly. Perhaps point out the possibilities and let SS decide for themselves. However, it is probably advisable for SS to have a separate section for these verbs in their vocabulary records. To review these verbs you can ask SS to think of all the phrasal verbs they can with a particular stem or particle. This may tell you how they are accessing the verbs. They often seem able to access them equally well or equally badly from either cue! Again, the secret seems to be review them frequently, consciously use them in class whenever possible and give praise when SS use them correctly.

Writing: biographies

- SS will need to use the verb *begin* or *start* in this activity. Although it can be followed by either the infinitive or the gerund, the exercise cues the use of the gerund. This should be pointed out to SS as they will probably need this construction when they write their own biographies.
- You could introduce some basic sequencing words such as *then*, *next* and *after that*.

Students' Book (page 67)

Exercise 3a) Ask SS if they have heard of Marilyn Monroe and what they know about her life. You could mention that Monroe was married to Arthur Miller the writer (see WB page 17 Unit 2). The exercise focuses attention on ordering biographical information.

1 sentences 1, 2 2 sentence 3–5 3 sentence 6

Exercise 3b) Ask SS if they know how the famous people in the photographs died. SS could do a biography for another famous person for homework (see *Extra material and ideas* 1 below).

Extra material and ideas

1 Biographies page 135, 6.2 Give SS the biodata for James Dean, Ayrton Senna, Martin Luther King or John Lennon. Ask them to write their biography from the information.

2 GW. SS are allowed 5 or 6 minutes to find out as much about your life history as they can. They think of questions then send a member of the group to ask you. They continue to do this until you say "Stop". Then they write your biography. These can be displayed around the room. SS read each other's and try to find extra information about you that their group didn't manage to get.

3 PW. Display various pictures of people round the room. Try to find pictures of people doing unusual things who look as if they have had interesting lives. SS invent a biography for one of the pictures. Correct them and read them aloud or redistribute them to different pairs. Other SS try to guess which biography goes with which person.

REVIEW

- Vocabulary.
- Past Simple.
- Linking words, *and, but, because, so, then, and.*

Students' Book (page 68)

Vocabulary

Exercise 1 Check SS understand they are aiming for a line from one side of the board to the other and they should try to block the opposing team from getting a line. The questions and answers are on SB page 129.

Using your grammar

Exercise 2a), b), and c) If you feel SS need extra help, you could do this as an oral picture composition with the class first. Ask questions to elicit the information about each picture and sound. Then tell SS to put that into the story, e.g. *One evening.* Continue with the next picture and sound. Review the first part of the story and ask SS to add the next part etc. As the new information is added encourage the use of linking words.

[6.4]
car crossing moorland slowly
eerie owl hooting
car stops
sound of dog and man saying "Good night Ben" and yawning
man falling asleep
sound of man waking up and yawning
man getting out of the car
man going into a castle (creaking door, footsteps on stone floor)
man sitting down and eating food
man going upstairs
man getting into bed, sleeping, screaming suddenly
man really waking up and starting, dog breathing.

(Suggested answer)

He drove into the forest and stopped the car. (It was foggy and he was hungry and tired.) Then he said "Goodnight Ben' to his dog and fell asleep in the forest. He woke up and saw a castle. The door was open so he went into the castle. There was a meal on the table but nobody was there. He ate the meal because he was hungry. He felt tired so he went upstairs and found a bed. He woke up and screamed because he saw a man with his head under his arm. Then he woke up and he was in the front seat of his car with Ben under his arm.

Extra material and ideas

1 GW. SS prepare their own vocabulary game, writing very simple clues. These can be played on different days and act as further review sessions. The group who wrote the clues should conduct the activity when their game is being played.

Practise and check key (Units 4-6)

PRACTISE

1 *Can* and *can't*

2 can't see 3 Can, cook 4 can't drink 5 Can, play 6 can meet 7 Can, go

2 Adjectives and adverbs

2 She's a good student.
3 It's a noisy hotel.
4 You sing beautifully.
5 Sylvie goes to sleep very quickly.
6 We eat a lot of fresh fish.
7 They play chess very slowly.

3 Past Simple (1)

a)
studied, married, went, wrote, left, worked, was/were, started, had

b)
2 was 3 married 4 had 5 started 6 left 7 went 8 worked 9 wrote

c)
2 He didn't go to school in London. He went to school in Stratford.
3 He didn't marry a 25-year-old woman. He married a 26-year-old woman.
4 Her name wasn't Mary. Her name was Anne.
5 They didn't have two children. They had three children.
6 He didn't write 156 plays. He wrote 36 plays.

4 Past Simple (2)

a)
2 Did you go to a restaurant? Yes, we did.
3 Did you see Big Ben? No, we didn't.
4 Did you take a taxi? No, we didn't.
5 Did you have a cup of coffee? Yes, we did.
6 Were you happy? Yes, I was.

b)
2 Who did you go with? 3 Why did you go with Carl? 4 When did you leave? 5 What did you do in the afternoon? 6 How much did you spend?

5 *An, the* or *no* article?

1 When she was **a** child she lived in India. She's got two sons.
2 Simon doesn't like writing but he likes computers. He loves **the** Toshiba T1000XE his son gave him for Christmas.
3 **The** first woman to swim **the** Channel from England to France was Gertrude Caroline Erdele from America.
4 Alex and Judy like football. On Friday, they go to London by train and stay in **a** hotel. On Saturday, they have breakfast in **the** hotel and then watch a match.

CHECK

1 Past Simple

1
2 went 3 did you see 4 saw 5 Did you like 6 did 7 loved

2
1 did you live 2 did your parents do 3 worked 4 lived 5 were you

2 Correct the mistakes

2 bored 3 so 4 a very good 5 yesterday morning 6 play 7 going 8 because 9 unusual 10 collecting 11 and

3 Prepositions

2 with 3 for 4 in 5 to 6 about 7 to 8 at 9 out 10 of 11 on 12 between 13 Opposite 14 down 15 to 16 for 17 to 18 at 19 after 20 out 21 of 22 in 23 for 24 to

4 Vocabulary

1 Clothes: sweater, socks, shoes, dress, cardigan, skirt, trousers
2 Adjectives to describe a person: kind, nice, attractive, noisy, quiet, sad, intelligent
3 Places in towns: church, hospital, travel agent, supermarket, railway station, library
4 Leisure activities: ballroom dancing, yoga, snowboarding, cooking, swimming, stamp-collecting, painting

TEST

There is a progress test, for Units 4–6 on pages 152 and 153 of this book for you to photocopy for your students. See page 158 for the Key.

Living in paradise

> ### Students' Book
>
> **General themes:** the country; a paradise island.
>
> **FOCUS ON VOCABULARY:** the country; descriptive adjectives; revision of Past Simple for narrative.
> **FOCUS ON GRAMMAR:** future plans: positive and negative sentences; questions and short answers; *when*, *if* and *going to*.
> **SKILLS:** reading (a paradise island – Vanuatu); vocabulary (noun and adjective suffixes); writing (a tourist brochure).
> **SOCIAL ENGLISH:** at a hotel; *can* and *can't* for permission; offers: *Shall I ...?*; decisions at the moment of speaking (*I'll*).
>
> ### Workbook
>
> **GRAMMAR:** future plans (*going to*); *when*, *if* and *going to*; questions in the present, past and with *going to*.
> **VOCABULARY:** the country and towns; parts of speech; compound nouns.
> **WRITING:** word formation.
> **PRONUNCIATION:** word stress on compound nouns; comparing sounds (/ɪ/ and /iː/).

FOCUS ON VOCABULARY

- Nouns and adjectives for describing the country.
- Verb and noun collocation.
- Revision of Past Simple.
- Preview of comparatives and superlatives to come in Unit 11.

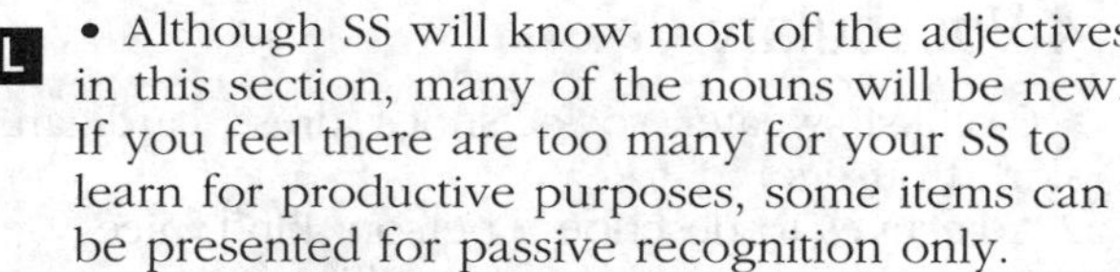

- Although SS will know most of the adjectives in this section, many of the nouns will be new. If you feel there are too many for your SS to learn for productive purposes, some items can be presented for passive recognition only.

Pronunciation: '*Mountain* is often influenced by L1 if there is a similar word e.g. /mɒntæn/ instead of /maʊntɪn/.

- There are three possible collocations with the verb *take*, e.g. *take a bike, the tent* and *a photograph*. SS may be confused by the more literal use of *to take a bike* or *tent* compared with *to take a photograph*. There is one example of *go* + *-ing* form (camping). This could be extended *go* → *fishing, swimming, climbing* etc.

The country

Exercise 1a) Establish the difference between ***a*** *country* (e.g. Russia) and ***the*** *country* vs. *a town* or *city*. Highlight the use of the indefinite and definite article. You could ask SS to guess in which country the photographs in the SB were taken. Is the SS' country similar or very different etc.? Make sure SS are familiar with the seasons and the meaning of *village*.

2 It is autumn in B.

Exercise 1b) Establish which of the words in the box SS already know. This will reduce the number of items they will need to check in their dictionaries. If the majority are unknown, divide the task among groups of SS, giving each group two or three words to look up in the dictionary. Each group then teaches their words to the other groups. Practise pronunciation as SS will be using these words in the following exercises. You could exploit the photographs for more vocabulary if you think SS can take it. Note that *bridge* came up in Unit 1 and *church* in Unit 5.

A: flowers, path, gate, village, tree
B: mountain, wood, tree, field
C: sheep, field, tree
D: fishing

Exercise 1c)

Sketch these on the board, the more humorous the drawings the better, and number them. (Adapt the drawings for your own country if necessary and prepare them as visuals in advance of the class.) Ask SS to look at the vocabulary and label the drawings and do the comparison of which is bigger. Note that students are only asked to *recognise* the comparative form (e.g. *bigger*) not produce it.

1 A river. 2 A mountain. 3 A forest. 4 A town. 5 A sheep.

Exercise 1d) Point to one of the drawings you have sketched on the board. Remind SS that all the words are nouns then ask them to list as many adjectives as they can that would go before the drawing you have indicated e.g. *a ______ town*. SS may offer *big, little, clean, nice* etc. Explore the meaning of the adjectives in the box then divide the class into Groups A and B. Assign one of the photographs in the book to each group. Allow SS to work with people from the same group to formulate ideas before pairing off with a member from the other group. This may allow for a more fluent description and encourage SS to improve simply by doing the exercise twice but with different people. Note the students are not required to produce comparatives although some may try, which will give you an idea of their awareness of comparatives before Unit 11.

Exercise 2 Highlight the language forms SS will need for this exercise, *Is there a _____ ? Are there any _____? What is /are _____ doing?* Encourage natural stress patterns and a rising intonation on the inverted questions and a falling or fall rise movement on the *What* questions. Practise, and tell the SS that you expect good pronunciation. There is a tendency among SS to be influenced by what is expected of them.

Student A
1 There are **five** windows in the house.
2 There are **four** trees.
3 There are **no** sheep.
4 There is a **woman** with the girl.
5 The girl is holding an **umbrella**.
6 The boy is riding a **bicycle**.
Student B
1 There are **seven** windows in the house.
2 There are **three** trees.
3 There are **four** sheep.
4 There is a **man** with the girl.
5 The girl is holding a **bag**.
6 The boy is riding a **horse**.

Exercise 3a) Note that except for the verb *take* which can collocate with *bikes, tent* and *photograph* (see L) there is only one possible collocation for the remaining verbs.

2g) 3f) 4a) 5b) or c) or f) 6b) 7e)

Exercise 3b) Elicit the crucial vocabulary in the Present Continuous, e.g. *What are they doing in the first picture? They're waking up,* before asking SS to use the Past Simple in the story. Having established which verbs are appropriate for each picture you can focus on irregular verbs.

A Two boys/men steal/take Henry's clothes, Barbara's camera, her rucksack/bag and the map.
B Henry is swimming in the river. Barbara is taking a photo(graph) of him.
C Barbara and Henry are setting off on their motorbike. They're going camping for the weekend. They're taking a picnic. It's a beautiful sunny morning.
D They put up their tent and have a picnic. Then they fall asleep.
E Barbara and Henry cross a bridge and stop by a river. It's very hot. There's a little path into a wood. Barbara is looking at the map.
F Barbara and Henry wake up. The boys/men run away into the wood. Barbara and Henry are worried. They are lost. It's starting to rain!

Exercise 3c)
C, E, B, D, A, F

Exercise 3d) If you think that SS need a change of pace and skill focus at this point, this could be a collaborative writing exercise which could then be a speaking activity as they read what they have written to other SS. There is also a gap fill version of the story if you think your SS need more structured guidance (see *Extra material and ideas* 3). However SS stories are just as valid. There is no right or wrong answer.

Exercise 3e) Play the cassette more than once if necessary.

[7.1]
Barbara: It was a lovely Saturday morning – bright and sunny – and Henry and I wanted to go camping for the weekend. We decided to set off early on the motorbike. We took a tent and something to eat and rode into the country. It was great. Then at about three o'clock we crossed a small bridge. It was very hot so we got off the bike and Henry went for a swim in the river. I took a photo of him. After that we decided to put up our tent and have something to eat. It was very warm and after lunch we both fell asleep. Well, some boys stole Henry's clothes, my camera, my bag and the map. It was terrible. We were lost and we didn't have any money so we decided to ...

Exercise 3f) Elicit suggestions from the whole class so that less imaginative SS have got some ideas to continue the story.

Exercise 4a and b) You could write this exercise on the board and as SS think of words they can write them up. Or after PW elicit all the words and write them on the board. You can then quickly check appropriacy and spelling. SS then choose the words they want to use in the next exercise.

Possible words: busy, industrial, noisy, dirty, work hard, go shopping, visit museums, cars, buses, houses, offices, buildings, factories, smoke.

Exercise 4c and d) Read the sentences out while SS follow in their books. If you think they have had enough pair work, they could work individually to write the lines. These could be put up round the room and SS then walk around reading each other's.

Extra material and ideas

1 WB page 46, Exercises 7–9.
2 Wordsearch page 136, 7.1. To remember the vocabulary, tell SS they are looking for seven words about the country and five words about the town or city.

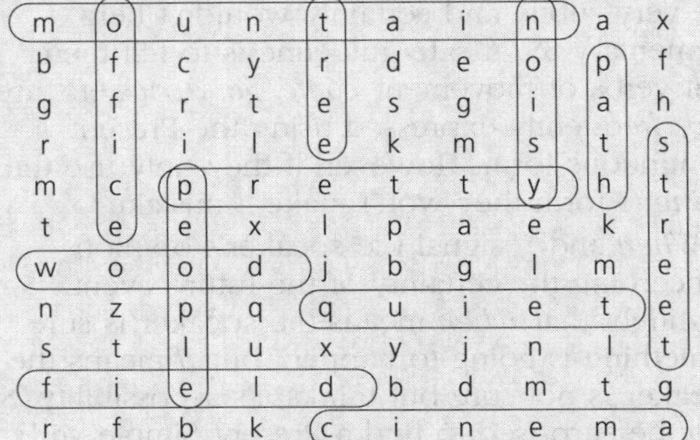

3 Gap fill, page 142, 7.2. Give SS a copy of the gap fill version of the picture story. The missing words are given in the box below. Ask SS to put the verbs in the correct form.

Barbara and Henry wanted to go camping for the weekend. They set off early on their motobike. It was a beautiful sunny day. They took a tent and something to eat and drink and rode into the country. Then at about three o'clock they crossed a small bridge and stopped by a river. It was very hot so Henry went for a swim in the river. Barbara took a photo of him. After that, they decided to put up the tent and had something to eat. Then they fell asleep. Some boys stole Henry's clothes, Barbara's camera and the map. It started to rain and Barbara and Henry woke up. They were lost and they didn't have any money.

FOCUS ON GRAMMAR

Future plans

• Future plans, *be going to* + infinitive, statements, questions and negatives.

• *Just* to mean *now* or *in a minute*.

• Present Continuous is mentioned as a possible alternative but this is **not** focused on in the exercises.

• *When* or *if* used with present + *be going to* + infinitive for future reference.

• Revision and extension of time expressions.

• Things that have been recently learnt can interfere with what was previously learnt. Because SS have just learnt the Simple Past of the verb *to be* you may need to focus again on the present form used as the auxiliary in the target structure.

• This structure is quite a long verb phrase for elementary SS and initially they may leave bits out, e.g. **I going to X, I'm going play X, I go to play X, What you going to do?* etc. Aim for accuracy in the initial stages of learning.

• The Present Continuous and *going to* are frequently interchangeable but not always. They both imply arrangements, they both include an element of time now, be it decision or action already taken for the future event. They both suggest a degree of certainty etc. However, they're generally not interchangeable when *going to* is a prediction for a non-personal event in the future e.g. **It's raining this afternoon.* The rules for when these forms are interchangeable are very subtle and certainly wouldn't help elementary SS. A safe guideline is to tell them that verbs of movement *come, go, arrive* etc. are very frequently expressed using the Present Continuous form. However, if they only use the *going to* form they won't make a mistake.

• *When* and *if* signal the speaker's opinion concerning the certainty of the future event. Highlight that *when* means the speaker is sure something is going to happen, but *if* means the speaker is not sure but thinks it's a possibility. SS may be surprised to find a Present Simple verb form follows *if* and *when* even though the structure refers to the future. This will need to be highlighted.

Point out that the order of this structure can be reversed e.g. *I'm going to X when I finish my work.* or *When I finish my work I'm going to X.* With the *if* sentence, point out that a comma is needed when the sentence begins with *if* but not when the *if* clause is the second clause in the sentence. *If he comes, I'm going to make a cake. I'm going to make a cake if he comes.* Note that SS will meet this structure in later levels more conventionally with *will* + infinitive referred to as the First Conditional.

Pronunciation The length of the phrase presents its own pronunciation problems. Initially, SS have problems getting their mouths around it. In isolation the velar sound /ŋ/ is used but in connected speech this is often realised as the alveolar sound /n/ in *going to* because of the following alveolar sound /t/. *To* is usually weakened: *to* before a consonant is often /tə/; *to* before a vowel is often /tʊ/.

Contracted forms are commonly used, *She's going to leave soon,* but only the negative can be shortened in short answers, **Yes, she's. (Yes, she is.)*

The intonation patterns for the question forms will need highlighting: the fall or fall rise on *Wh*-questions; e.g. *When are you going to see Max?* the rise on the straight inverted question(e.g. *Are you going to watch TV?*) and the rise followed by a fall or fall rise rise on the *either/or* inverted questions (e.g. Are you going to have lunch now or later?) You could write the following examples on the board to help SS.

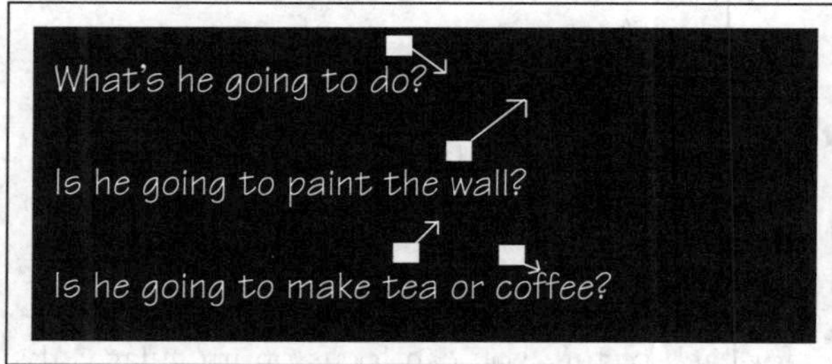

• *Just* is introduced to mean *in a minute, now.* As any dictionary will testify *just* is a complicated item of vocabulary with a plethora of meanings and uses. However, it is introduced here because it is so frequently used with the *going to* future to emphasise the nearness of the future time. It often signals the person is actually on their way to begin the action e.g. a person going out of the front door might say, *I'm just going to see Paul for a minute. Bye.* It has an equivalent use with the Present Perfect to emphasise the nearness of time past e.g. *I've just seen her, she went that way.* Some SS may have come across the latter but we recommend that you avoid reference to any other use than the one highlighted in the SB.

Future plans: *going to*

Students' Book (page 74)
Exercise 1a) The illustrations will help you to establish the idea of the future. Elicit what each person is holding (*dog lead* will probably be unfamiliar).

B She's holding a towel and some shampoo.
C He's holding a dog lead.
D She's holding a telephone.
C He's holding a dog lead.

Exercise 1b) Establish the idea of future plans. Repeat this concept as often as is reasonable. For each picture you could ask, *What's he/she holding in his/her hand now? Why is he/she holding it? What is his/her plan? What's he/she going to do next? What time are we talking about? The future?* With *I'm just going to wash my hair, just* is used to express immediate future. To give visual support draw this time line:

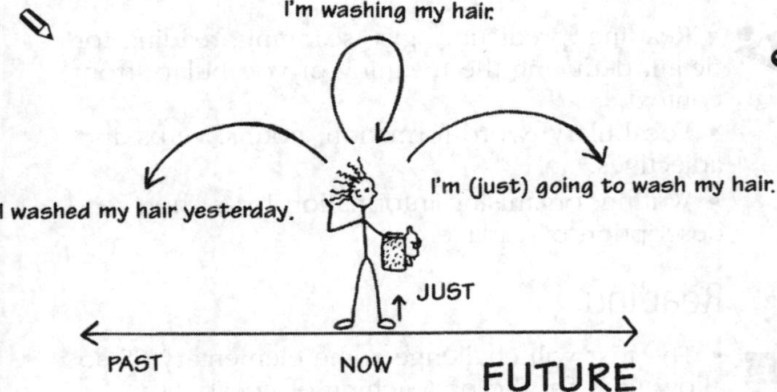

Practise the individual sentences and highlight features of pronunciation (see L).

Bb Cc Da

Exercise 1c)
a2 b3 c4

Exercise 1d)
[7.2]
MALE: I'm going to join a health club next week. Has yours got a good gym?
FEMALE: I'm going to phone John. Do you want to speak to him?
FEMALE: I'm just going to wash my hair. Would you like to use the bathroom first?
MALE: I'm not going to watch TV. I'm going to take Rex out. Do you want to come for a walk?

Elicit some possible responses to the questions, positive and negative replies. Allow SS time to practise the short dialogues in closed pairs. Encourage them to use a rising intonation on the questions. Then ask a few of the more confident SS to say the dialogues for the whole class.

Exercise 2a) Quickly establish the meaning of the verbs and check that SS know the vocabulary *ceiling* and *wall* before practising the question form. Note the woman has white paint on her brush, the ceiling is blue. She's *just* going to paint the ceiling white.

B feed C watch D order

Exercise 2b) Practise the question forms. Encourage SS to use the contracted form *What's* and a medium fall or fall rise intonation in *What* questions (see below) and a rise in *Is/Are* questions.

What's she going to do?

Exercise 3 After SS have had a moment to digest the idea of the exercise, ask one or two pairs to do one example for the whole class. Highlight the intonation pattern involved in an *either/or* inverted question form which perhaps breaks the rule they are familiar with (see L pronunciation). Monitor SS and stop the exercise if similar mistakes are being made by the majority of the class. Focus on the problem, form, pronunciation or vocabulary and then allow SS to continue. This suggests to the SS that your expectations are high and they will probably rise to the occasion.

2 A: Is Tom going to play tennis or football?
B: He's going to play football.
3 A: Is Sally going to have a cup of tea or a cup of coffee?
B: She's going to have a cup of coffee.
4 A: Is Adam going to be a teacher or a policeman?
B: He's going to be a teacher.
5 B: Is Sue going to travel by plane or by train?
A: She's going to travel by train.
6 B: Is Jim going to listen to a cassette or a CD?
A: He's going to listen to a cassette.
7 B: Is Kate going to cook rice or spaghetti?
A: She's going to cook spaghetti.

Exercise 4a) and b) To change the interaction focus you could do this as a whole class activity.

[7.3]

1
A: Where's **she going** for her holiday?
B: To **Portugal**.
2
A: **Is she going** by train?
B: No, by **plane**.
3
A: **Is she going** to stay in a hotel?
B: No, she's going **to camp**.
4
A: What's she going **to do on the beach**?
B: **She's going to read, sunbathe, swim and listen to her walkman.**

Exercise 4c) and d) As a demonstration, begin by writing things you would take on holiday. You could include some humour, e.g. You're going to take SS' homework, your teacher's book, a dog lead etc.

Establish the question form for the second person singular *Are you going to X?* Encourage SS to use a rising intonation. (See *Extra material and ideas* 2 for a possible lead in to Exercise 4d.) Note that holidays are dealt with in Units 3 and 12.

When, if and *going to*

Exercise 5a) Check the meaning of *take, pass* and *fail* an exam. If you want to explore the concept of *if* vs. *when* before doing the exercise use examples that are real for your situation e.g. *When we finish today I'm going to X. If you do your homework tonight, I'll check it tomorrow.*

Ask SS which of these you're sure about. Establish *when* suggests certainty, *if* suggests maybe yes, maybe no, it's a possibility.

Play the cassette, establish what SS understand and if necessary, play the cassette again. Focus on concept and form of *if* and *when* with *going to* (see L). Note that the long negative for *going to* is introduced in these sentences.

[7.4]

NICK: When I **get out of** here next year, I'm going to **see** my friends and **we're going** to have a party. Then I'm **going to** look for a job.

ALEX: If I **pass** my driving test, I'm going to **drive** my brother's car. I'm **not going to** buy a car because I haven't got enough money.

Exercise 5b) Use these questions to reinforce the concept of *if* and *when.*

1 Yes, he is.
2 We don't know.
3 Future.
4 Present Simple.

Exercise 6 Consider the interaction patterns and skills focus that have occurred in the class up to this point and ensure there is a balance. It may be time to allow the SS to work individually or do this exercise with the whole class or change the focus from oral to written practice.

1 He's going to get married **when he's** 30.
2 She's going to New York this summer **if she has** enough money.
3 **When I finish** at univiersity next year, I'm going to work in a bank.
4 Are you going to have private lessons **if you don't do** very well in your exams?
5 What's she going to do **when she gets** home?

Exercise 7 Do one or two examples with the class before pairwork. Examples: *When I leave school/university ... If I pass my exams ... When I'm old ... When/If I get married ... If I become rich ...*

Ask SS to choose interesting examples for the feedback at the end. Monitor SS and correct errors of form and use.

Extra material and ideas

1 WB page 43, Exercises 1–2, page 44, Exercises 3–5, page 45, Exercise 6.

2 PRACTISE AND CHECK, page 96 for more work on *going to, when* and *if*.

3 PW. As a forerunner to Exercise 4d), you could collect the lists SS have made of things they're going to take on holiday. You could read some out and other SS try to guess whose list it is.

4 Let's have a meeting page 136, 7.3. Photocopy the diary extracts for SS working in groups of three. Establish that the three people all work for a Travel Agency called Sun Holidays. They are all managers and the company has several offices in London and Paris and they are going to open a new office in Berlin. Their objective is to arrange a time to have a business meeting about the new office in Berlin. This must happen before Susan Lock flies to Berlin on Wednesday afternoon. There is only one time in the week that they can all meet (Wednesday morning) but don't tell them! They will need language for making suggestions, you could write the following on the board: *Can we meet on .... at...... ? Are you free on ...... at ....? What are you doing on .... at ....?* Highlight polite responses and the use of *going to* + infinitive for future plans, e.g. *I'm sorry I can't have a meeting then because I'm going to visit the office in Paris.* Tell them not to go from Monday am through to Wednesday evening in that order. It's better and more realistic if they jump around.

SKILLS

• Reading: prediction, gist, scanning, reading for detail, deducing the meaning of vocabulary from context.
• Vocabulary: word formation: nouns, verbs and adjectives.
• Writing: organising information for a short description of a place.

Reading

• The text will challenge some elementary SS so allow time for the preteaching of vocabulary.
• Adjectives which may be unfamiliar: *hard'working, 'sandy, soft, fresh, de'licious, 'tiny, 'hurricane.*

Pronunciation: SS frequently mispronounce *de'licious* /dɪlɪʃəs/. Highlight the word stress.

Students' Book (page 76)

Exercise 1a) Ask SS to look at the photograph of Vanuatu for a minute, then they close their books and have one minute to write down or draw as many things as they can remember from the photograph. Show them where Vanuatu is on the map. Which country is it near? (Australia).

Suggested answer:
I can see the blue sea, some (palm) trees, a beach, the sand, blue sky etc.

Exercise 1b) Establish the senses: *hear, smell* and *taste*, before returning to the photograph. Declare your opinion and join in the discussion.

Suggested answer:
I can hear the sea, the wind in the palm trees, birds in the trees. I can smell the tropical flowers and the sea. I can taste the salt of the sea. I feel good, warm, relaxed.

Exercise 1c) If all of the words are unfamiliar, divide the class into two groups and give half the words to each group to check. Each group then teaches the other the words they were responsible for.

Exercise 1d)
Ask SS to say whether they think Brian was happy or not. Tell them they will have the chance to read this twice so you want them to read it as quickly as they can the first time to see if their predicted answer about Brian was correct. If you want to check how quickly SS are reading, you can ask them to put up their hand when they reach the end of the second paragraph. Not all of them will remember to do this, but many do and it certainly gives a teacher an idea of the average reading speed. Alternatively set a time limit. A useful guideline is for you to read it twice at a relaxed speed. After reading, ask SS if they guessed correctly about Brian's attitude to living in Vanuatu.

Yes, he was.

Exercise 1e) This requires more detailed information so allow sufficient time for SS to locate the information and formulate their answers. To ensure that the activity doesn't flag because SS are somewhat slow, you could ask some SS to begin at the end of the exercise and find answers for questions 6, 5 and 4. This ensures that all the questions will be answered in the feedback even if some SS are slower than others.

1 Vanuatu is in the Pacific Ocean. The capital is Port Vila. Ten thousand people live there. The weather is tropical / beautiful / hot.
2 On foot or by boat.
3 He was probably a teacher.
4 Seafood.
5 He was once very ill. There were hurricanes. There was an earthquake. A plane crashed before it took off from the airport.
6 The colour and the sunlight.

Exercise 1f) The focus is now on vocabulary rather than the information in the passage but it does require SS to scan the text again to pinpoint the words they need. It would be beneficial to establish that the focus is on adjectives and, in this exercise, adjectives of colour some of which are new.

1 blue 2 white 3 green 4 fire-red 5 grey

Exercise 1g) In this exercise SS are given the adjectives and they have to find which noun they describe.

1 The beaches.
2 The people of Vanuatu.
3 Life in Vanuatu/Port Vila.
4 The seafood.
5 Britain.
6 The fruit.
7 The flowers.

Exercise 1h) Allow SS to work in pairs. Each pair is writing to another pair in the class. It would save time if you tell them who they are writing to. In an attempt to keep them to a similar time schedule, you could tell them the "post" is going in 10 minutes and they should all have their cards ready by then. Ask some SS to read out the cards they received. Encourage them to use the Present Continuous to describe what they're doing.

Extra material and ideas

If you have a collection of postcards you have received and you wouldn't mind them being read by SS, take some in and let SS have a look at them. Alternatively you could ask SS to bring in postcards they have received.

Vocabulary: suffixes

L • To raise awareness of common suffixes for nouns: *-ness, -sion*, and for adjectives: *-ful, -able, -(l)y, -ive, -ous* and words which can be both nouns and verbs, e.g. *cook*.

Pronunciation No stress changes occur on the vocabulary in the noun formation exercise. However, the diphthong in the second syllable of *de'cide* /dɪ'saɪd/ changes to /dɪ'sɪʒən/ in *de'cision*. SS often misplace the stress in *'comfortable* and *a'ttractive* e.g. **comfor'table, *attrac'tive*.

Students' Book (page 77)

Exercise 2a) Establish what a suffix is by reminding SS of the adjectives and adverbs in Unit 4, e.g. *quick* → *quick**ly***. Then do this exercise with the whole class.

sweetness, freshness

Exercise 2b) If you think it wouldn't overload your SS, you could extend the vocabulary of words which like *cook* have the same form as verbs and nouns by introducing the phrase *to go for a* and adding *walk/ride/drive/swim*.

decision kindness cook
Kindness has the same ending.

Exercise 3a) To focus attention write the suffixes for adjectives on the board. Ask SS if they can think of any adjectives with these endings. List any correct suggestions and write the nouns next to them. SS then do the exercise and any new items can be added to the board. Highlight the doubling of the consonant in *su**nn**y* and the fact that *friendly* is an adjective in spite of its adverb-like suffix.

friendly sunny attractive comfortable dangerous beautiful

Exercise 3b)

[7.5]
friendly
sunny
attractive
comfortable
dangerous
beautiful

'sunny at'tractive 'comfortable 'dangerous 'beautiful

Exercise 4

1 dangerous 2 decision 3 beautiful 4 kindness

Extra material and ideas

1 WB page 47, Exercise 10, page 48 Exercise 14.
2 Team game Divide the class into teams. Divide the board into columns according to the number of teams. Include suffixes for nouns, adjectives and

adverbs, e.g. *-ed, -ing, -sion, -ly*. Write one of the suffixes on the board e.g. *-ive*. Establish whether it's used to make a noun or an adjective, then allow the teams one minute to make a list of as many adjectives with that suffix as they can. One member of each team then writes the words on the board. Meanwhile you give out the next suffix to the remainder of the teams. They have a minute to think of words with that suffix. When the minute is up, another team member writes the second group of words on the board while the others work on the next suffix you have given and so on.

Give four or five suffixes. When you're checking the words on the board, give one point for an acceptable noun, adjective or adverb and an extra point if it's spelt correctly. Teams lose a point if the word is unrecognisable. Examples which you can expect from this level: *examination, happiness, kindness, slowly, quickly, attractive, expensive, dangerous* etc.

P **3 Word formation crossword** page 137, 7.4. Ask SS to quickly look back at SB page 49 to review the section on adverbs before they begin. The exercise also includes adjectives, verbs and nouns.

1 b							2 k				3 f	a	s	t	
4 a	t	t	r	a	c	t	i	v	e		r				
d							n			5 d	i	r	t	y	
l		6 w	e	l	l		d				e				
y											n				7 e
				8 c	h	o	i	c	e		d				x
			9 d								l				a
	10 b	e	a	u	t	i	f	u	l	l	y				m
			n												i
11 s			g					12 n			13 d				n
l			e				14 c	o	r	r	e	c	t		a
o			r					i			c				t
w			o					s			i				i
l		15 q	u	i	c	k	l	y			d				o
y			s								e				n

Writing: a tourist brochure

L • The following items will probably be unfamiliar: *'sea level, 'foothills, plan'tations, cool 'climate, bells, 'racecourse, 'produce* (n).

Students' Book (page 77)

Exercise 5 Preteach key vocabulary. Read the text aloud while SS follow in their books so that all SS can begin the writing activity at the same time.

Exercise 5a

1B 2C 3A

Exercise 5b) Make sure SS realise that these questions form a framework for them to follow when they write their paragraphs.

Exercise 5c) In monolingual classes, SS who know the same places could work together. SS could exchange papers for 'proof reading'. Ask them to look for word formation mistakes with adjectives and nouns or any spelling mistakes. They then return the papers and the original S corrects anything they agree is a mistake. Collect the written work and focus your correction on the same aspects (word formation and spelling) but also encourage SS to use colourful adjectives to persuade people to choose their place to visit. When the brochures have been corrected display them round the room and SS then choose the most tempting.

Extra material and ideas

1 The corrected descriptions from Exercise 5c) could be stapled together to make a brochure and displayed on the wall. If SS have pictures of the places they have described these could be added.

2 Take in various pictures of places e.g. beaches, cities, the countryside. Put them up around the room and number them. SS choose one to describe but don't remove it from the wall. When they have finished, they exchange papers with another pair of SS who try to guess which picture they were describing.

3 In multilingual classes, you could extend 2 into a small project. Different nationalities are asked to prepare a short talk on their country, produce a poster and write a short description covering main aspects such as weather (Unit 3, page 40), population, popular places etc. Five minutes at the beginning or end of the next few lessons could be set aside for the presentations. SS listening to the presentations could be asked to take notes and encouraged to ask questions.

SOCIAL ENGLISH

At a hotel

A • Vocabulary and lexical phrases commonly used in hotels.

• Revision and extension of functional exponents for requests, asking for and giving permission, offers, spontaneous decisions. *Shall* for offers and *can't* for prohibition are new.

• Speaking: fluency practice.

L • The following may be unfamiliar vocabulary: *double/single room, to book, guests.*

• *Shall* for offers and *can't* for prohibition are the only new exponents. The other exponents have been covered in FOCUS ON VOCABULARY in Units 1–6. We recommend that functional exponents shouldn't be treated as grammatical points because there are too many. It's more useful for SS to know that these are lexical phrases they can use to perform certain functions. It's important to associate the responses with the exponents, e.g.:

A: *Can I have ...?*
B: *Yes, of course. / Sorry, I haven't got one/any.*
A: *Shall I help you?*
B: *Oh, yes, please. Thank you very much. / No thank you. It's alright.* etc.

Pronunciation *Can* (see L Unit 4 page 40.) Remind SS that the weak form mat be used in the question and the strong form is always used in the short answers. Encourage SS to use the consonant vowel links which occur with the pronoun *I* e.g. *Could‿I ..., Shall‿I...; 'll* + consonant, e.g. *I'll‿think about it....*, creates a consonant cluster which many learners of English find difficult and consequently reduce to *I think.*

Students' Book (page 78)

Exercise 1a) SS are familiar with *can* and *can't* to express ability. However, this is the first time *can't* has been used for prohibition. Highlight the different uses. To establish the idea of public notices ask SS to think of any public notices in the school. Allow them time to read the notices in the SB then do the matching exercise with the whole class.

1G 2E 3A

Exercise 1b)

B You can't smoke in the (bed)rooms.
C You can't have dogs in the (bed)rooms.
D You can pay by credit card.
F You can swim from 7 (seven) o'clock in the morning until 10 (ten) o'clock in the evening.

Exercise 1c) Other suggestions may include; you **can't** have visitors in your room or make a noise after a certain time. You **can** make tea, coffee, hot chocolate etc. in your room in some hotels and it's quite common in British hotels to have your clothes washed and ironed and your shoes cleaned (note this requires a causative construction so don't expect accuracy of form) etc.

Exercise 2a) Let SS work individually first then check their questions with a partner. Write the correct question forms on the board so they can refer to them in the roleplay in Exercise 4. These questions will also act as a prediction exercise for the listening.

1 How much is a double room with a shower?
2 Do we/you pay extra for children?
3 Do they serve dinner in the hotel?
4 What time is breakfast?
5 Is there a car park?
6 Do you take credit cards?

Exercise 2b), c) and d) Make sure SS realise they are listening for the answers to the questions on the board. Ask SS to explain why they think Ron does or doesn't like the hotel. Pause the cassette to allow SS time to fill in the gaps.

[7.6]

RECEPTIONIST: Good morning, the Regency Hotel. Can I help you?
RON: Yes. Could you give me some information, please? My wife and I are looking for a hotel near the airport. How far are you from the airport?
RECEPTIONIST: Only five minutes by taxi. Or you can get the hotel bus. It leaves every half an hour.
RON: Can you tell me the cost of a double room with shower?
RECEPTIONIST: A double room... Let me see, that's eighty pounds Monday to Friday and sixty pounds on Saturday and Sundays.
RON: Oh, and we have two children. Do I pay extra for the children?
RECEPTIONIST: Ah... I'm sorry. You'll need a family room. You can't have children in a double room. They're too small.
RON: Oh dear... Mmmm... Do you serve dinner?
RECEPTIONIST: Yes, of course. Until ten o'clock every evening.
RON: And what time's breakfast?
RECEPTIONIST: We start at seven and finish at ten.
RON: We're coming by car. Is there a car park?
RECEPTIONIST: Yes, there's a large one behind the hotel.
RON: And can I pay by credit card?
RECEPTIONIST: Yes, that's OK but you must send a ten per cent deposit. Or you can give me your credit card number when you book. Shall I book a room for you now?
RON: No. Thanks very much. We'll think about it.
RECEPTIONIST: Thank you, sir. Good bye.

Exercise 2c)

1 £80 (eighty pounds) Monday to Friday, £60 (sixty pounds) on Saturday and Sunday.
2 Yes. They need a family room, not a double room.
3 Yes, they do.
4 From seven until/to ten (o'clock in the morning).
5 Yes, there is.
6 Yes, they do.

Exercise 2d)

No, not very much.

Exercise 2e) Note that *will* was introduced in Unit 3 for decisions. This is the first time SS have come across *shall* used for offers. Ask SS to look at the grammar box before they start the exercise.

1 **Can** I help you?
2 **Could** you give me some information, please?
3 You **can** get the hotel bus.
4 **Can** you tell me the cost of a double room with shower?
5 You **can't** have children in a double room.
6 And **can** I pay by credit card?
7 ... or you **can** give me your credit card number.
8 **Shall** I book a room for you now?
9 We'**ll** think about it.

Exercise 3 You may want to do this as a whole class activity first to establish the correct functional exponents for each example and to practise appropriate stress and intonation. SS could then have further practice in closed pairwork.

1
A: Can you lend me a dictionary?
B: Yes, of course. Here you are. OR No, I'm afraid/sorry I haven't got one.
2
A: Can I open the window? It's very hot in here.
B: Yes, of course. OR No, I'm cold.
3
A: I'm very thirsty.
B: Shall I get you a drink? OR I'll get you a drink.
4
A: This bag is very heavy.
B: Shall I carry it for you? OR I'll carry it for you.

Exercise 4 Establish that Watford is near London and Edinburgh is in Scotland. Divide the class into two groups A and B. Allow them time to read through their rolecards and ask you questions about things they are unsure of. To encourage SS to practise enough so that they improve upon their first attempt, tell them they will perform the roleplay for another pair of SS. This is less daunting than performing it for the whole class but it should still act as a stimulus for them to try and make it as good as they possibly can. Monitor and help individual SS to attain a higher standard of fluency in pronunciation, again showing them that you have high expectations and confidence in their ability.

Food and drink

Students' Book

General themes: food and jobs.

FOCUS ON VOCABULARY: food and drink; revision of countable and uncountable nouns; revision of *a/some*, *one/s* and frequency adverbs.
FOCUS ON GRAMMAR: *a*, *some* and *any*; *much*, *many* and *a lot*.
SKILLS: reading (an article about Waris, a model from Somalia); vocabulary (jobs); listening and writing (applying for a job and a letter of application).
REVIEW: vocabulary (a word snake); using your grammar (snakes and ladders game).

Workbook

GRAMMAR: countable and uncountable nouns; *how much* and *how many*; *any* and *some*.
VOCABULARY: food and drink; jobs, positive and negative adjectives.
WRITING: talking notes; correcting mistakes.
PRONUNCIATION: sound and spelling: *a*.

FOCUS ON VOCABULARY

Food and drink

- Review: things we eat and drink.
- Review: countable and uncountable nouns introduced in Unit 3, *a* and *some*, zero article when talking about things in general, the use of *one/ones* to avoid repetition of the noun, adverbs of frequency.
- Review of functional exponent *Would you like ...?* used for offers.
- Some of the vocabulary was introduced in Unit 3, e.g. *'orange juice, 'yogurt, cheese, 'chicken, 'biscuits, 'salad* etc. Therefore the vocabulary load isn't as heavy as it might first appear.

Pronunciation There is a strong secondary stress on the first word in the following; *green beans, frozen peas, ice cream, olive oil, Diet Coke*, but the tonic stress is on the second word. Compare this with the compound noun, *'orange juice*, where the primary stress is on the first syllable.

Encourage the use of the weak form of *some* /səm/ and *a* /ə/ in statements and questions but point out that in short answers the strong form of *some* is used /sʌm/.

Students' Book (page 80)

Exercise 1a) As a warmer ask SS to write down everything they ate and drank before coming to class or on the previous day. This will give you some idea of which vocabulary they know. In feedback you could establish who ate the most/ the least, the healthiest, the unhealthiest, etc. This will act as a preview for Unit 10, comparatives and superlatives. Or, SS could try to find another S who ate and drank similar things. Alternatively, make sure that SS know what a fitness teacher is and ask them to predict what such a person would and wouldn't eat and drink. Ask them to name the items of food in the photograph. Supply vocabulary where necessary. Allow them time to read the caption about Mr Motivator and with the whole class, identify which of Mr Motivator's favourite foods is not in the fridge. Mr Motivator is a popular television personality who presents early morning fitness programmes and appears on chat shows and in advertisements. His high profile wedding in 1996 was attended by a lot of TV celebrities.

chicken, cream, brandy, orange juice

Exercise 1b) Highlight the word stress patterns and practise pronunciation.

a onions b mushrooms c garlic d carrots e potatoes f bread g beefburgers h wine i butter j grapes k jam l melon

Exercise 1c) SS could do this individually and then check with a partner before you do feedback.

1 FRUIT grapes melon
2 VEGETABLES garlic carrots potatoes mushrooms onions peas
3 MEAT chicken beefburgers steak
4 DRINK wine Guinness milk orange juice brandy
5 OTHER jam bread cream eggs fish butter rice

Exercise 1d) The idea of uncountable and countable nouns was introduced in Unit 3 FOCUS ON VOCABULARY so *some* v. *a* should be familiar. However, you shouldn't expect a real understanding of the concept or use of **countable** and **uncountable** nouns which is the main teaching point in FOCUS ON GRAMMAR in this unit. This section aims to review Unit 3 and preview FOCUS ON GRAMMAR. Write countable and uncountable on the board establishing that this refers to things we can and cannot count. Refer to the dictionary extract and clarify why *lamb* can be both countable and uncountable. Then ask SS to give you one item of food for each column on the board. Let them continue with the exercise working with a partner. If you have some confident SS, you could ask them to do the exercise on the board so that you have an efficient reference point when you do feedback. If you think SS need and could tolerate more dictionary practice you could give them other words *beef, pork, aubergines, peaches* etc.

COUNTABLE: grapes, carrots, potatoes, mushrooms, onions, peas, beefburgers, eggs

Exercise 2a) and b) Ask SS to say which they think is correct but don't give the answer before playing the cassette. Highlight the weak form of *a(n)* and the weak and strong form of *some* (see L) and that *some* is used with uncountable nouns and plural countable nouns.

[8.1]

1
A: Would you like **a** banana?
B: Yes, please, I'd love **one**.
2
A: Would you like **some** bananas?
B: No, thanks. I never eat **bananas**.

Exercise 2c) Monitor and correct pronunciation mistakes.

Exercise 2d) Allow SS time to digest the information on their rolecard then do one example with the whole class to make sure they understand what they have to do.

Exercise 3a) and b) Ask SS to copy and complete the chart. You could fill in the chart for yourself and then join in the class mingling activity allowing you to monitor SS less obtrusively.

Exercise 3c) Write *NEVER, SOMETIMES* and *EVERY DAY* on the board. Ask SS to name items on their lists. Take a hand count of how many SS do or don't eat that food and write the food and the number of SS under the appropriate column to find out which food is popular and which is unpopular.

Exercise 3d) and e) SS could do this individually and then check with a partner before listening to the cassette. From the first listening SS should get an idea of how close they got with their guesses.

[8.2]

JUDITH: In the day I haven't got time to eat much so I eat things that are quick and give me energy, like crisps, bananas and chocolate. When I go out I eat steak or beefburgers.
GEORGE: I work long hours so I can't spend a lot of time shopping and cooking. I always have bread, eggs and rice in the house. And I eat a lot of cheese and biscuits.
WILLIAM: I love chips and chicken and bread and apples but I don't like vegetables, except for peas. I like peas.

Exercise 3f) Make sure SS understand that J= Judith, G= George and W= William. You could pause the cassette after each speaker to allow SS time to write the person's initials next to the food items. Note that some of the food items in the list are not mentioned on the cassette. As follow up ask SS which of the food listed do they like/don't like.

beefburgers =J
eggs = G
bananas = J
cheese = G
chicken = W
bread = W, G
biscuits = G
steak = J
crisps = J
rice = G
chocolate = J
apples = W
peas = W

Exercise 4a) Write *PLACE, WHEN, GOOD* or *BAD* on the board. Then invite SS to ask you the questions about a memorable meal you have had. This will act as a demonstration and add personal interest value as SS are often keen to know more about their teacher. Emphasise that the memorable meal can include bad meals as well as good.

SS may need to ask you or refer to a dictionary for vocabulary.

Exercise 4b) You could quickly feed back in class. Ask about any particularly interesting meals, bad as well as good.

Extra material and ideas

1 WB page 52, Exercise 9, page 53, Exercises 10 and 11.

2 What was in the fridge? page 137, 8.1. Tell SS they are going to look at a picture for one minute. Then with a partner they have to recall as many items as they can and make a list of them. Tell them to note whether there was more than one of any item e.g. *some apples*. When SS have recalled as many items as they can, they feed back. To practise countable and uncountable nouns and the past of the verb *to be*, write the following on the board:

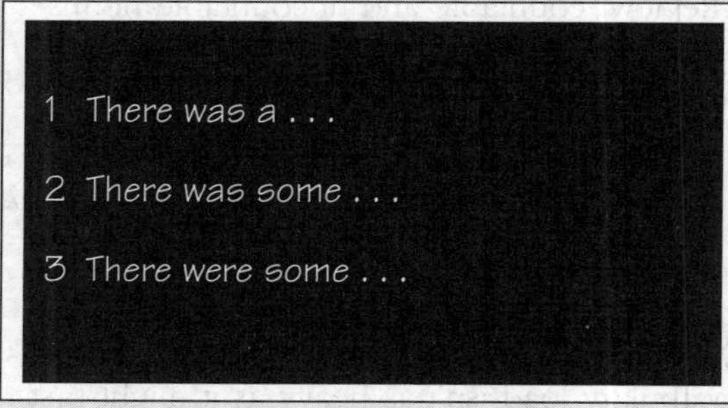

1 There was a . . .
2 There was some . . .
3 There were some . . .

In the feedback ask each pair to tell you two things on their list. They also have to say which of the sentences on the board they correspond to. Write the items next to the correct sentence. Don't write up any incorrect grammar, e.g. if SS say *milk* should be in 3, correct it and add to 2. However, if they suggest an item that wasn't in the fridge, add it to the board. When you have written all the items they can remember, allow them to look at the picture again. They should check to see if any of the items on the board are incorrect. You could preview the grammar for the FOCUS ON GRAMMAR by asking the following when you're doing the feedback *Were there any ...? Was there any...?*

3 In a multilingual class you could have a cultural information exchange about eating customs, e.g. biggest meal of the day, times of meals, does the family eat together, typical meals, do they often eat in restaurants? etc.

FOCUS ON GRAMMAR

Countables and uncountables

- Revise and give further practice of *there is, there are, a* and *some* used with countable and uncountable nouns.
- Review of quantifier *How many* introduced in CHECK YOUR ENGLISH and Units 1 and 3.
- To introduce quantifiers: *any* used in negatives and questions, *(How) much/many*, and *a lot of* + countable and uncountable nouns.

L

- At this level SS find the whole area of quantifiers, countable and uncountable nouns, confusing. For example they have to learn that the word *money* is uncountable which might fly in the face of logic for many SS. It is confusing that *some* can be used with *there is* and *there are.* They then have to match the correct quantifier with the noun in positive and negative sentences and questions. To reach any level of accuracy this whole area will need patience on the part of everyone! You should look for improvement rather than accuracy in the early stages while SS assimilate this area of grammar and it will need frequent revision.
- SS are further confused by the use of a countable noun before an uncountable noun which then changes the quantifier, e.g., *How **much** water..?* but *How **many** bottles of water...?*
- The use of *some* is **not** limited to positive sentences e.g. *Would you like some...?*, and *any* is **not** limited to questions and answers e.g. *I'll take any you have.* However, considering the problems the SS at this level already have to face, we recommend you suggest that if they follow the guideline, *some* with positive sentences and *any* with negative sentences and questions they won't make a mistake. However, it would be unwise to offer this as a hard and fast rule.

Pronunciation Encourage the use of weak forms, *some* /səm/, *a* /ə/ and *of* /əv/ in *a lot of.* The intrusive soundlink /j/ occurs after *many* and *any* if a vowel follows, e.g. *How many apples* /haʊmenijæplz/.

Other consonant/vowel sound linking will occur after *some* and *much* e.g. *How‿much oil ... Some‿apples.* If SS use these features of sound linking when speaking this will help them to achieve a better sense of rhythm and sentence stress.

Students' Book (page 82)

A, some and *any*

Exercise 1a and b) Copy the table onto the board and elicit which two columns are for countable nouns and which is for uncountable. You may wish to write the following on the board to support this.

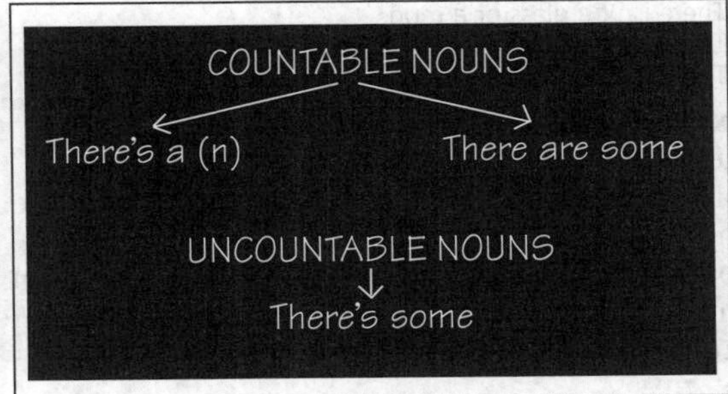

Highlight that the verb before *some* can be singular or plural depending on whether the noun is uncountable or countable plural. Underline the examples on the board. Focus on the examples in the SB and ask SS to give you one more example for each column before they continue the exercise working individually. Note that all the vocabulary should be familiar apart from the items used in the examples, *egg, spoons* and *toast.*

THERE A/AN: egg melon orange newspaper
THERE ARE SOME: cups spoons letters knives apples tissues
THERE'S SOME: sugar some milk butter coffee toast bread

Exercise 1c)

[8.3]
There's an egg, a melon, an orange and a newspaper on the table. There are some spoons, some cups, some knives, some apples, some tissues and some letters. There's also some toast, some bread, some sugar, some milk, some coffee and some butter.

After checking and correcting their lists SS practise the use of the weak forms indicated. See L for pronunciation.

/ə/, /ən/, /səm/, /ðərə/

Exercise 1d) You could get SS to predict where the stress occurs and then check by playing the cassette again or saying the words yourself. Allow time for SS to practise saying the words with the correct stress.

'melon 'newspaper 'coffee 'orange 'letters 'apples 'sugar 'butter 'tissues

Exercise 2a) Ask SS to read the information about *any* in the grammar box. While they read, write the following on the board:

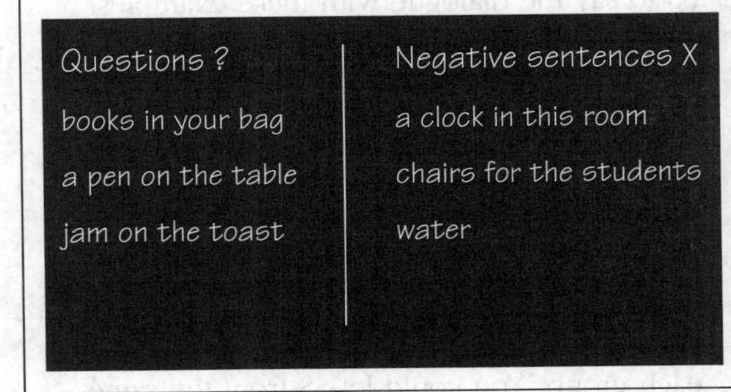

Ask SS to make questions and negative sentences using the cues on the board to check they have understood what they have read. Then ask them to complete the exercise working individually.

1 There isn't a glass or a mug.
2 There isn't any jam or any rice.
3 There aren't any forks or any mushrooms.

Exercise 2b) Do two or three examples with the whole class then monitor the pair work. If mistakes of form are frequent, stop the exercise and focus on the problem before letting SS continue. Aim for accuracy of form at this point. Only focus on pronunciation mistakes if they are causing problems of understanding.

Much, many and *a lot*

Exercise 3a) Again allow SS time to read the information in the grammar box. Write the following on the board to check they have understood the use of the quantifiers:

sandwiches/sugar
How much ______ do you want?
How many ______ do you want?

students/noise
There are a lot of ____ in the room.
There's a lot of ____ in the room.

Support this by asking questions:
1 Do we use *much* or *many* with countable nouns?
2 Can we use *a lot* with countable and uncountable nouns?

Let SS do the exercise in the SB individually then check with a partner before you do feedback.

1 How many 2 How much 3 How many 4 How much
5 How many 6 How much 7 How much

Exercise 3b) Ask two confident SS to say the dialogues. Then ask check questions *Why do we say, How* ***many*** *letters? Why do we say, How* ***much*** *toast?*

Take another example of a countable and uncountable noun e.g. *apples* and *coffee*, and ask SS to say the dialogue with these examples. Then let them work in pairs asking and answering questions about the kitchen. Monitor and stop the activity if mistakes of form are frequent. Focus on the problem then continue with the exercise.

Exercise 4 Make sure SS realise that they are going to exchange roles and that the activity is in two parts. SS should both prepare a) and the questions before beginning the roleplay to ensure that the preparation time is the same for each group. You could let SS from the same group work together in the preparation stage to help each other. Before feedback SS from the same group could check to see if they have the same shopping lists.

Student A needs **a** large lemon, **a lot of** eggs, **a lot of** sugar, **some** butter, **some** flour and **a lot of** milk.
Student B needs **an** onion, **some** olive oil, **some** butter, **a lot of** mushrooms, **some** wine, **a lot of** cheese and **some** rice.

Extra material and ideas

1 WB page 49, Exercise 1, page 50, Exercises 2–5, page 51, Exercises 6–7, page 52, Exercise 8.
2 PRACTISE AND CHECK, page 96 for more work on *any, how much* and *how many.*
3 Board game page 138, 8.2. Divide the class into groups of five. You will need a dice, a copy of the board game and a copy of the questions cut up for each group. Each person throws the dice and moves forward on the board. If they land on a ? square they then pick up a question from the pile and answer it. They move backward or forwards accordingly. The winner is the first to the finish.
4 Card game page 139, 8.3 Photocopy the worksheet and cut it up into cards for each group of four SS. (If you can enlarge the cards on the photocopier then this is recommended.) The cards are face down on the table. The SS take it in turns to turn over a card. If the card has a + symbol, the S should make a positive sentence with *there is/are*, using the countable or uncountable noun on the card. If the symbols are – or ?, they form negatives or questions using *there* and the noun on the card, e.g. *Is there any sugar? There's some sugar. There isn't any sugar.* If the group agree that the sentence is correct, the original S keeps the card. The winner is the one who has the most cards at the end of the game.

SKILLS

- Reading: prediction, gist and reading for detail.
- Vocabulary: jobs, common suffixes used with these nouns.
- Listening and writing: listening for detail, note taking, writing a simple job application letter.

Reading and vocabulary

- Some elementary SS may find the passage quite long. However, apart from the vocabulary which is checked in Exercise 1a), the majority of the lexis should be familiar.

Students' Book (page 84)
Exercise 1a) Preteach *model* by mentioning the names of some current supermodels (e.g. Kate Moss, Naomi Campbell, Claudia Schiffer). After you have established that SS are going to read about why Waris left Somalia, ask if anyone knows any of the words in the speech bubbles. This will cut down the number of items they have to look up. If SS are taking a lot of time to check the vocabulary in their dictionaries, it may be better for you to explain a few items rather than waiting for them to check every word.

Exercise 1b) The extracts from the text used in Exercise 1a) can form the basis of this exercise. Ask SS to look at the sentences in Exercise 1a) and make questions about Waris's life. Ask some SS to tell the class what questions they have written.

Example questions:
Why did you decide to run away?
What was frightening?
Where did you work as a builder?
How many children did you look after in London?
What did the photographer do?

Exercise 1c) Check which of SS' questions were answered. Note that this passage is recorded on the class cassette for your use after the silent reading as a sound/spelling reinforcement. See *Extra Material and ideas* 2.

Exercise 1d) You could set a time limit to encourage SS to scan the text quickly to complete this exercise.

2F 3B 4A 5D 6E

Exercise 1e) Ask SS to correct the false sentences.To make sure all the questions can be covered in feedback, you could have half the class work from question 9 backwards.

1T 2T 3F 4T 5F 6T 7F 8T 9F

Exercise 2 So that both groups are occupied in the preparation stage, ask them both to work out their questions as journalists before beginning the mock interviews. If you have a surplus of males in the class who are unwilling to play the part of Waris, they could be Waris' brother being interviewed about his sister.

Vocabulary: jobs

Exercise 3a) In small groups ask SS to make a list of as many jobs as they know before they look at the photographs. This will give you an idea of how much help they will need to complete the crossword. Ask one group to write their list directly onto the board. Correct any spelling mistakes and add any words that other groups have which aren't on the board. SS can do the crossword individually, in pairs or small groups.

2 receptionist 3 doctor 4 electrician 5 dentist 6 actor 7 hairdresser 8 musician 9 footballer 10 businesswoman

Pronunciation Two of the items illustrate a word stress rule you could introduce. Words ending with the sound /ʃən/ i.e., the stress usually falls on the preceding syllable e.g. *'station, elec'trician.* The sound /ʃən/ can be spelt in various ways: *-tion, -cian , -sion, -tian, -sian.* Note the stress change in *elec'trician* and *e'lectrical.*

Exercise 3b) Point out that these suffixes often signal that the word is a noun describing the person who does the job.

-er hairdresser, footballer
-ist receptionist, dentist
-ian electrician, musician
-man/woman policeman, businesswoman
-or doctor, actor

Exercise 3c) Give SS time to make a list of jobs they would like and wouldn't like to do before expecting them to talk about it.

Extra material and ideas

1 WB page 53, Exercise 12.

2 When the SS have completed the reading exercises, ask them to close their books and then read the passage aloud to them or play the cassette. The advantages are that they will now be familiar with the meaning and content and they can assess how good they are at associating the spoken with the written word. They usually have a great sense of achievement if they can follow the information as they hear it.

3 Spidergram page 139, 8.4. Divide SS into two groups A and B. Each group completes their spidergram with the words from their box using a dictionary or asking you the teacher for meaning. When they have finished they teach their words to a S from the other group. He/She then completes the other two spidergrams on the worksheet. Remind SS of useful questions for the PW, e.g. *How do you spell that? Is it a noun/verb etc? Where's the stress?*

Group A
DOCTOR pills (n), a patient (n), an appointment (n), a prescription (n), a nurse (n), a surgery (n)
TEACHER a student (n), teach (v), a board (n), a classroom (n), homework (n), mark (v)

Group B
HAIRDRESSER a comb (n), scissors (n), a client (n), cut (v), a tip (n), a hairbrush (n)
ACTOR a play (n), an audience (n), a theatre (n), a film (n), a director (n), act (v)

4 Jobs page 140, 8.5.Photocopy the worksheet for SS. They first match the stem to the suffix and then write the job under the picture. Encourage them to use dictionaries to access the word and add phonemic transcriptions and word stress information on the worksheet. In feedback highlight stress and pronunciation. SS could interview each other about which of the jobs they would or wouldn't like.

1 gardener, 2 scientist, 3 guitarist, 4 drummer, 5 waiter, 6 politician, 7 jeweller, 8 engineer, 9 photographer

Listening and writing

- Make sure SS understand : *'salary, responsi'bilities, 'driving licence.*

Students' Book (page 85)

Exercise 4 You may need to explain what job Roy is applying for if SS are not aware of what social organisers in a private language school in Britain actually do. Explain that they arrange sightseeing visits and trips to the theatre and the cinema. They also organise sports and sports competitions, discos etc. SS can work in pairs to form the questions from the cues. These will help them to predict the content of the listening. If SS are having problems, they can read the tapescript and listen at the same time. Check one or two question forms with the whole class before dividing the class into two groups.

 [8.4]
ANDY: Hello.
ROY: Is that Andy?
ANDY: Yes, speaking.
ROY: I'm phoning about the job in the paper – about summer work.
ANDY: Oh yes, right. Are you a student?
ROY: Yes, I'm at university here in York. I'm studying French and drama.
ANDY: OK. So you know York quite well, do you? (Yes). Can I ask how old you are?
ROY: Yes, I'm nearly twenty-two. How old are the students at the school?
ANDY: In the summer they're between seventeen and about twenty-five. Do you speak any languages?
ROY: Well, French, of course, and some German.
ANDY: And do you play any sports? Sports are quite an important part of the job, really.
ROY: Well, football and tennis.
ANDY: What else do you like doing?
ROY: I can play the guitar – if that's any use.
ANDY: Oh, very, because we have musical evenings. By the way, have you got a car?
ROY: No, but I've got a driving licence.
ANDY: Because we need someone to drive the minibus when we go on trips.
ROY: No problem. What are the hours?
ANDY: From three in the afternoon to eleven or even midnight.
ROY: What about weekends?
ANDY: Saturday, yes, but you get Tuesday off.
ROY: When does the job start?
ANDY: From the first of June until the end of September. Ah, look, if you're interested, why don't you put all this in writing? I'll let you know by the end of the month.
ROY: OK – thanks very much. Er – one last thing – the salary.
ANDY: Ah, yes – around one thousand five hundred pounds a month.
ROY: Thanks very much. Bye.

a) When does the job start? (1st June)
When does the job finish? (end of September)
What are the hours of work? (3 pm–11pm/ midnight, Monday–Saturday with Tuesday off)
What is the salary? (£1,500 a month)
What do I have to do? (play sports, drive the minibus, organise musical evenings)
How old are the students? (17–25 years old)

b) How old are you? (21)
What do you do? (student)
What languages do you speak? (French, some German)
Can you drive? (Yes)
Do you play any musical instruments/any sports? (guitar/ football, tennis)

Exercise 5 Note that there is no input on how to write a formal letter as we feel it is unlikely that SS at this level would be expected to write such a letter unaided either in real life or for an examination suited to their level. When SS have finished their letters ask them to exchange with another pair and check for spelling and grammar mistakes. They then return the letters to the original pair who correct anything they agree is a mistake. Collect these and indicate any mistakes not identified. Return these for the SS to correct. (Give corrections which you think SS wouldn't know.) Ideally SS should end up with a neat piece of written work with no mistakes. This is often a good psychological boost for low level SS.

REVIEW

Vocabulary

- Review of Units 7 and 8.

- Vocabulary: country, animals, food, phrasal verbs.
- Using your grammar: *going to* + infinitive, quantifiers *when* and *if* etc.

Students' Book (page 86)

Exercise 1a)

sweet, take, eggs, set off, fish, hill, lamb, bridge, get, tomatoes, steak, knives, sugar, river, ride

Exercise 1b) Let SS work in small groups and set a time limit. There could be a competition between groups for the most words.

Exercise 1c) and d) Invite SS to ask you what you ate before they begin the pair work.

Exercise 1e)

1 take a photograph
2 set off early in the morning
3 get lost
4 ride a motorbike

Exercise 2a) If you have a multilingual class, try to arrange the groups according to nationalities. If this isn't possible, then within the groups SS from different countries could be responsible for different courses of the meal; starters, main course and dessert. Tell SS to make notes because they will tell other SS about their menu and dinner guests.

Exercise 2b) Rearrange the class into new groupings so there is a representative from each of the original groups in the new group.

Using your grammar

This activity will need at least fifteen minutes depending on how long it takes SS to grasp the rules of the game. Allow them time to read the instructions and check they understand them. You could quickly draw part of the game onto the board and use this as a demonstration. There shouldn't be a need for feedback as SS have the corrected sentences.

Extra material and ideas

SS prepare their own correction worksheet. In pairs, SS write ten sentences. Some should be correct, some wrong. Encourage them to write questions and negatives as well as positive sentences. They then exchange with another pair who try to find and correct the mistakes. The original SS then mark it. You could set areas you want to target, e.g. Past and Present Simple, or allow SS to choose the areas they want to test.

Are you feeling OK?

Students' Book

General themes: the body and health; pets.

FOCUS ON VOCABULARY: the body and health; parts of the body, illnesses; giving advice.
FOCUS ON GRAMMAR: *have to* and *don't have to*; inviting and making excuses; infinitve of purpose.
SKILLS: reading (pets and health); vocabulary (meaning from context); listening and writing (giving advice by phone and letter).
SOCIAL ENGLISH: getting around by train and plane.

Workbook

GRAMMAR: *have to* and *don't have to*; infinitive of purpose; giving advice.
VOCABULARY: the body; clothes and illness.
WRITING: pronouns.
PRONUNCIATION: word stress; sound and spelling (dipthongs).

FOCUS ON VOCABULARY

The body and health

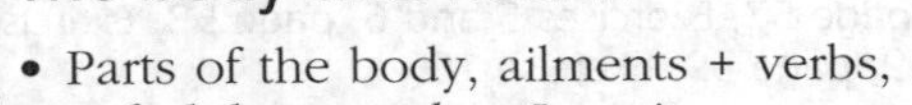

A • Parts of the body, ailments + verbs, *have/has got, feel, hurts, aches, I can't ...*

• Functional exponents for giving advice: *You should... You'd better(not)...* + infinitive.

• Review of offers, *I'll... Shall I...?*

• Review of verbs *have got* and *can't*.

L • **The indefinite article** We say *I've got a 'headache*, but we don't use *a/an* with *'earache, 'backache, 'toothache*.

Pronunciation The spelling of the following words usually causes pronunciation problems: *ache* /eɪk/, *cough* /kɒf/, *knee* /niː/, *'stomach* /stʌmək/, *throat* /θrəʊt/.

SS often wrongly stress the word *'temperature*. Encourage them to reduce the word to three syllables /tem|prɪt|ʃə/ or /tem|prət|ʃə/.

• Remind SS that *teeth* is an irregular plural form but that we don't say **teethache* even if we are referring to more than one tooth.

• ***Should*** has the same formal characteristics as *can*, a modal which they already know i.e., no third person *-s*, no auxiliary in the question and negative; and it's the first verb in the verb phrase, followed by the infinitive of the verb. The negative can be a contracted form, *shouldn't*.

Pronunciation The weak form of *should* /ʃəd/ is commonly used in statements and questions. In short answers it is commonly pronounced /ʃʊd/.

• Highlight that the uncontracted form of *you'd better* is *you had better*. There is no third person *-s*, it's followed by the infinitive of the verb and the negative does not have a contracted form, only *'d better not*. This expression usually carries the suggestion that there would be negative consequences if the advice wasn't followed.

Pronunciation SS tend to avoid the glottal stop and pronounce this structure as **you better*. Highlight the weak form of *you* as in /jəd'betə/ with the stress on *'better*.

• *Advice* is uncountable. SS often say **advices*.

Students' Book (page 88)

Exercise 1a) and b) You could tell SS things about your body that you like and don't like.

1 My eyes are too small.
2 I'd like a thin waist.
3 I quite like my hands.
4 My legs are short.
5 I don't like my nose.
6 My hair is nice.
7 I've got big feet.

[9.1]
ANGELA: There's a lot I'm not happy with. My eyes are too small, for a start. Then I'd like a thin waist. I quite like my hands, but my legs are short and I don't like my nose at all. My hair's nice but I've got big feet.

Exercise 1c) With the whole class establish which words in the box SS already know. This will limit the number of items they have to look up in the dictionary.

Exercise 1d) You could draw a body outline on the board (see below) and write the body parts in a list to the side of the drawing. Use a ruler and point to a word and ask SS to pronounce it. Gradually move the ruler faster and faster. Then remove the words and just point to the body part on the drawing. You could again gradually increase the speed to the point that it's almost impossible to keep up with you.

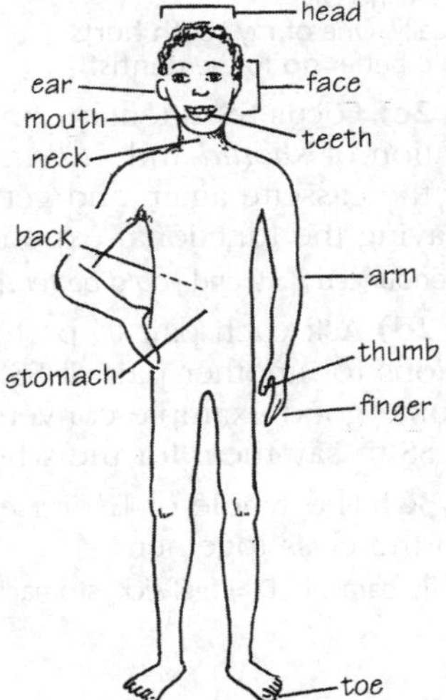

Exercise 1e) You could begin this by declaring what you would like to change about your body. Beware of this activity provoking embarrassment. Leave it out if you think it might be too sensitive.

Exercise 2a) To help SS predict the language in the listening you could ask them to read the information in the grammar box. Check to see if they know what problems the photographs represent but don't indicate whether they are right or wrong before they listen to the cassette.

[9.2]
1
A: What's wrong?
B: I can't read the board from here.
A: I think you should see an optician.
2
A: What's the matter?
B: I've got a bad cold and a cough.
A: You'd better not go out then.
3
A: Are you feeling OK?
B: No, not really. One of my teeth hurts.
A: Well, you'd better go to the dentist.

1 B 2 A 3 C

Exercise 2b) Pause the cassette to allow SS time to write their answers. Write the word *advice* on the board. If SS don't understand the word, pretend to have a bad headache and say, *Give me some advice.* Then paraphrase this e.g. *give me a good idea, tell me what to do, give me some advice.* This should elicit a suggestion of some kind, in which case respond by saying, *Yes, that's good advice, that's a good idea.* Then ask SS to identify the advice in each of the three conversations. Isolate the exponents *should* and *'d better* and write them on the board. Highlight grammatical features (see L). SS may supply exponents *Why don't you ...?* and *How about ...?*

A: What's **wrong**?
B: I can't **read** the board from here.
A: I think you should **see** an optician.
2
A: What's the **matter**?
B: I've got a bad **cold** and a **cough**.
A: You'd better not **go out** then.
3
A: **Are you** feeling OK?
B: No, not really. One of my **teeth hurts**.
A: Well, you'd better **go** to the **dentist**.

Exercise 2c) Focus SS' attention on the pronunciation of *should* and *'d better* (see L) then play the cassette again and get them to practise saying the functional exponents.

Should is pronounced /ʃəd/ and *you'd better* /jəd'betə/.

Exercise 2d) Ask each pair to perform their conversations for another pair of SS. Try and identify some good example conversations and ask these SS to say them for the whole class.

Exercise 3a) The whole of Exercise 3 can be done with the class together.

B = flu C = flu earache D = feel sick, stomachache
E = cough

Exercise 3b) Encourage SS to offer more than one piece of advice.

(Suggested answers)
Go to bed if you've got flu.
I'll give you some antibiotics for your earache/flu.
If you feel sick/have stomachache, you shouldn't eat for a day or two.
Shall I get you some medicine for that cough?

Exercise 3c) Play the cassette through completely and check the SS' answers. Only play the cassette again to establish the correct answer if there is disagreement.

[9.3]
1 You'd better take an aspirin for that headache.
2 If you feel sick, you shouldn't eat for a day or two.
3 Go to bed and keep warm if you've got flu.
4 I'll give you some antibiotics for your earache.
5 Shall I get some medicine for that cough?

1 A 2 D 3 B 4 C 5 E

Exercise 4 An alternative approach to this exercise would be to divide the class into doctors and patients. Half the patients get one problem the other half get the second problem. The patients should try to see as many doctors as they can within a time limit. They then decide on who is the best and worst doctor. This is all meant to be light-hearted, of course.

Extra material and ideas

1 WB page 57, Exercises 5 and 6, page 58, Exercises 8 and 9, page 59, Exercise 10.

2 Divide the class into two groups A and B. Using the problems in the box below, give one problem to group A and one problem to group B. The problems should be written on the board.

Problems
Group A
1 Jane can't sleep.
2 Jack hurt his back.
3 Pauline's got flu.
Group B
1 Simon's got spots.
2 Gillian feels tired all the time.
3 David's got a high temperature.

Group A have to write 4 pieces of advice using *She/He should ...* Group B are given a different problem and they have to write 4 pieces of advice for that problem using *She/He shouldn't ...*
SS from A and B form pairs. Remind the SS of their partner's problem. They have one minute each to guess what advice their partner wrote down. You should be the time keeper to avoid disputes! The winner is the one who guesses the most sentences their partner had written down. In the next round Group A uses the *You shouldn't ...* and Group B uses *You should ...*

3 GW. Divide the board into two. Draw a large outline of a body on each side (see Exercise 1d). Alternatively draw one on the board and ask SS to copy it, one per group. It should be quite big. You call out a part of the body and SS write the word next to the appropriate part either on the board or on their papers. If they spell the word correctly, they get extra points.

4 GW. Give students sticky labels with parts of the body written on them. Divide the class into two groups. One SS from each group comes to the front of the class. The other members of the group stick the labels on this S. The winning team is the one with the most labels in the correct place.

FOCUS ON GRAMMAR

A
- Introduces: *have to* + infinitive, positive, negative and question forms.
- Functional exponents for inviting and making excuses.
- Infinitive of purpose.

L
- *have to* + infinitive is used for external obligation, cf. *must*, or the imperative e.g. *leave now* used to express obligation from the speaker. If your SS already know *must*, we recommend you offer this as an alternative rather than trying to explain the subtle difference in meaning. The SB doesn't emphasise the externality of the obligation. However, you can point out that while *mustn't* remains an obligation, *don't/doesn't have to* removes the obligation.
- Highlight that *have to* has a third person form *has to*, and uses the auxiliary verb *do* and *does* in negatives and questions. Also the verb *has* in the third person reverts to *have* in negatives and questions, *He doesn't have to go*. Note that a common alternative form is *have/has got to* + infinitive. We recommend that you don't mention or practise this until you feel SS have achieved reasonable accuracy with *have to* + infinitive.

Pronunciation The weak form of *to* is used /tə/ + consonant and /tʊ/ + vowel e.g. *I have to leave* /aɪhæftəli:v/ *I have to eat* ... /aɪhæftʊwi:t/. Note that *have to* is frequently pronounced /hæftə/. See SB page 90.
The weak form of *do* /də/ and *does* /dəz/ is commonly used in questions, but the strong form is used in the short answers /du:/ and /dʌz/.

- *Would you like to* + infinitive is introduced as a functional exponent for a polite invitation. Highlight that because of *would*, *like* has to be followed by the infinitive form of the verb in this structure. *Like* + *-ing* was covered in Unit 6 FOCUS ON VOCABULARY. Therefore SS may think that it's possible to use the *-ing* form with this structure. Point out that *like* + *-ing* refers to a general situation, *would like to* refers to one occasion/specific situation. Use the following to highlight the difference.

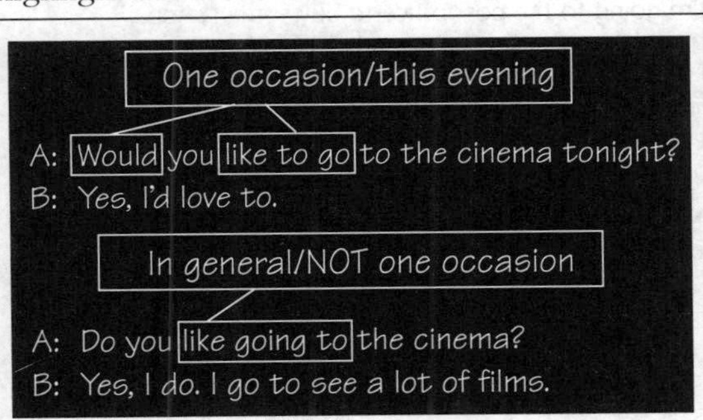

Pronunciation Highlight the pronunciation of *Would you like to* /wədʒəlaɪktə/ which includes assimilation, linkage and weak forms.

- **Making excuses** Note that although in the SB they are kept separate we can combine *I'm sorry* and *I'm afraid* in the following way; *I'm sorry but I'm afraid I can't.* However, it would be wrong to reverse the order **I'm afraid but I'm sorry I can't.* This literally means *I'm frightened.*
- **Infinitive of purpose** SS often try to express this by using *for* + *to* + infinitive or *for* followed by the *-ing* form e.g. **I came here for to learn English*, **I came here for learning English.*
Highlight that the infinitive is used after certain verbs expressing reason e.g. *I came here to learn English*.

Students' Book (page 90)

Have to and *don't have to*

Exercise 1a)
[9.4]
HELEN: What's the matter, Mark? You look awful.
MARK: It's OK. I've got a headache, that's all, and I feel sick.
HELEN: Why don't you go home? You should be in bed.
MARK: No, there's too much to do. I have to interview a new assistant at eleven.
HELEN: OK, well, go home after that and go to bed. You don't have to work this afternoon, do you?

To immediately focus attention on meaning put the following on the board:

Tell SS they're going to listen to two recordings. You want them to think about which things the people say are necessary and which are not necessary. Set the scene for the first recording so SS can predict the content and focus on the language: two people who work together in an office. Mark has a headache and Helen is giving him some advice. Why doesn't Mark take Helen's advice? See if they understood that Mark has to interview a new assistant and that this is why he doesn't take her advice. Alternatively, you could elicit the situation after they listen.

Exercise 1b) Focus attention on *I have to interview a new assistant,* and add this to the appropriate column on the board under *It's necessary.* Focus on the pronunciation (see L).
have to /hæftə/

Exercise 1c) Before playing the cassette ask SS to predict how we can say something isn't necessary. After the recording elicit the example, *I don't have to go to lunch with the bank manager*, and add to the board under, *It isn't necessary*.

[9.5]

MARK: Well, I've got a lunch appointment with the bank manager but I suppose I don't have to go. I can phone him and see him another day. But I have to phone Germany at two o'clock – it's the only time I can speak to Herr Fischer. I can phone the new Sales Director and change our meeting to another day. I don't have to see him today – and I don't have to write the report on my visit to Brazil – I can do that tomorrow. But then there are our important visitors from Argentina – I have to take them out to dinner tonight – they're going home tomorrow.

HELEN: Shall I take them out for you?

MARK: That's very nice of you, but really I have to go – there are a lot of problems.

1✗ 2✓ 3✗ 4✗ 5✓

Exercise 1d) Ask SS to read the information in the grammar box. Meanwhile, add the following to the board:

I have to interview a new assistant.
You
We
They
She
He

I don't have to have lunch with the bank manager.
You
We
They
She
He

Ask SS to use the sentences on the board but to change the pronoun and change the verb if necessary. This is to highlight the third person *-s*. Write up the sentences for *has to* and *doesn't have to*. Ask them to form the questions, again using the sentences on the board, for *you* and *he* : *Do you have to interview a new assistant? Does he have to interview a new assistant?* Practise these with the SS and encourage them to use the weak forms of *do you* /dʒə/ and *does he* /dəz(h)ɪ/.

A: Does he have to phone Germany at 2 o'clock?
B: Yes, he does.
A: Does he have to meet the new Sales Director?
B: No, he doesn't. He can change the meeting.
A: Does he have to write a report?
B: No, he doesn't. He can write it tomorrow.
A: Does he have to take the visitors out to dinner?
B: Yes, he does.

Exercise 2 Before the pair work practise the pronunciation of: *Would you like to go to the cinema tonight?*

Then focus on the polite way of making excuses and practise: *I'm afraid I can't. I have to visit my aunt.*

Encourage SS to use appropriate facial expression e.g. furrowed brow and disappointed eyebrows! Check that the SS can express the excuses cued by the pictures.

(Suggested answers)
A I'm afraid I can't. I have to go and see the optician.
B Thank you very much but I have to work this evening.
C I'm sorry but I have to babysit for my sister at 9.
D I'm afraid I can't. I have to fly to Madrid.

Exercise 3a) and b) As a lead-in for the quiz you could begin by asking SS to write down as many things as they can think of about Britain (including any rules/laws) in two minutes and get feedback. There are also answers to the quiz on page 131 of SB.

2T 3F 4T 5F 6T 7T 8F 9T 10F

Exercise 3c) If you have a multilingual class, allow SS of the same nationality to work together.

Exercise 4 Check that SS can say the names of the professions/jobs. SS could write the sentences saying what each profession *has to* or *doesn't have to* do. These sentences could be collected, read out and the other SS guess the profession being described.

Taxi drivers have to drive, get up early, work long hours, work Sundays. They don't have to wear a uniform or use a computer.
Nurses have to wear a uniform, be nice to people, use a computer, work long hours, work on Sundays, look after people.
Shop assistants have to be nice to people, work with money, work long hours and look smart. They don't usually have to wear a uniform.
Vets have to study for a long time. They have to look after animals. They have to work long hours and on Sundays. They don't have to look smart.
Politicians have to be nice to people, get up early, look smart, work long hours and on Sundays. They have to travel a lot.

Infinitive of purpose

Exercise 5a) You could begin by asking SS to tell you where the nearest post office, supermarket etc. is. When you have checked the answers highlight the infinitive form. You could anticipate the common error of, **I went to the garage for buying some petrol*, and write it on the board. Then put a "dramatic" cross through *for buying*, and write *to buy* above it.

to buy
I went to the garage ~~for buying~~ some petrol.

2 c) 3 a) 4 b) 5d)

Exercise 5b) Play the cassette once to check the answers. Then play each sentence in isolation and identify where the main stresses occur. Tell SS to mark them in their books and then practise the sentences.

[9.6]

1 I'm going to the post office to buy some stamps.
2 I want to go to the supermarket to get some bread.
3 I have to go to the garage to get some petrol.
4 I have to go to the library to borrow a book on China.
5 I'm going to the gym to do some exercise.

to is pronounced /tə/

Exercise 6 Do one of the question and answers with the whole class to demonstrate the activity.

Monitor SS and correct mistakes as they occur. If the same mistakes are repeated, stop the exercise and focus on the problem before letting SS continue.

Student A
A: Do you have to wear glasses to read?
B: Yes, I do./No, I don't.
A: Do you have to use a diary to remember birthdays?
B: Yes, I do./No, I don't.
A: Do you have to use a calculator to add up?
B: Yes, I do./No, I don't.
Student B
B: Do you have to get a bus to school?
A: Yes I do./No, I don't.
B: Do you have to take sleeping pills to go to sleep?
A: Yes I do./No, I don't.
B: Do you have to stand on a chair to touch the ceiling?
A: Yes, I do./No, I don't.

Extra material and ideas

1 WB page 55, Exercise 1, page 56, Exercises 2 and 3, page 57, Exercise 4.

2 PRACTISE AND CHECK, page 96 for more work on *have to* and *don't have to*.

3 What's my job? As a whole class or in small groups a S is secretly given the name of a profession. The other SS have to guess what it is but they are only allowed ten questions. They should ask questions with, *Do you have to ...?* as well as other structures. Then another S is given another profession and so on. Example questions: *Do you have to wear a uniform? Do you have to work in an office? Do you have to have a secretary? Do you have to work with other people? Do you make a lot of money? Do you have to work at night? Do you have to work in the evening? Do you have to travel? Is your job dangerous? Do you help people?*

4 Playlet. The family 1 page 140, 9.1.
SS should be in groups of five for the sketch. One S is the director.
1 SS read the sketch. Ask if they understand all the vocabulary. Then ask a few comprehension questions e.g. *What does the mother want? What are the children doing? What does the father offer to do?* etc.
2 SS choose which roles they want to play and who will direct the scene.
3 SS read out their parts giving eye contact to the person they're addressing. Monitor the group's pronunciation, sentence stress and intonation. If you think they could all benefit from some guidance from you, stop the proceedings and focus on one aspect. Ask them to try again.
4 Tell the directors they now have to think about the environment: Where are the people? What are they all doing? etc. The SS should now be acting as well as speaking their parts. The directors should get the group to repeat the conversation until they think it's the best it can be.
5 SS should then act out their scene for the other SS. Encourage the others to applaud after each group has performed.

SKILLS

- Reading and vocabulary: reading for gist and detail, word formation, deducing meaning from context.
- Listening, vocabulary and writing: listening for detail, pets, creative writing.
- Functional exponent: giving suggestions using *Why don't you...?*

Reading and vocabulary

- There are a number of items that will be unfamiliar. However, don't preteach the following as they form the basis of the vocabulary exercise: *com'plain, de'lay, 'common, the hold* (in a plane or ship).

You may want to check the following before the reading: *to stroke* (an animal), *'blood pressure, 'heart beat, 'absent, take 'off, to land, to a'gree.*

If you feel that your SS' comprehension of the text will be blocked by the unknown items in the vocabulary exercise which follows the reading, you could help SS to locate the words in the text and do the exercise **before** the reading. However, if you think they can tolerate the uncertainty, don't use it as a preteaching activity.

Students' Book (page 92)

Exercise 1a)
Check that SS understand the word *pet*. To aid prediction you could begin by eliciting the names of as many animals as the class can think of. Ask about pets in their country, which animals are popular and which are not, whether people keep unusual pets e.g. tarantula spiders etc. Tell SS to do the matching exercise as quickly as possible, pointing out that they don't need to read the whole text to do this. These texts are recorded on the Class cassette if you want to exploit them further.

A=3 B=1 C=2

Exercise 1b) Read the headlines out and again encourage SS to scan the texts to match the headlines.

A=5 B=4 C=6

Exercise 1c) This will require SS to read in more detail so allow more time for this exercise.

pets, health

Exercise 1d) SS should be fairly familiar with the texts at this point and should be able to locate the information quite quickly. However, they will require time to digest it and relate it to the question.

2b) 3b) 4b) 5a) 6b) 7a)

Exercise 1e) Ask SS to give an example of a noun, a verb and an adjective before you begin the exercise.

1v 2n 3v 4 adj

Exercise 1f) Ask SS to refer back to the text to help them match the words and definitions and encourage them to guess the meaning of words from context. In monolingual situations the definitions could be in L1.

1a) 2d) 3c) 4b)

Exercise 1g) If the earlier exercises were mainly done individually or in pairs, change the interaction pattern and do this as a class discussion. Nominate SS to respond to the questions rather than waiting for volunteers, making sure the quieter members of the class are involved.

Listening and writing

L

• Quickly check that SS can recognise and pronounce the names of the animals to facilitate the exercises that follow.
• The following items may be unfamiliar: *to feed, neighbour.*

Students' Book (page 93)

Exercise 2 Do this with the whole class. (A=snake, B=stick insect, C=parrot, D=hamster, E=fish, F=dog, G=cat)

Exercise 3a) SS should be ready to go straight into the listening now without prediction exercises. If you feel they need time to write the notes, pause after each speaker. Feed back, and if there is disagreement, play the cassette again to establish the correct answer rather than supplying the answer yourself. This approach gives the second listening a very clear focus.

[9.7]

CALLER 1: Hi, yes. I'd like a pet – I think I'd like a snake because they're different and I suppose they're easy to look after. I work very long hours and sometimes go away on business so I can't have a dog.

CALLER 2: My mother lives by herself now and wants some company in the house. I thought a bird would be a good companion for her because they sing and seem happy. Is that a good idea?

CALLER 3: My son wants a pet. I thought of a hamster because they're quite cheap to feed and you don't have to take them to the vet a lot. Also we live in a flat so the pet has to be quite small. What do you think?

	PET	WHY?
Caller 1	a snake	because they're different and easy to look after
Caller 2	a bird	because they sing and seem happy
Caller 3	a hamster	because they're cheap to feed, they're small and you don't need to take them to the vet a lot.

Exercise 3b) and c) Remind SS of their choices in Exercise 2) and play the cassette once to see if their suggestions were the same as Zelda's. SS should copy the table onto a piece of paper and then fill in the second column under Zelda's advice (there's no advice for the third person). Play the cassette again, pausing for them to make notes after each speaker.

[9.8]

CALLER 1: Hi, yes. I'd like a pet. I'd like a snake because they're different and I think they're quite easy to look after. I work very long hours and sometimes go away on business so I can't have a dog.

ZELDA: Yes, snakes are different, but you need to look after them. They need small dead animals to eat and this will be a problem if you are away or working late. Lots of people don't like snakes so they aren't always happy to help you. Also snakes die if they aren't warm so that's a problem if you aren't there and the electricity goes off. Why don't you get a cat? They can come in and go out when they like. And I'm sure a friend or neighbour would come in and feed it while you're away. You can get cats that are very unusual.

CALLER 2: My mother lives by herself now and wants some comany in the house. I thought a bird would be a good companion for her because they sing and seem happy. Is that a good idea?

ZELDA: Well, yes, but a bird isn't very loving. What about a small dog? If your mother's alone, a dog usually barks when someone comes to the door, so it'll make her feel safer. Also a small dog doesn't have to have very long walks but at the same time it'll be nice for your mother to go out for a short walk.

CALLER 3: My son wants a pet. I thought of a hamster because they're quite cheap to feed and you don't have to take them to the vet a lot. Also we live in a flat so the pet has to be quite small. What do you think?

PROBLEM	ZELDA'S ADVICE
1 Works long hours, goes away on business.	A cat. (They come and go as they like, the neighbours can help you, they are unusual.)
2 Mother lives by herself.	A dog. (They are loving, they bark when someone's at the door, they need short walks.)

Exercise 4 You could do this orally with the whole class first if you think SS need more guidance.

(Suggested answer)
I think hamsters are nice animals but they are not very good for young children because they sleep all day and wake up at night. Sometimes they bite too.
You should get a goldfish/stick insect. They don't do very much but they are cheap, small and easy for children to look after.

Extra materials and ideas

Find someone who page 141, 9.2. GW. Hand out the worksheets and check that SS can form questions from the cues e.g. *Do you like cats?* The questions are the same for groups A and B. Check that the SS are forming correct questions: *Did you ... Have you ... Are you ...* When a S from group A and a S from group B have completed the worksheets feed back with the whole group. You should be able to locate SS with opposing opinions and experiences so you can turn this into a mini discussion. For example, locate a S who didn't have pets as a child and a S who did. You could ask further questions or invite the other SS to ask further questions e.g. *Did you want pets? Why didn't you have any pets? What pets did you have? Did you want other pets?* etc.

SOCIAL ENGLISH

Getting around

• Vocabulary and lexical phrases related to airports and railway stations.

• The following vocabulary may be unfamiliar. You may wish to precheck them: '*platform, day 'return, flight, aisle.*

• **Present Continuous for fixed arrangements in the future** This may confuse SS who expect this verb form to relate to time now. Point out that *going to* + infinitive is an acceptable alternative. (This also came up in Unit 7.)

• **Present Simple** for timetabled future (trains/planes) and itineraries is also used but not focused on.

Students' Book (page 94)

Exercise 1a) Elicit *railway* and *airport* from the photographs. Introduce *to catch a plane/train.* Set the scene by asking SS about the last journey they took by train and/or plane. Join in the discussion and tell them about yourself. Does anyone have a good travel story to tell? Ask SS which form of transport they like best etc. Play the cassette and allow time for them to decide where each phrase might be heard.

[9.9]
1 Last call for passengers travelling to Miami on BA flight one nine six.
2 Can I see your passport and ticket, please?
3 Customers are advised that the train from Edinburgh, due to arrive on platform seven, is running approximately ten minutes late.
4 Thank you. Here's your boarding card. Have a good flight.
5 Smoking or non-smoking?
6 Passengers travelling to Frankfurt are advised that BA flight one five six is now boarding at Gate sixteen. We apologise for the delay and any inconvenience this may have caused.
7 Single or return?
8 Have you got any hand luggage?
9 Yes, madam. There's a buffet car at the other end.
10 Passengers are asked to fasten their seatbelts and extinguish their cigarettes.

A AIRPORT 1, 2, 4, 5, 6, 8, 10
B RAILWAY STATION 3, 7, 9

Exercise1b) Get SS to practise saying the phrases. Model the pronunciation for them first.

1B 2A 3B 4A

Exercise 2a) and b) Do this with the whole class so that all the SS are ready for the practice at the same time. You can also model the suggestions which are appropriate for the gap fill and make it clear that there are possibilities other than the ones on the cassette.

[9.10]

1 AT THE RAILWAY STATION
A: Good morning. Can I help you?
B: Good morning. **I'd like a ticket** to Newcastle, please.
A: Single or return?
B: **Return**, please. I'm coming back tonight. **What platform does it leave** from?
A: Platform eight.
B: **What time does it** leave?
A: 9.15 and it arrives in Newcastle at 10.30. Here's your ticket.

2 AT THE AIRPORT
A: Can I see your passport and ticket, please?
B: Yes, here you are. Is **the flight on time?**
A: No, I'm sorry. There's a half hour delay.
B: Oh, dear. **Do I have to change planes** in Frankfurt?
A: No, you stay on the same plane.

Exercise 2c) Monitor the pair work and correct any mistakes as they occur.

Exercise 2d) After allowing time for practice, ask for volunteers to say the conversations for the whole class. Ask the others to listen and see if they had different examples of how to finish the dialogues. Try to create an atmosphere where SS aren't embarrassed about speaking in front of the class. This is often helped by giving praise and asking the others to acknowledge the "bravery" by applauding, and it isn't usually helped by launching immediately into the mistakes. The more SS do this in front of others, the less threatening it becomes.

1 AT THE RAILWAY STATION
B: How much is the ticket?
A: Seventeen pounds fifty. How do you want to pay?
B: By credit card.
A: Sign here, please. Thank you. Here's your ticket.

2 AT THE AIRPORT
A: How much luggage have you got?
B: Just this suitcase.
A: Would you like smoking or non-smoking?
B: Non-smoking, please.
A: Would you like a window or an aisle seat?
B: (A) window (seat), please.
A: Here's your boarding card. The flight will board at Gate 22 from/at one thirty. Have a good flight.
A: Thank you.

Extra material and ideas

1 Aiming high! This activity is better if you have access to cassette recorders and blank cassettes but they're not essential. Ask SS to practise the conversations from Exercise 2a). Monitor their progress. If you find a common error occurring, e.g. inappropriate intonation on question forms, stop the SS and practise intonation on question forms. When SS have reached a point where they really don't think they can further improve the conversations they have been practising, they record them. Write the following on the board and as they listen to their cassette ask them to consider the following points to help them assess their performance:

• Is my pronunciation clear?
• Do I speak too slowly?
• Do I stress important words in the sentence or do I stress every word?
• Is my intonation on questions good?
• Is my intonation monotone?

When they think it's as good as they'll be able to get it, they hand it in for your assessment. If you couldn't record them, ask them to do their conversation for another pair of SS who then reciprocate. The objective is to get SS to see that they can improve but it does take some effort on their part. The more they practise the better they can get.

Practise and check key (Units 7-9)

PRACTISE

1 *Going to*

2 A: I'm going to get married next year.
B: Who are you going to marry?
3 A: They're going to buy a new car tomorrow.
B: Which car are they going to buy?
4 A: He's going to study Japanese at university.
B: Why is he going to study Japanese?
5 A: We're going to travel round the world next year.
B: Which countries are you going to visit?
6 A: I'm going to watch a video this evening.
B: Which video are you going to watch?

2 *Going to* and *if* or *when*

2 **When I leave** school **I'm not going to work** in my father's business.
3 **I'm not going to take** the children out **if** it **rains** tomorrow.
4 They**'re going to phone when** they**'re** ready.
5 **I'm going to make** your dinner **when I finish** work.

3 Countable and uncountables

a)
1 Countables: apple, biscuit, egg, grape, carrot, melon, banana
2 Uncountables: cheese, butter, garlic, milk, jam, bread, sugar

b)
1 some 2 a 3 any 4 any 5 some 6 any 7 any

c)
2
2 How much coffee 3 How many CDs 4 How many books 5 How much

4 *Have to* or *don't have to*

a)
VANESSA: If I'm going to New York or Singapore, yes, I **have to** be away for two days or more. But we **don't have to** do long flights.
INTERVIEWER: **Do** air stewardesses **have to** do a lot of training?
VANESSA: We **have to** do about two months.
INTERVIEWER **Do** you **have to** wear a blue jacket?
VANESSA: Yes, when we're flying we **have to** wear a blue jacket.

b)
She has to work very long hours, be away for for two days or more on long trips and has to do a lot of training. She also has to wear a uniform.

She doesn't have to do long flights if she doesn't want to.

CHECK

1 Verb forms: past, present or future

2 went 3 don't like 4 want 5 go 6 can 7 doesn't cost 8 found 9 had 10 met 11 did 12 played 13 sat 14 read 15 started 16 didn't stop 17 decided 18 are planning 19 are going to stay 20 are going to fly

2 Correct the mistakes

2 When 3 Does he have to 4 any, some 5 pass 6 don't have to pay 7 to go 8 lamb 9 help 10 you'd better not 11 a lot of 12 can't 13 drive

3 Prepositions

1 of, with, at, of, of
2 on, about, for, at
3 in, with
4 out, on, from

4 Vocabulary

1 The body: face, toe, 'finger, arm
2 Travel: 'luggage, de'lay, flight, 'platform
3 The country: field, wood, path, 'mountain
4 Illness: hurt, cough, 'aspirin, 'backache
5 Jobs: 'builder, elec'trician, 'businessman
6 Food: steak, rice, fish, 'mushrooms

TEST

There is a progress test, for Units 7–9 on pages 154 and 155 of this book for you to photocopy for your students. See page 159 for the Key.

Staying in

Students' Book

General themes: rooms and furniture.

FOCUS ON VOCABULARY: rooms and furniture; verb/noun collocation.
FOCUS ON GRAMMAR: comparative adjectives and superlative adjectives.
SKILLS: listening (song – *My girl's mad at me*); vocabulary (meaning from context); speaking and writing (roleplay and diary writing).
REVIEW: vocabulary (quiz and odd words out); using your grammar (an imaginary life and comparing two language schools).

Workbook

GRAMMAR: comparative and superlative adjectives.
VOCABULARY: rooms and furniture; words which go together; prepositions.
WRITING: description of a place.
PRONUNCIATION: comparing sounds (/æ/ and /ʌ/).

FOCUS ON VOCABULARY

Rooms and furniture

- Vocabulary: rooms and furniture, verb and noun collocation.
- Review prepositions of place from Units 2 and 5.
- Word stress is fairly consistent on the new vocabulary, including compound nouns, and occurs on the first syllable in most words, e.g. *'sofa, 'washing machine.*
- Point out that the word *'furniture* is uncountable. SS often say **furnitures.*
- The exercises which require SS to describe a room will include revision of prepositions of place.
- Although the verbs *think* and *should* are not new to SS, they may not have used them together as in *I think it/they should go …*
- The verb and noun collocation exercise includes three phrasal (multiword) verbs: *turn on, off* and *hang up.* They are all separable and transitive in this context.

Students' Book (page 98)

Exercise 1a) Begin by eliciting the names of the rooms in a house. Before asking SS to use their dictionaries, establish if any of the words are familiar. If SS aren't very efficient users of dictionaries and they don't know the words, divide the task by asking each half of the class to look up four words. They can then work in pairs and teach a S from the other group.

1 toilet 2 washbasin 3 bath 4 shower 5 curtains 6 wardrobe 7 bed 8 carpet

Exercise 1b) If you can quickly sketch the items on the board, you could ask SS to close their books and point to the drawings during the practice stage. This will act as an aid to memory and your drawings may add some humour.

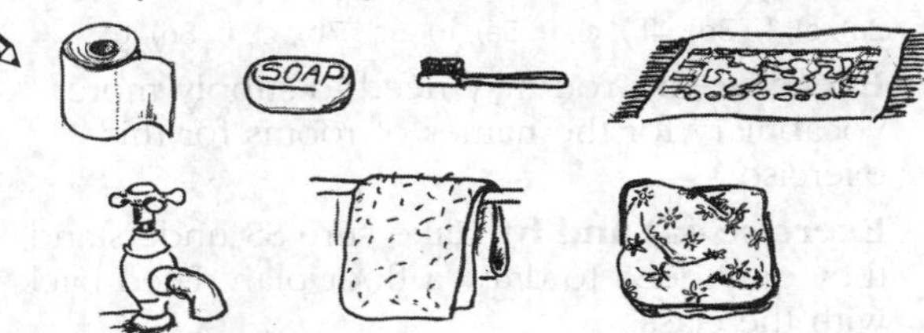

9 toilet roll 10 towel 11 toothbrush 12 soap 13 tap 14 rug 15 cushion 16 duvet 17 sheet 18 pillow

Exercise 2a) and b) These could be done with the whole class.

The sink and the cooker are in the kitchen.

Exercise 2b)

1 sitting room 2 kitchen 3 sitting room 4 kitchen 5 kitchen 6 sitting room

Exercise 2c) Quickly revise prepositions of place and write them on the board so SS can refer to them. Practise the structure: *I think the X should go _____.* SS could now work with a partner.

Exercise 2d) You could copy the drawings on SB page 98 on the board and after the listening ask SS to tell you where to put the furniture. This will be an efficient way of checking and offer more speaking practice.

[10.1]

REMOVAL MAN: Where do you want the things for the sitting room?
JESSICA: We want the sofa in front of the window. I need a lot of light for reading.
TOM: And I'd like the armchair next to the sofa.
JESSICA: No, I don't like that idea. Put the armchair on the other side of the room and the coffee table next to it.
REMOVAL MAN: What about this washing machine?
TOM: Oh, I don't know. What's the best place for it...?
JESSICA: Oh, next to the fridge, I think. Then we can put the microwave under the cupboard, on the table next to the cooker.
REMOVAL MAN: What about the dishwasher?
TOM: Well, I think it should go between the table and the sink.
REMOVAL MAN: OK...

Armchair: on the opposite side of the room to the sofa
Coffee table: next to the armchair
Washing machine: next to the fridge.
Microwave: under the cupboard, on the table next to the cooker
Dishwasher: between the table and the sink

Exercise 2e) SS should be able to suggest items such as TVs, CD players, chairs, tables etc. You could have a group competition to see how many items each group can think of.

In the sitting room: TV, radio, CD player/stereo/music centre, cupboard, bookshelf/shelves, table, chair, carpet, rug, cushion, curtains
In the kitchen: table, chair, stool, curtains

Exercise 3a) Use *turn on the lights*, *the tap* and *the TV* to illustrate that there may be more than one possible collocation. Note that students will often try to say **open/close the tap*. To allow for more practice and to aid memory you could ask SS to put the nouns and verbs in sentences e.g. *Can I make a phone call? Can you turn on the lights, please?*.

2a), e), f) 3g) 4b), c), i) 5a), h) 6c) 7b), c), i) 8d), g)

Exercise 3b) You may need to supply more vocabulary for the names of rooms for this exercise.

Exercise 4a) and b) Make sure SS understand they only need to draw a floor plan. Feed back with the class.

Exercise 5a) Check the meaning of *a dream house*, *location* and *building*. Play the cassette through once. Then check SS answers. Where they agree and are correct, acknowledge that they're right. Where they disagree, write the heading e.g. *Location*, on the board and play the cassette again. This way there is a focus and real reason to listen again.

[10.2]

JESSICA: I like my house in England but my dream house is by the sea in Spain. I'd like good restaurants and a café or bar nearby. The house of my dreams is also large, very modern and made of glass. There are large sofas, glass tables and a lot of plants everywhere. I'd like three very big bedrooms and one big sitting room. I'd paint all the walls cream. A big kitchen is not important because of the local restaurants and I don't want a garden. My only luxuries when I win the lottery are going to be a private beach with a place for barbecues and a swimming pool.

1a) 2b) and c) 3a) large, b) modern, c) made of glass 4a) large sofas, b) glass tables, c) a lot of plants 5a) very big bedrooms, b) one big sitting room, c) small kitchen 6b), c)

Exercise 5b) SS should use the same headings as in Exercise 5a) to guide them. Again you could join in by telling them about your dream home. This, perhaps, offers more realistic listening practice than listening to a cassette because of all the visual paralinguistic features which accompany 'authentic' listening. It also has the added value for SS of finding out more about someone they actually know.

Exercise 5c) Read out the advertisements. Point out that Jessica doesn't use verbs in her advertisement. Feedback could be based on *Who could you share a flat with?* trying to find SS who have similar ideas about their ideal home.

Extra material and ideas

1 WB page 64, Exercises 9–11, page 65, Exercises 12 and 13, page 66, Exercise 15.

2 Our ideal classroom SS could have any equipment and furniture they want, e.g. *coffee machine*, *CD player*, *computers*, *curtains*, *a balcony* etc. They should consider the colour scheme, too, and this information should be included on the plan. In groups they design their perfect classroom. The plans could be displayed around the room. Then SS walk around to see which they think is the best design. If you have any furniture catalogues, take them in as reference material.

3 If you're teaching outside the UK and you have any pictures of homes or buildings in Britain, take them in for SS to look at and comment on. If you're teaching in an English-speaking environment, ask SS how homes in their country of origin are different or similar. If you're teaching a multilingual class, SS could describe typical types of dwellings in their country and list the furniture they would have in each room. You may need to supply vocabulary such as *flat roof*, *single storey*, *block of flats* etc.

4 Picture dictation SS draw two plans of their bedroom. On one they draw where the furniture is and they use this to dictate to the other S who receives the floor plan only. When they have both finished dictating to each other, they compare their picture with the originals to revise prepositions of place.

FOCUS ON GRAMMAR

Comparative and superlative adjectives

L

• Conceptually comparatives and superlatives don't usually cause any difficulty. However, this area of grammar brings up problems of form and spelling. It is also an area of language which is changing in spoken English.

• **Form** SS have to have an awareness of syllables in order to understand the rules of form. Without this they have to memorise each individual adjective and its comparative and superlative form. There are added complications with two-syllable adjectives: some add *-er than* and *-est*, -others use *more than* and *the most* and some are acceptable in either form, e.g. *simpler, more simple* and *simplest, most simple*. There are also irregular forms which usually cause difficulty, e.g. *bad, worse, worst*. Note that there are a few monosyllabic participle adjectives which don't take the *-er* or *-est* ending e.g. *scared* → **scareder*, *bored* → **boreder*.

• **Spelling** SS have to learn spelling rules which again require that they understand the internal form of the adjective, e.g. when a single syllable word ends in a short vowel + a consonant, the consonant is doubled e.g. *bigger*. When there is a long vowel + a consonant, the consonant is not doubled e.g. *cheaper*. Two-syllable words ending in *-y*, change the *-y* to *-i* and add *-er* and *-est* e.g. *happier/est*. However, remind SS they have met similar spelling changes in the context of the Present Simple and Continuous, e.g. *begin* → *beginn ing*.

As we digest this information we can appreciate the complications this area of grammar presents for elementary SS. Immediate assimilation is unlikely and the need for revision and practice is imperative. Try consciously to use the forms in lessons whenever it seems natural or possible, e.g., *The weather's better/worse today. This exercise is easier than the last one.* etc. This incidental exposure will help SS to assimilate the various forms. It's also advisable to include them in quick spelling tests at the beginnings and ends of lessons.

Comparatives

Students' Book (page 100)

Exercise 1a) Establish the concept and form of comparative adjectives before looking at the two brothers. Draw two circles on the board of similar size, one slightly bigger than the other. Label them A and B. Don't draw a large one and a small one as this could elicit *that's big* and *that's small.* We need to establish we are comparing **similar** features. Write the words big and small on the board. Ask SS to tell you about the two circles using the adjective *big.* If they can't, supply the sentence A is bigger than B. Write this on the board. Underline the *gg* in bigger. Then ask them to tell you about the circles again using the adjective *small.* Highlight the form 1 syllable + -er + than. Then write two sums on the board e.g. A 12x6x8=? B 12x16x13=?. Write the adjectives *easy* and *difficult.* Ask SS to compare the sums using *difficult.* Again supply the structure if they can't and again highlight the form. Repeat the exercise with the adjective *easy,* again highlighting the form and spelling rule. Then go to the SB and compare the lives of Derek and Pete. Note this is a recognition not a production exercise.

1 T 2 F 3T 4 T 5 F

Exercise 1b) As you check the answers keep asking why the comparative form is *-er* or *more than* in each sentence. This should help SS to assimilate the 'rules'.

Exercise 1c) Tell SS there is extra information in the grammar box and give them time to read it. Then ask them about the irregular adjective forms *better* and *worse.*

Pete has longer hair than Derek.

Exercise 1d) Do this with the whole class to vary classroom interaction. As a student gives an answer ask the others if they agree before you declare it correct or incorrect. This will help to keep all SS involved.

(Suggested answers)
Pete's richer than Derek.
Pete's more attractive than Derek.
Derek looks younger than Pete.
Derek's friendlier than Pete.
Pete looks more interesting than Derek.
Derek is happier than Pete.

Exercise 1e) Tell SS to make a list of the names of six members of their family. They then give this to their partner so there is a natural cue for the questions.

Exercise 2a) This could be a written exercise where SS exchange papers to check and correct.

1 The River Seine is shorter than the River Nile.
OR The River Nile is longer than the River Seine.
2 Rio de Janeiro is older than Brasilia.
OR Brasilia is newer than Rio de Janeiro.
3 Mount Everest is higher than Mont Blanc.
OR Mont Blanc is smaller than Mount Everest.
4 Capri is prettier than Naples.
OR Naples is more expensive than Capri.
5 Mexico City is more crowded than Reykjavik.
OR Reykjavik is colder than Mexico City
6 New York is more exciting than London.
OR London is safer than New York.
7 The Caribbean is more beautiful than the Irish Sea.
OR The Irish Sea is greyer than the Caribbean.

Exercise 2b) Allow time for feedback. This will help you to assess how well the grammar has been assimilated. Of course, SS won't be completely accurate but there should be evidence that they have understood the rules. If there are a lot of mistakes, focus again on the rules and ask SS to look at their sentences again and correct any mistakes before continuing with the exercise.

Exercise 3 Try to make sure this is kept light-hearted!

(Suggested answers)
Women are quieter than men. Men are luckier than women.
Men are more untidy/untidier than women.

Superlatives

Exercise 4 Before doing the matching exercise in a) ask SS to tell you what is in each picture and elicit or teach *'lottery* and *'wedding.* This will help them to predict the content of the texts. After you have checked the answers, focus on the meaning of superlative adjectives. Draw three tall buildings on the board labelled A, B and C. Ask SS which is the highest and which is the smallest. Alternatively, take in photographs of people, sport etc. and write adjectives on the board to act as a stimulus, e.g. *tall, short, fast, dangerous.*

2 = B 3 = A

Exercise 4a)

1 the highest 2 the most expensive 3 the luckiest

Exercise 4b) Get SS to practise the pronunciation.

[10.3]
1 The highest building in the world.
2 The most expensive wedding in the world.
3 The luckiest man in the world.

-est /əst/

Exercise 4c) Ask SS to focus on the way we form superlative adjectives and relate it to the way we form comparative adjectives. Include the similarities in spelling; doubling consonants and *-y* changing to *-i* . Highlight the use of *the* in superlative sentences.

1 *-est* 2 *-iest* 3 *the most*

Exercise 5 Let SS work individually on this exercise so they can quietly concentrate on the form and spelling of superlative adjectives. The answers are also in the SB, page 134.

1 the smallest 2 the most popular 3 the hottest 4 The oldest 5 The driest

Exercise 6 Don't do feedback at this point as it forms the basis of Exercise 8.

Exercise 7 Do the first one with the class as a demonstration. Check the question forms but don't deal with answers as these are the basis of Exercise 8.

1 Who's the most attractive person you know?
2 What's the most popular make of car?
3 What's the most dangerous sport?
4 Where's the most interesting place to visit in your country?
5 Who's the most famous fashion designer at the moment?
6 What's the nicest food you can eat?

Exercise 8 Join in the feedback by giving your opinions. If SS make mistakes, reformulate the sentence and say it as if you were just repeating the sentence. Only ask SS to self-correct if you're sure it won't block them in any way.

Extra material and ideas

1 WB page 61, Exercises 1 and 2, page 62, Exercises 3–5, page 63, Exercises 6–8.

2 PRACTISE AND CHECK, page 122 for more work on comparatives and superlatives.

3 Class questionnaire page 141, 10.1. PW. Photocopy the questionnaire. The SS could complete the questionnaire individually and then the class could feed back while you collate the answers on the board. Alternatively the quesionnaire could be used for a class mingle where SS compare their answers with each other.

3 Spot the mistakes In pairs SS write ten sentences using comparative and superlative adjectives. Most of the sentences should have a mistake but a few should be correct. When they have finished they exchange papers with another pair who try to find and correct the mistakes.

SKILLS

- Listening and vocabulary: prediction, listening for detail, inference, guessing the meaning of words from context, rhyming sounds, homonyms.
- Speaking and writing a diary entry.

Listening and vocabulary

- Note that the singer has a slight London Cockney accent.
- Although there are quite a few vocabulary items and phrases in the song which will be unfamiliar to SS, they form the basis of the vocabulary exercises and shouldn't be pretaught. Assure SS that they will explore the meaning of the vocabulary so that they don't panic! However, you could preteach/check *'realise, 'argue, 'cause* (short for *because*), *to talk something out* (to talk about a problem and try to find an answer).
- The rhyming exercise is an opportunity to continue highlighting the sound and spelling differences which occur in English.
- The homonym (words which have the same spelling and pronunciation but have a different meaning) exercise aims to make SS aware of the need to check which dictionary definition is appropriate for the context. The dictionary extracts offer two meanings for *light, mad* and *watch*.

Students' Book (page 102)

Exercise 1a) Check the meaning of *'argue.* Do the exercise with the whole class.

Exercise 1b) You may need to play the song twice if SS have difficulty with the accent.

[10.4]
See SB page 143 for the words to *My girl*.

Linda's angry and Richard's worried.

Exercise 1c) Allow time for SS to read through the sentences before you play the cassette again. This will help them to understand the lyrics and locate the sentences more easily. Because it's a song it would spoil the enjoyment of the activity to pause after each line so play the recording through and repeat as often as is necessary.

1a) 2f) 3i) 4d) 5g) 6b) 7c) 8h) 9e)

Exercise 1d) Let SS work individually on this then feed back with the whole class. In a monolingual situation the definitions could be in L1.

1 every now and then 2 on my own 3 in 4 I'd had enough of her

Exercise 1e) Copy the following onto the board.

1 Turn on the <u>light</u>, please.

2 Have you got a <u>light</u>, please.

Ask SS to match the drawing with the sentence. Highlight the homonym *light* to introduce the focus of this exercise.

hard = difficult mad = angry watch = look at

Exercise 1f) Other homonyms you could expect them to know include: *to play/a play, fly, coach, bat, change.*

Exercise 1g) Take a vote before giving the correct answer. How many SS chose 1, 2 or 3? Ask SS to say why they chose the one they did.

2

Exercise 2a) In a monolingual situation get SS to translate the idioms into L1. However, you could equally ask multilingual classes to tell the other SS how they would say this in their language. This often causes surprise, interest etc., as SS note the differences in languages. Some will be able to express the idioms in one word, others seem as though they need a paragraph to express the idea. It will also act as a memory aid to the individual SS who are able to associate the idiom with an L1 equivalent. In either situation, it will raise awareness that idioms are rarely a word for word translation between languages.

1 She doesn't understand.
2 He's not interested.

Exercise 2b) To illustrate the aim of the exercise write go on the board and ask for words that rhyme. To clarify, supply *no.* Other words they should be able to supply are *slow, so, snow, toe* etc. To reinforce or encourage recognition of phonemic script, write the words from the exercise on the board with their phonemic script: 'explain /eksplem/, speak /spi:k/, word /wɜ:d/, say /seɪ/, night /naɪt/ care /keə/. Model the pronunciation of these words and get SS to practise saying them. To check their answers say the verse but let them supply the gapped word. Don't say whether they are right or wrong before playing the cassette.

[10.5]
See SB page 143 for the words to *My girl*.

Exercise 2c) You could ask SS if this is a love song, if it's a common situation etc.

[10.6]
See SB page 143 for the words to *My girl*.

Extra material and ideas

1 Sound and spelling SS could begin to make lists of sound and spelling relationships, e.g. a vowel sound is put at the head of a column and words with that sound are listed beneath the phonemic symbol (see below). Underline the target sound, e.g. person. SS will begin to realise that one sound has many possible spellings and that there are patterns of sound/spelling relationships. The lists could be personal records or class lists which are kept on posters in the classroom. As new spellings for a sound occur they are then added to the lists.

/e/	/i:/	/eɪ/	/aɪ/
pet	leave	cake	ski
letter	reading	examination	flying
head	meet	paper	nice

2 Rhyming words How many rhyming words can SS think of? This will sensitise SS to the sound/ spelling difficulties. As a warmer or end of class activity you could call out a word and in pairs SS list as many words as they can that rhyme with it. Do this over a series of lessons but make sure that there are some rhyming words that SS are likely to know.

3 Sound/spelling sorting cards page 142, 10.2. Copy and cut out the cards of the thirty words with target sounds underlined. SS are asked to group them according to vowel sounds. They can be asked to discover how many different sound columns they need or they can be given the phonemic symbols and asked to group the words under the correct symbol.

schwa /ə/ police, better, telephone, address, today, after
/ʌ/ comfort, hungry, under, up, butter, son.
/ɜ:/ furniture, word, heard, early, her
/ɪ/ him chicken, dictionary, pretty, ill, gym
/i:/ cream, he, tree, field, please, people

4 Homophones PW. As SS have practised working with homonyms this might be a good opportunity to introduce the idea of homophones. Give *pair/pear* as an example. Point out that the pronunciation of each word is the same but the spelling is different. Tell SS to write two words for each word you say.

/sʌn/ (*son, sun*)
/raɪt/ (*right/write*)
/aʊə/ (*our/hour*)
/mi:t/ (*meet/meat*)
/sɪ:/ (*sea/see*)
/weə/ (*wear/where*)

Speaking and writing

Exercise 3a) Establish that *to split up* means to end a relationship. If you have males and females in your class, put them in groups according to their sex to discuss the questions in Exercise 3a). In the feedback write their answers up in note form, e.g.

women	men
1 stay together	split up
2 etc.	

This will highlight similarities and differences but keep it light-hearted!

Exercise 3b) Try to assign roles to the appropriate sexes but if numbers don't allow this, assign roles arbitrarily so that some females are playing males and vice versa.

Exercise 3c) Make sure SS understand the context of the diary entry. Saturday is the day they had the argument and **Sunday** is what happened next. SS should continue with the roles they played in Exercise 3b). Ask them to write their diary entry on a separate piece of paper so you can collect them later.

Exercise 3d) You could ask a few SS to read out their diary entries for others to comment on in the feedback.

Extra material and ideas

Diary project This could be the opportunity to begin a diary project with the class. You could ask SS to use a notebook as a diary and write a five-minute entry each day. To encourage this to become a habit you could allow them to write their entries in the first or last five minutes of the next few lessons. Periodically collect the diaries and, if SS agree, you could respond to their entries, e.g. *It sounds like you had a great evening. Do you go dancing very often?*

REVIEW

- Vocabulary: parts of the body, furniture, professions, illnesses, adjectives describing human characteristics.
- Using your grammar: superlatives, *have to* + infinitive.

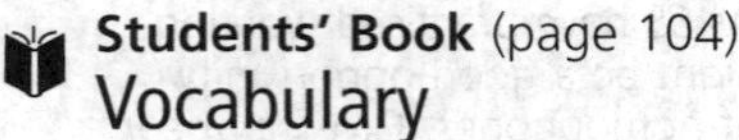

Students' Book (page 104)

Vocabulary

Exercise 1a) and b) Invite SS to ask you the questions which could add some humour and demonstrate the activity. Ask SS to report back for their partner in feedback. They usually report it all wrong which again adds humour.

Exercise 2a) and b) PW. Feed back with the whole class to check their answers.

2 neck 3 director 4 sofa 5 tired 6 lights 7 ache 8 clothes

Using your grammar

Exercise 3a) and b) Write this as an example on the board: *I'm smaller than a dog. I don't have to find my own food. A person gives food to me. Sometimes I kill birds. I sleep a lot. I have to be careful of dogs. I don't like them. (a cat).* This will show SS that they don't have to write a lot. Give them a time limit of four or five minutes. If you think they need a different interaction pattern from pair work, this could be done as a whole class or small group activity.

Exercise 4a) Before SS actually write or say the comparative sentences, allow sufficient time for them to read and digest the information. Check they have understood the advertisement by asking a few check questions, e.g. *Which school doesn't have a restaurant?* etc.

(Suggested answer)
Communication Incorporated (CI) is nearer the centre of London than International Friends (IF). It's more expensive and bigger than IF. It has more courses than IF. Classes are smaller. IF is further from the centre of London than CI. It is cheaper and smaller than CI. IF has bigger classes than CI. CI has more modern technology and better facilities than IF. IF is friendlier than CI.

Exercise 4b) If the last exercise was conducted as a speaking activity ask SS to write their sentences in this exercise or vice versa. Take the opportunity to revise informal letter layout: where the address is, how the date is written and opening and closing phrases. Encourage SS to exchange and proofread each other's work so they can eradicate as many mistakes as possible before handing them in to you.

Extra material and ideas

1 Gap and picture dictation Dictate the following paragraph to SS. Where there is a gap draw the appropriate sketch (see above for example sketches). The SS have to fill the gap in with the word for the drawing.

Yesterday John woke up with a sore _______ (throat). He got up and went to the _______(wardrobe) to get his _______ (trousers) and his _______ (shirt). He fell and hit his _______ (arm) and his _______(leg) on the _______ (chest of drawers). He went to the bathroom and hit his _______ (head) on the _______(mirror) and hurt his _______(nose). John decided it was a bad day and he went back to _______ (bed) etc.

2 Wordsearch page 144, 10.3. There are seven words for body parts, five for illnesses, five for furniture and three for jobs.

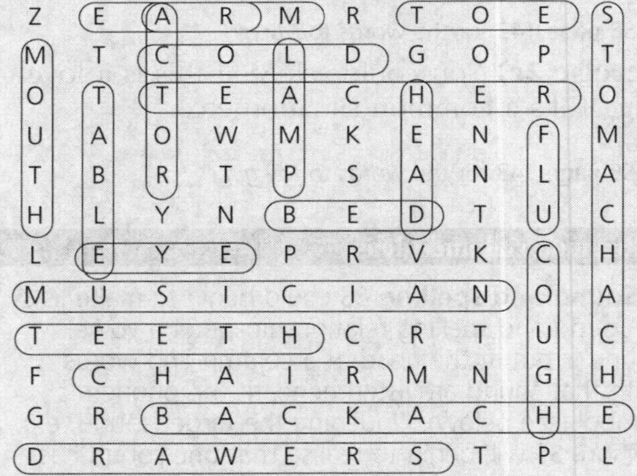

Z	E	A	R	M	R	T	O	E	S
M	T	C	O	L	D	G	O	P	T
O	T	T	E	A	C	H	E	R	O
U	A	O	W	M	K	E	N	F	M
T	B	R	T	P	S	A	N	L	A
H	L	Y	N	B	E	D	T	U	C
L	E	Y	E	P	R	V	K	C	H
M	U	S	I	C	I	A	N	O	A
T	E	E	T	H	C	R	T	U	C
F	C	H	A	I	R	M	N	G	H
G	R	B	A	C	K	A	C	H	E
D	R	A	W	E	R	S	T	P	L

Unit 11

Song and dance

Students' Book

General themes: music and entertainment.

FOCUS ON VOCABULARY: music and entertainment; making arrangements for an evening out.
FOCUS ON GRAMMAR: verb patterns (1) (verbs with *-ing* or *to*); verb patterns (2) (verbs + two objects).
SKILLS: reading (*The Phantom of the Opera*); vocabulary (meaning from context, parts of speech); listening, vocabulary and writing (*Sunset Boulevard*, relative pronouns).
SOCIAL ENGLISH: shopping for clothes.

Workbook

GRAMMAR: verb patterns (1) and (2); *would like to do* and *like +-ing* ; mixed verbs.
VOCABULARY: music and entertainment; word formation (noun endings); opposites (verbs).
WRITING: punctuation lists and linking words.
PRONUNCIATION: word stress in nouns and verbs; sound and spelling (/s/ or /z/ and /θ/ or /ð/).

FOCUS ON VOCABULARY

Music and entertainment

- Review of functional exponents for invitations, suggestions, offers, accepting and refusing.
- Review of Present Simple questions.
- Vocabulary associated with music.
- SS may be familiar with a lot of the vocabulary but will probably have difficulty with the pronunciation, particularly if there is L1 interference. Focus on the use of the definite article in *I play* ***the*** *piano/violin* etc.

Pronunciation SS often misplace the stress when naming instruments, e.g., *'*guitar* instead of *gui'tar*, *'*piano* instead of *pi'ano*. Note the stress changes to the first syllable in the word *'pianist*. Similarly, a stress change occurs in *'music/mu'sician*.

- Functional exponents for invitations and suggestions *Would you like to* + infinitive, *Why don't we* + infinitive, *Let's* + infinitive.
- In the conversation the refusal of invitations is specific to entertainment. You may feel it would be useful to give more general examples for refusing, e.g. *I'd like to but I'm busy. I have to ... Sorry I'd like to X but I can't X on Thursday* etc.
- When accepting an invitation, point out *That would be great*, is considered to be more enthusiastic than *That would be good*. Also highlight the use of *That* ... SS often say *This would be great*. *That* is used to acknowledge that the suggestion/invitation is complete and is seen in the past. We would use *This* to refer to something we see as still being in the present, e.g. *This is an interesting suggestion*. Perhaps only the speaker knows what the suggestion is at this point but will no doubt inform the listener/s.

Pronunciation Make sure the SS pronounce the *d* in *I'd*. Because this often creates a consonant cluster SS avoid it and say *I like*. Also encourage the use of the weak form and assimilation /'wədʒə/ in *Would you*.

Students' Book (page 106)
Exercise 1a) Any questions focused on what kind of music SS like, listen to, don't like, don't listen to etc. will act as a useful prediction for the questionnaire. You may need to explain the meaning of *to be mad about* something in the sense of being enthusiastic, really liking something. It's important that SS shouldn't feel ignorant if they don't perform well in answering the questionnaire, so, if necessary, change the names of musicians, types of music etc. to reflect more closely your SS' knowledge of music. You could approach the questionnaire by checking that they understand the questions and then leaving them to fill in the answers, or looking at one section at a time and letting them answer that section before going on to the next one. The answers to question 2a) and b) are also in SB, page 131.

Questionnaire
Question 1 Practise the pronunciation of the instruments.

The guitar and drums are in the photo of the pop group. The violins are on the left hand side of the orchestra photo, flutes are in the centre and the trumpets are on the far right at the back.

Question 2a) Make sure SS are aware of the different types of music. They won't necessarily know the names of the musicians.

1 jazz: Louis Armstrong
2 classical: Chopin, Vanessa Mae
3 pop/rock: Ringo Starr, Vanessa Mae, Jimi Hendrix

Question 2b) Emphasise that the question refers to past as well as present. Highlight the definite article, *He played* ***the*** *piano* etc.

Louis Armstrong: trumpet
Chopin: piano
Vanessa Mae: violin
Ringo Starr: drums
Jimi Hendrix: guitar

Question 3 Perhaps SS had music lessons when they were children. If there are SS who don't play any instruments, ask them if they would like to learn an instrument.

Question 5 Make sure SS understand this is about actually sitting down to listen to music and not using it as background to another activity.

Question 6 This doesn't have to exclude the financially less well off. It could be a free concert, a children's school concert etc.

Exercise 1b) To save face it might be better to let SS discreetly check their scores with other SS rather than having a whole class feedback.

Exercise 2a) and b)

Copy the sketch to help establish what a desert island is. Focus attention on the chart and make sure SS realise they can only take a person and four things even though there are seven categories listed. Invite SS to ask you about things you would take which should clarify vocabulary.

Exercise 3a) Because most of the required functional exponents are known SS could try to do the exercise before listening. However, if you choose to go straight into the exercise, let SS follow the conversation in their books as they listen. This will help them to locate the language they have to write down in the next exercise.

[11.1]
CHRISTINE: (Answering the phone) Hello.
RAY: Hello. It's Ray.
CHRISTINE: Hi! How are you?
RAY: Fine. How are you?
CHRISTINE: I'm OK.
RAY: I was wondering. It's your birthday tomorrow. Would you like to go out?
CHRISTINE: Mmmm... That would be nice. Where do you want to go?
RAY: **Why don't we go and see** that new film at the Odeon?
CHRISTINE: Well, actually, I saw it last week. It's great, but I don't really want to see it again.
RAY: Well, **let's go** to the pub by the river. There's a jazz band there.
CHRISTINE: Ray, I'm sorry, I really don't like jazz.
RAY: **Would you like to** see *Miss Saigon*?
CHRISTINE: Yes, I'd love to.
RAY: **Shall I ring up and book** for tomorrow evening?
CHRISTINE: That would be great.
RAY: OK, if I get tickets, **I'll pick you up** at six o'clock.
CHRISTINE: OK, thanks. Bye.
RAY: Bye.

Miss Saigon

Exercise 3b) Pause after each gapped phrase to allow SS time to write. You could ask a more confident pair of SS to work at the board – an efficient and effective focus for checking and correction.

Exercise 3c) SS have to be familiar with the names of functional exponents in order to do this exercise but the words *offer* and *invitation* have been covered in earlier units. You may need to establish the meaning of *suggestion* if it wasn't introduced in Unit 10.

1 Shall I ring up and book for tomorrow evening?
2 That would be nice. OR Yes, I'd love to. OR That would be great.
3 Would you like to go out? OR Would you like to see *Miss Saigon*?
4 Why don't we go and see that new film at the Odeon? OR Let's go to the pub by the river.
5 It's great but I really don't want to see it again. OR I'm sorry I really don't like jazz.

Exercise 3d) This aims to raise awareness of main sentence stress and rhythm. It would be beneficial to point out that main stress usually occurs on content words, e.g. nouns, adjectives, adverbs and main verbs, rather than grammatical words e.g. articles, auxiliaries, pronouns and prepositions in the middle of an utterance etc. Of course this is a very simplified description of English rhythm and stress but it may help SS to make better informed decisions about where to place the main stresses in sentences.

1a) river b) jazz c) like
2a) Saigon b) love
3a) evening b) great

Exercise 3e) Practise with the whole class before pairwork.

Exercise 3f) If you think SS will need more guidance, you could elicit an example dialogue and tell them they can use this or create their own. Tell them they will perform their conversation for another pair and should practise until it's as good as they can get it.

Extra material and ideas

1 WB page 69, Exercise 9, page 70, Exercises 10–12.
2 Try and get hold of current local entertainment guides which SS could refer to when practising the conversations in which they invite each other out.
3 If SS are interested in pop/rock music, you could take different songs into the next few lessons and ask SS to vote and comment on which they like the best. This could also be done with other types of music.
4 SS present or write a short biography of their favourite singer, group, composer, musician etc. giving the following information; dead or alive, dates, age, nationality, most famous pieces of music/songs/books/poems/paintings, anything interesting about their lives.
5 PW page 143, 11.1. Photocopy worksheets A and B. SS read the biographies and prepare six questions on their passage for SS in the other group. They exchange biographies, read them and answer their partner's questions. The worksheet is then returned to the original S to be marked. Most of the vocabulary should be familiar. If there are any items SS don't know, encourage them to use their dictionaries.

FOCUS ON GRAMMAR

- Verb patterns 1: verb + *to* + infinitive e.g. *I want to go*, verb + infinitive + *-ing* e.g. *I enjoy sleeping*, verb + infinitive e.g. *I can stay*.
- Verb pattern 2: verb + two objects e.g. *Please lend me a pen.*
- Functional exponent for requests.

L

- SS often feel a sense of relief when this area of grammar is highlighted. They may have realised that certain verbs seem to dictate one pattern while other verbs dictate another. They have already met the following modals, *can*, *will*, *would* and *should* followed by the infinitive without *to* and *would like* followed by the infinitive with *to*. When this grammatical area is addressed and verb patterns are compared, SS can begin to make sense of something which previously seemed to have no logic. Once they are aware of the different patterns, they then have to cope with learning which verb dictates which pattern. This is an ongoing process as new verbs are introduced.
- Verbs such as *like*, *love*, *hate* can be followed by either *to* + infinitive or the *-ing* form. The choice may be dictated by the speaker's perception of whether this is a general state or a specific situation e.g. *I love swimming*. (general) but *I love to swim in cold water* (specific). However, we could equally say, *I love swimming in cold water*. The *-ing* form is considered to be the most frequently used when the above choice is available. This is not the case when *like* follows the modal *would* where the *to* + infinitive must follow. The SB focuses on the use of *like* as in *would like to*. If SS try to say **would like* + *-ing*, point out that it is *would* which dictates the use of the infinitive.

Pronunciation Encourage SS to use the weak forms of *to* + infinitive: /tə/ + consonant (*to go* /təgəʊ/) and /tʊ/ + intrusive soundlink + vowel (*to open* /tʊwəʊpən/) encourage any consonant vowel links which occur, e.g. *I hate‿eating fish.*

- **Present Perfect** is previewed in Exercise 1. This is the grammatical focus of Unit 12. Don't focus on the meaning or the form unless SS ask questions. They should be able to understand the concept of *before now* from the context and neither *decide* or *finish* are new verbs and shouldn't cause comprehension difficulties.
- **The second verb pattern** in the unit is verb + two objects, e.g. *Please pass me that pen* (verb + indirect object + direct object). Highlight that the indirect object can be a noun, a name or an object pronoun: *Give the dog some water. Give Kim some water. Give her some water.* You may need to revise object pronouns again (see SB page 113) to gain accuracy of form. Note that the pattern *Please pass that pen to me* (verb + direct object + *to* + indirect object) is not introduced in *Elementary Matters* but it is in *Pre-Intermediate Matters*, SB Unit 19 page 117.
- **Functional exponents** SS have met the verbs *can* and *will* in earlier units to express ability, offers and spontaneous decisions. Remind SS that *can* and *will* are also used for informal requests and *could* is considered to be slightly more formal/polite. However, *could* is frequently used in informal situations. Also remind SS of possible replies to requests, both agreeing and refusing politely, e.g. *Yes, of course./Certainly./No problem.* and *I'm very sorry, I can't. I'm very busy/late* etc.

Pronunciation Encourage SS to use assimilation and the weak form /kədʒə/ *could you*. Remind them of the weak form of *can* /kən/ in statements and questions and encourage the use of the weak form /kəd/ *could*. Encourage appropriate sentence stress and point out that a rising intonation is commonly used (see below).

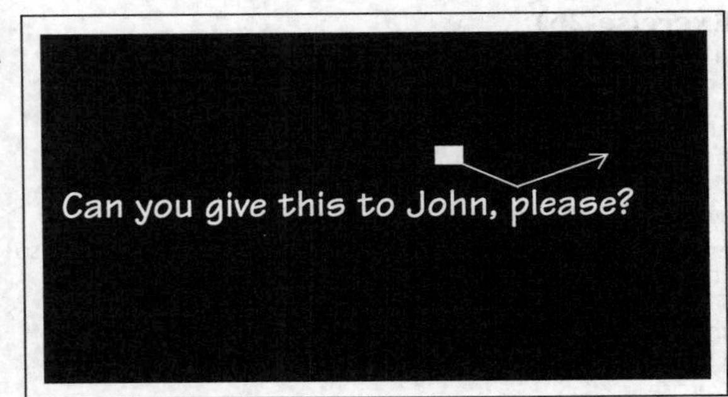
Can you give this to John, please?

Students' Book (page 108)

Verb patterns (1)

Verbs with *-ing* or *to*

Exercise 1a) The letter is meant to be humorous. Ask SS not to complete the gaps until they have read through the letter.

Not really. He wants Emma to think it was difficult but in fact it probably wasn't difficult for him. He's having a wonderful time in Australia!

Exercise 1b) The letter distinguishes between verbs which are followed by the *to* + infinitive or the *-ing* form. Do the first example with the whole class then let SS work in pairs to complete the exercise.

Exercise 1c) This gives SS time to reflect on the *Language reference* section which gives more examples. If possible, allow them to go at their own pace so you could ask SS who finish early to do further exercises in the WB or carry on with the next exercise.

1 to stay 2 to come back 3 living 4 to try 5 to find 6 to see 7 thinking 8 to go out 9 to hear 10 to tell

Exercise 1d) If some SS did finish the previous exercise early and have already completed this exercise, they could write their lists on the board.

to + verb
decide
promise
would like
hoping
want
wait
forgot

Verb + *-ing*
like
stop

Add verbs from the *Language reference* on page 113 which are following by *-ing*: *enjoy, hate, don't mind* and *finish*.

Exercise 2a) This includes examples of modals + infinitive, e.g. *can't find*... After checking the answers, highlight the verb pattern used with modals in sentences 1, 4 and 6, (*can't, will* and *should*). Add another list to the board with the heading 3 verb + infinitive, write *can, will* and *should* under the third column. Ask SS to read the grammar box and add the other modal auxiliaries to this list.

See tapescript below.

Exercise 2b)

[11.2]

1 I **can't find** a job in this country, so **I'd like to go** to America and look for work there.
2 **I've decided** to travel abroad when **I finish studying**.
3 I **like cooking**. One day I **hope to have a** restaurant of my own.
4 I **want to take** my mother to Australia. She **hates flying** so I think **we'll go** by boat.
5 I **promise to work** harder because I **want to go** to university.
6 I **want to stop smoking** soon and I **should do** more exercise.

Exercise 3a) Before SS start you could ask SS to identify which of the three patterns on the board is needed with each sentence e.g. *I like* → verb + *-ing*.

Exercise 3b) You could join in and encourage SS to ask you questions.

Verb patterns (2)

Verb + two objects

Exercise 4a) Ask SS to guess what they think is happening in each picture before playing the cassette. After checking the answers, point out that *kids* is an informal word for *children*.

[11.3]
1 Please buy us an ice cream.
2 Could you tell the kids a story?
3 Will you lend me a pen?

1 = B 2 = C 3 A

Exercise 4b) Pause the cassette to allow SS time to write the dictated sentences. Note that we can use the first part of the core structure in the exercise with all object pronouns except *you*. If you wish to give a possible sentence for *you*, add, *Can I buy you a drink?* to the sample sentences.

Exercise 4c) Again this allows SS time to reflect quietly on the grammar. SS who need less time to absorb the information could be asked to list the other verbs on the board.

Exercise 4d) Do this with the whole class.

1 I bought her a present.
2 Can you get me a dictionary?
3 Can you tell me the time?
4 He showed us the photographs.
5 Shall I bring you a newspaper?
6 Pierre taught me French.

Exercise 5a) and b) Ask SS to describe what's happening in the pictures before the pair work. Monitor SS and correct mistakes as they occur. Encourage SS to use a rising intonation on the requests using inverted question forms e.g. *Can you read me the letter?* and weak forms of *can* /kən/ and *could* /kəd/. Feed back by asking pairs to say the two-line dialogues for the whole class. Note that this gives more revision practice of accepting and refusing.

B A: Can/Will/Could you bring me a glass of water?
B: Yes, of course./No, I'm sorry.
C A: Could/Can/Will you show us the way?
B: Yes, of course./No, I'm sorry.
D A: Can/Could/Will you send us a postcard?
B: Yes, of course./No, I'm sorry.
E A:Could/Will/Can you buy me this motorbike?
B: Yes, of course./No, I'm sorry.

Extra material and ideas

1 WB page 67, Exercises 1–3, page 68, Exercises 4–7, page 69, Exercise 8.

2 PRACTISE AND CHECK, page 122 for more work on verb patters (1) and (2).

P **3** Page 144, 11.2. GW. Make a photocopy of the material for each group. Cut the verbs up and hand a pile to each group face down. Write do/to do/doing /my homework? on the board. To demonstrate turn over the top verb and complete the sentence with the correct form of *do* e.g. if you turn over *I want* the sentence is I want to do my homework, if it's *I enjoy* the sentence is I enjoy doing my homework etc. SS take it in turns in to complete the sentences. If you think it wouldn't slow the proceedings down too much, you could ask one member of the group to be the scribe and you could collect the sentences and check them. However, this isn't essential. If you think the cue *love* wouldn't be offensive SS could use it instead of *do* + *homework* e.g. *I love loving you, I want to love you, I don't mind loving you* etc. This activity could be used as a review activity in the next lesson.

4 Make cards for the different verbs in pattern 1. These should be big enough to be seen at a distance. On the board write, 1 = -ing, 2 = *to* + infinitive, 3 = infinitive ~~to~~.
Divide the class into two teams down the middle of the room. Try to create a space between the teams so they're clearly defined. Flash the verbs up and the first team to shout out the correct number 1, 2 or 3 (according to whether the verb is followed by *-ing* / *to* + infinitive or just the infinitive) is given that card. At the end the teams add up how many cards they have won. Certain nationalities will find shouting out uncomfortable but others will turn this into a deafening experience! If you have the latter, warn teachers in neighbouring classrooms.

5 Spot the mistakes page 145, 11.3. Photocopy the story and give it to SS for individual or pairwork.

Pictures 1, 3, 6 and 8 don't belong to the story.

1 I wanted to be 2 correct 3 I decided to be 4 I'd like to be 5 I'm waiting to get 6 correct 7 I finish studying 8 I hope to get 9 I like going 10 they give you 11 I enjoy learning 12 correct 13 he stopped working 14 he always gave us 15 I wanted to be 16 correct

SKILLS

- Reading and vocabulary: simple inference skills, reading for gist and detail, parts of speech, working with a dictionary.
- Listening, vocabulary and writing: relative pronouns *who* and *which*, pre-checking vocabulary for listening, prediction for the listening, listening for detail.

Reading and vocabulary

- This is a fairly long text for the level. You may want to inspire confidence by preteaching/ checking the following but only do so if you feel your SS have difficulty in tolerating unfamiliar vocabulary: *mask*, *part* (as in *role*), *'ugly*, *'broken heart*; *box* (as in a private seating area in a theatre), and *chande'lier* are illustrated in the photographs in Exercise 2. Check that SS realise *sang* and *heard* are past forms of *sing* and *hear*. Write the new words on the board so SS will recognise their written form when they read them.
- The following words form the basis of the vocabulary exercise therefore shouldn't be pretaught: *di'rector*, *hide*, *'enemy*, *'accident*, *e'normous*.

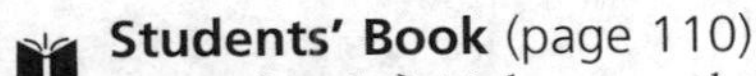

Students' Book (page 110)

Exercise 1a) Make sure the SS know the meaning of *a musical* though it will have come up earlier in the unit. Ask if SS can name any musicals. Then focus on the pictures in the SB. If anyone has seen one of the musicals illustrated in the pictures, ask them about it, *Where did they see it, Did they like it?* etc.

Exercise 1b) The pictures should help SS to guess even if they don't know the musicals.

A *Miss Saigon*
B *Sunset Boulevard*
C *The Phantom of the Opera*

Exercise 2a) Preteach the vocabulary (see L) and write the words on the board so SS can recognise them when they read them. Encourage them to read the story through very quickly. It will be easier to persuade them if you have pretaught unfamiliar vocabulary as this will no longer present a potential block to comprehension. Their objective at this point is to establish whether this is a happy or sad story so they're only reading for gist. Assure them they will have time to read it again. You could set a time limit to motivate SS to read quickly.

It's sad.

Exercise 2b) This could be done with the whole class if you want to change the interaction pattern at this point.

hides (line 8) (verb) = to put something in a place where people can't find it
enemy (line 12) (noun) = a person or people who hate you and want to hurt you
accident (line 33) (noun) = when something (often something bad) happens but no one planned it or wanted it to happen
enormous (line 33) (adjective) = very, very big

Exercise 2c) You could relax the pace here and allow SS to work in their own time. Those who finish early can always go on to the next exercise. In feedback it is important that they explain why they chose their answers. This will help you to focus on the process, i.e., how they came to that conclusion.

1a) 2b) 3a) 4b) 5b)

Exercise 2d) This asks SS to react to the text. It usually takes time for low-level SS to express their opinions, so give them time to think before asking them to declare their opinions. Feedback could be based around who had similar ideas. Ask one S to give her/his opinion and ask the others if they agree or have different ideas. If SS really are struggling to express their ideas ask direct questions rather than tolerating uncomfortable and unproductive silences which can negatively affect the pace of the lesson. E.g. *Do you think the phantom was an actor who had a bad accident? Do you think Christine and Raoul had a happy marriage?* etc.

Extra material and ideas

If you have a multilingual class, you could ask SS to write or tell a traditional story from their country. This could be corrected and collated into a book, 'Stories from Around the World.'

Listening, vocabulary and writing

- SS are aware that *who* and *which* are question words. Make sure they realise that these words aren't introducing questions in the relative clauses. Highlight that they link sentences e.g. *That's the woman. She lives here.* → *That's the woman **who** lives here.* It's important to highlight that *who* is for people and *which* is for things. Expect SS to include the subject pronoun as this is a common mistake e.g. **I like the man who he lives next door.* Although *that* can replace *who* or *which* in defining clauses, we recommend that you only deal with this if SS bring it up. Note that both defining and non-defining relative clauses are included in the exercises but the difference is not focused on in the exercise. The objective is to differentiate between *which* and *who*. However, if the question of defining v. non-defining relative clauses comes up, explain/elicit that the information between commas (non-defining clauses) isn't necessary for us to understand the meaning of the sentence. It's extra information.

• The following vocabulary occurs in the listenings and will probably be unfamiliar: *'memories, to be'lieve, 'prisoner, strange.* Don't teach the following items because SS are asked to find their meaning in a dictionary: *script, 'butler, once, 'close-up, the screen, a scene.*

Students' Book (page 111)
Exercise 3a) Be sensitive to the timing of this. If SS are taking too long checking the definitions in a dictionary, supply them with the last few or divide the class and give each group one or two to check.

1 *a script* – the written form of a film or play
2 *a butler* – a man servant in a house; *once* at a time in the past but not now
3 *a close-up* – a photograph taken very near
4 *the screen* – literally, the large white place where films are shown in a cinema, but here it means films in general, i.e., the actress wants to be in films again
5 *a scene* – part of a film or play when there is no change in time or place

Exercise 3b) You could do this with the whole class. You'll need to play the cassette more than once.

2 d 3 e 4 a 5 c 6 h 7 g 8 f

[11.4]
At the beginning of the film a young scriptwriter, Joe Gillis, is driving through Los Angeles. He has no work and no money, and he can't pay for his new car. Some people are looking for him because they want to take his car back so he hides it in a garage of a big house on Sunset Boulevard. The house belongs to an old film star called Norma Desmond. She lives there with a butler who was once her husband and who also directed her films. She lives with her memories of the time when she was famous, watching her old films and reading letters which she believes are from her fans, but which her butler writes.
She wants to return to the screen and become famous again so when she meets Joe she asks him to write a filmscript about her. She also wants him to live at her house while he is writing it.
Joe doesn't want to live like a prisoner in this strange house, but he is happy to have a job and to take money and expensive clothes from Norma.
Soon there are problems. Norma falls in love with Joe. Also, the man who she wants to direct her new film, Cecil B. de Mille, does not like the filmscript.
Then Joe fallls in love with a young writer and tries to leave Norma. She shoots him, saying: 'No one ever leaves Norma Desmond.'
In the most famous scene at the end of the film the police come to take her away. The photographers and journalists are waiting as she walks down the stairs, and her last words are 'All right, Mr de Mille. I'm ready for my close-up.'

Exercise 3d) Allow SS time to reflect on the information about the relative pronouns *who* and *which* in the grammar box at the foot of the page. Meanwhile write the following on the board:

1 I know a man. He only drinks water.
2 That's the book. It's got the answers in it.

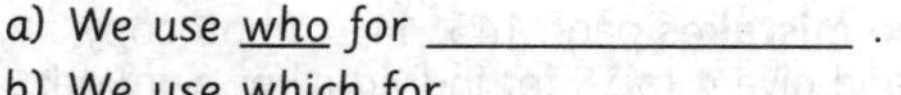
a) We use <u>who</u> for ____________ .
b) We use <u>which</u> for ____________ .

Ask SS to join the sentences in 1 and 2 and to complete a) and b). If the issue of defining and non-defining relative clauses comes up, see L.

1 who 2 which 3 who 4 which 5 who 6 which

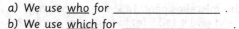

Extra material and ideas

Relative pronouns page 146, 11.4. Photocopy the paragraph about Andrew Lloyd Webber and Tim Rice. SS complete it with *who* or *which*.

who which which who

SOCIAL ENGLISH

• Vocabulary and lexical phrases commonly used for shopping.
• Functional exponents for stating opinions about the future.
• Revision of other functional exponents: offers and refusing and accepting offers.

• Preteach the meaning of vocabulary for the gap fill. This includes two phrasal verbs, *bring 'back* and *try 'on* which are separable and transitive. If your SS are keeping a separate list for these verbs, allow time for them to note them down.

Pronunciation Point out the silent letter in the word *recei(p)t.* Highlight word stress; a *'refund, re'ceipt, ex'change, a 'cheque card, a 'present.*

• *Will* and *won't* are introduced as grammatical exponents for stating opinions/predictions about the future. The form is not new but the function is different. It was introduced in Units 3 and 7 for offers and requests.

Pronunciation SS often pronounce *won't* /wəʊnt/ the same as *want* /wɒnt/. It might help to compare the vowel sound in *no* /nəʊ/ then get the SS to say *wo* /wəʊ/ and finally *won't* /wəʊnt/.

Students' Book (page 112)
Exercise 1a) Tell SS to read the conversation through before trying to fill in the gaps. Feed back with the class but don't indicate whether they are right or wrong before playing the cassette in Exercise 1b).

Exercise 1b) Focus SS' attention on the functional exponents *will* and *won't* in the grammar box to express opinions about the future. Practise pronunciation of the sentences in the conversation with examples of this function. Monitor the practice phase and correct any pronunciation mistakes as they occur.

[11.5]

SHOP ASSISTANT: Can I help you?
WENDY: No, it's all right, thanks. I'm just looking.
SHOP ASSISTANT: Would you like to **try** that jacket **on**?
WENDY: No, thanks. It's a **present** for my sister, actually.

SHOP ASSISTANT: What **size** is she?
WENDY: Twelve. This one looks a bit big, and I'm sure she won't like the colour.
SHOP ASSISTANT: What about this red one?
WENDY: Yes, that's better. Can I **bring** it **back** if it doesn't fit?
SHOP ASSISTANT: Yes, we can **exchange** it for something else or give you a **refund**. But don't forget to keep your **receipt**.
WENDY: OK. I think it'll be fine anyway.
SHOP ASSISTANT: How would you like to pay?
WENDY: Oh, by **cheque**, I think. Or do you take Visa?
SHOP ASSISTANT: Yes, both. Visa, or a cheque's fine if you have a cheque card.

Exercise 1c) Before the roleplay you may want to use *Extra material and ideas* below. Make sure SS understand they will be roleplaying two characters, the customer and the shop assistant. Tell them to begin with Student A being the customer. Student B is the customer in the second situation. Monitor SS and correct mistakes as they occur. Tell SS they are going to perform their conversations for another pair. If any SS are confident enough, they could perform their roleplays for the whole class.

Extra material and ideas

1 Match the pictures to the words page 147, 11.5. To review and extend clothing and accessory vocabulary. Hand out the worksheet before the roleplay to review and extend vocabulary which the SS can then use in their conversations.

2 Conversion table page 146, 11.6. SS may well appreciate this activity. You could use the chart as a reading comprehension and ask questions like: *What size shoes do you take in the USA? What size do you take in Europe?*

Unit 12

Two of a kind

> ## *Students' Book*
>
> **General themes:** describing things; family relationships.
>
> **FOCUS ON VOCABULARY:** describing things; order of adjectives.
> **FOCUS ON GRAMMAR:** past experiences (Present Perfect with *ever* and *never*); Present Perfect or Past Simple?
> **SKILLS:** reading and vocabulary (an 'only child' and identical twins); review of question forms; listening, speaking and writing (brothers and sisters).
> **REVIEW:** vocabulary (describing and comparing pictures); using your grammar (a grammar auction and asking about past experiences).
>
> ## *Workbook*
>
> **GRAMMAR:** Present Perfect, Past Simple or Present Perfect?
> **VOCABULARY:** describing objects, opposites (adjectives), negative adjectives with *un-*.
> **WRITING:** spelling, a letter of invitation.
> **PRONUNCIATION:** sound and spelling (silent letters).

FOCUS ON VOCABULARY

Describing things

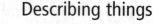

- Vocabulary: shape and material.
- Order of adjectives.

- **Order of adjectives** Highlight that opinion comes before more factual descriptions: a ***beautiful*** *red leather bag.*
- Highlight the questions: *What does it look like?* and *What's it like?* Point out the contraction of *is.* To clarify meaning you could compare it with *Do you like it?* The question, *What's it made of?* is included in the grammar box. Although this is a passive construction we recommend you present it as a lexical phrase rather than going into its passive form.

Pronunciation SS don't usually use the syllabic /n/ in the final syllable of *'cotton*: /kɒtn/ *'wooden* /wʊdn/ *'leather* /leðə/ and they often stress the second syllable and the final schwa in */kɒ'tɒn/wʊ'den/le'ðeə/. Encourage the consonant vowel link in the question *What's it like?*

Students' Book (page 114)
Exercise 1a) and b) As a 'warmer' activity you could ask SS to draw a sketch of their favourite possession. They then exchange drawings with a partner and they ask each other questions. The questions should be elicited and written on the board to facilitate a well-paced activity, e.g. *When did you get it? Did you buy it or was it a present? What's it like?* etc. Alternatively, SS could write the name of their favourite object on a piece of paper. Collect these and pick a few out. SS try to guess whose favourite object it is and then you and they ask questions about the object. Try to include the question, *What's it like?* as this will help to preview the following exercises.
Write, *SIZE, SHAPE, COLOUR* and *MATERIAL* on the board. Ask SS to suggest words to put in each column. Then focus attention on the adjectives in the exercise. Practise pronunciation of the words, highlighting stress and the use of the syllabic /n/ and schwa where appropriate (see L). Note the nouns for the things in the photographs are not required.

(Suggested answers)
A=1, 5, 9 B=5, 6, 9 C=8, 9, 10 D=1, 11 E=3, 4, 9
F=1, 5, 7, 9 G=2, 5, 7, 9 H=3 I=3, 5, 12 J=2, 5 K=3, 4, 9

Exercise 1b)
Note that it is not necessary to add the different nouns at the end of each list.

Personal opinion	Size and shape	Colour	Material
beautiful	big	red	leather
useful	round	grey	plastic
______	square		wooden
	oblong	______	cotton
modern	______		glass
wonderful		green	leather
pretty	small	blue	gold
		orange	

Exercise 1c) If you have already established the columns on the board add the new adjectives. Don't forget to allow time for SS to make the lists in their books for a personal record. If they have bilingual dictionaries or it's a monolingual class, ask SS to think of words they would like to know in English that could be added to the lists and add them. Of course they won't be able to produce all the new words immediately, but it will facilitate recognition of many of the adjectives. At this point you could return to the 'warmer' activity, *My favourite thing,* and ask SS to ask for more information to elicit the adjectives they have been focusing on: *What's it made of? What colour is it? How big is it?* etc.

Exercise 2a) Focus attention on the pictures and ask SS to try and describe the objects. This will act as prediction for the listening. Again, it is not necessary to name the objects. Then play the cassette.

[12.1]
1
A: I've got a new futon at home.
B: Oh, what's that?
A: It's Japanese. You can sit on it or sleep on it.
B: What's it made of?
A: The base is made of wood and the other part is cotton.

2
A: My cousin sent me this wonderful mask from Africa.
B: What's it like?
A: It's made of brown wood – it's the face of a man. It's beautiful.
B: What do you do with it?
A: Well, I hang it on the wall.
3
A: I bought a poncho in Mexico.
B: What's it for?
A: It's a kind of coat. It keeps you warm.
B: What does it look like?
A: It's white with a hole for your head.
1=B 2=I 3=H

Exercise 2b) Pause after each conversation to let SS consider their answers.

1 2c) 3a) 4e) 5b) 2 1b) 2d) 3c) 4e) 5a)
3 1c) 2e) 3b) 4a) 5d)

Exercise 2c) This could be an opportunity to focus on sound linking and its effect on rhythm. Take the first conversation and point out and practise features of linkage, perhaps limiting it to consonant/vowel links. To give visual support write the conversation on the board and draw lines to show the links.

A: I've got‿a new futon‿at home.
B: Oh, what's that?
A: It's Japanese. You can sit‿on it or sleep‿on it.
B: What's‿it made of?
A: The base is made of wood and the other part is cotton.

Ask SS to look at either the second or third conversation and mark consonant vowel links before practising it. Encourage SS to say their conversation to other pairs. If they work with pairs who practised the same conversation, they could see if they agreed on the linkage points.

Exercise 3a) There should be no need to demonstrate this activity but check that SS have understood the instructions. Don't let this go on too long. Its purpose is to offer practice of the language in the examples based on already familiar items.

Exercise 3b) This exercise requires SS to listen intensively to their partner with no visual reference to look at as they try to guess what the item being described is. Monitor and focus on mistakes of form and pronunciation of the target lexis. If you think SS will accept more practice, they could describe something they own and others guess what it is.

Student A: two plastic pens, one green, one red; a round, wooden clock; a brown leather bag and a white cotton bag; a pair of green plastic beach (jelly) shoes.
Student B: a blue leather wallet; a gold ring; two cotton shirts, one blue, one red; an oblong wooden picture frame.

Extra material and ideas

1 WB page 75, Exercises 10 and 11, page 76, Exercises 12–14.

2 Dictate the following three jumbled sentences. When you have finished dictating them all, SS put the words in the right order. It could be a competition, the winner being the first person to get the correct order.

a) really I small that ring next box brown like wooden wedding the to
b) cotton sister my me birthday for gave wonderful a blue shirt my
c) that oblong table really ugly hate wooden I me bought you

a) I really like that small brown wooden box next to the wedding ring.
b) My sister gave me a wonderful blue cotton shirt for my birthday. For my birthday, my sister gave me a wonderful blue cotton shirt.
c) I really hate that ugly, oblong, wooden table you bought me.

3 Draw the following chart onto the board and ask SS to copy it down.

	size	shape	colour	material	price
Jacket					
Jumper					
Bedside table					
Curtains					
Trainers					
Ring					

Read the following text. The SS should fill in as much of the chart as they can. Tell them you will read it twice.

I'm really tired. I went shopping this morning. I bought a lot of things and spent a lot of money. I got a lovely jacket. It's blue and made of cotton. It wasn't very expensive, only £40. I also bought a big, red, woollen jumper from the same shop. I haven't got a nice jumper. It was in the sale and it was really cheap, £5.99p. There was a sale on at the furniture shop too, and I just had to go in and look. I didn't plan to buy anything but I found a small, square, bedside table made of wood. It was cheap, too. And I also got some new curtains for my bathroom. They were more expensive, £35.50. They're yellow and white. They're nice. They look good. I then went to the shoe shop on the corner of Devon Street, near the bus station. I needed some new trainers but I didn't have much money left so I bought some very cheap ones. I don't think they're real leather. I'm sure they're made of plastic, but they're OK. Next to the shoe shop there was a jeweller's shop. Again, everything was on sale. I saw a gorgeous gold ring. It was only £16.25 but I didn't have any money left. Yes, spending money is very tiring!

SS should compare with a partner while two, more confident SS, fill in the chart on the board. Ask SS if they agree. Put a question mark next to anything that SS don't agree on. Read the passage again and see which information was correct. Note that price is not normally used as an adjective before the noun. However the other adjectives follow the normal order of adjectives.

	SIZE	SHAPE	COLOUR	MATERIAL	PRICE
Jacket			blue	cotton	£40
Jumper	big		red	woollen	£5.99
Bedside table	small	square		wooden	
Curtains			yellow and white		£35.50
Trainers				plastic	
Ring				gold	£16.25

FOCUS ON GRAMMAR

- Present Perfect Simple.
- Adverbs *ever* and *never*.

Past experiences: Present Perfect

• The concept of the Present Perfect is limited to past experiences. The obvious confusion for SS lies in the perception of time. Both the Past Simple and Present Perfect (used to talk about experiences) clearly refer to actions completed in the past. However, with the Present Perfect there is some link to the present whereas the Past Simple distances the event, action or state, pushing it away from time now. The Present Perfect views the past from time now and signals **before now**. Past Simple signals **then**. To guide SS towards this rather subtle difference in perception of time is very difficult indeed if there is no equivalent in L1. However visual support can help.

Establish that you are standing on 'time now', your left is 'past' and your right is 'future time'. Raise your left arm to the side and to shoulder height bring it back towards the body in a circular movement placing it sharply back against the side of your body. Do this a few times repeating ***Before time now***. Next, in a very determined way stretch your left arm out to the side and point your index finger at some imaginary distant time. Again do this several times repeating ***Then***. Repeat these gestures at every reasonable opportunity. After a while it becomes a humorous element in the lesson which SS often mimic, but it does begin to drive the difference home!

As teachers and SS we all have to accept that it will take quite some time before this verb form will be used with any real confidence or accuracy. Therefore, it's important to acknowledge any progress you observe. When it's used appropriately, congratulate the S and highlight the example. Also be prepared for a temporary disappearance of the Past Simple.

Recent learning often interferes with what was learnt before and because both verb forms refer to the past, SS seem to view the Past Simple as being superfluous when the Present Perfect is introduced. This is often because it is the form that is used in many languages to express the past. It's important to compare the two verb forms frequently, both concept and form. You may like to draw the following on the board to reinforce this.

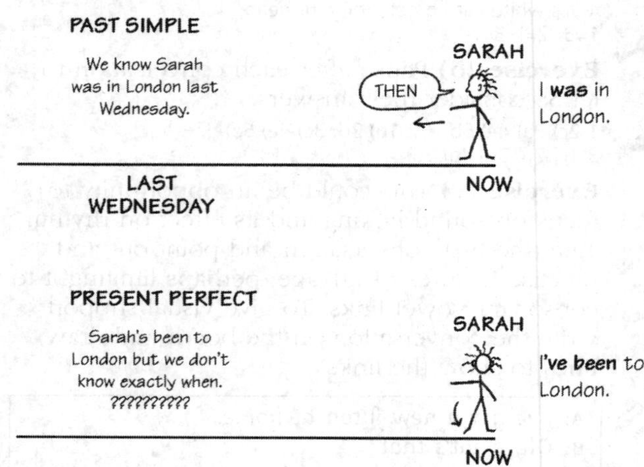

The good news is the Present Perfect Continuous can't be used to list past experiences which have been completed/finished. Therefore whether the continuous or simple form of the verb should be used isn't relevant for the use being introduced here. So, elementary SS are spared the problem which occurs with other uses of the Perfect aspect.

• SS will be familiar with the auxiliary verb *have* but past participle forms of irregular verbs will probably be new to most and will need constant reviewing. Highlight that in short answers we only need to use the auxiliary verb, e.g. *Yes, I have. No, I haven't.*

• Adverbs *ever* and *never* are practised. They were both introduced in Unit 3 with the Present Simple. Remind SS that *ever* **does not** mean *at all times* or *always*, it means *at any time*. With the Present Perfect it means *at any time before time now*. Point out that *ever* is usually restricted to questions. Also highlight that we don't use *never* and *not* together **No, I've not never been.*

Pronunciation Encourage the use of contracted forms *I've, She's* etc. but point out that in positive short answers we don't use the contracted form **Yes, she's.*

Weak forms of *have* /həv/ and *has* /həz/ are used in questions but in short answers they revert to their strong form /hæv/, /hæz/.

The pronunciation of *-ed* endings in regular past participles will need continued monitoring. Aim to eradicate overuse of /ɪd/ e.g. *cleaned* /kliːnd/ (not */kliːnɪd/).

Students' Book (page 116)

Exercise 1a) Ask SS if they know the band U2 and where they come from (they are an Irish rock band from Dublin). Ask them to close their books and listen to the whole song. Tell SS to write down any or as many words as they can as they listen to the song. Elicit these words and write them on the board. Then ask SS to consider the words which might help them to answer the question. Notice that the singer uses 'poetic licence' and omits some of the official words that are printed in the SB, page 143. He also clips parts of words, so like many songs it is not a perfect model of English. However, the motivational value of giving SS an authentic song by a band they may recognise should offset these difficulties. Note that there is also some vocabulary support for the song in the illustration.

[12.2]
See SB, page 143 for the words to *I still haven't found what I'm looking for*

It's a love song.

Exercise 1b) Ask SS the direct questions before referring to the questions in the SB, *When did he climb the mountain? When did he run through the fields?* This should elicit, *We don't know*. Then ask, *But was it in the past or is it in the present?* We need to establish it was completed in the past, before time now and we don't know the exact time. Then ask SS to answer the questions in the book. This means that the concept and use will be immediately reinforced.

[12.3]
See SB, page 143 for the words to *I still haven't found what I'm looking for.*

1 No, he doesn't. 2 No, he doesn't.
3 Past Simple. I **climbed** the mountain last night. I **ran** through the fields yesterday.

Exercise 2a) and b) Allow SS time to digest the information in the grammar box and then begin to focus on the form of the Present Perfect. Once they have checked their answers in the Irregular verbs list at the back of the book, ask SS to close their books, say the infinitive of one of the verbs and to supply the past form and the past participle. Take every opportunity to review concept and use as you continue through the exercises. Repeat the questions and gestures, (see L) wherever you can.

found kissed felt spoken held was
kissed is regular

Exercise 2c) Focus attention on the pictures and the words and make sure the meanings are understood. (The vocabulary could be translated if necessary as it is a means to an end and not a vocabulary exercise in itself.) This exercise could be done with the class as a whole but don't give the answers if you intend to play the cassette for checking. Check the exercise with the students before they listen because Bono (the lead singer of U2) sounds as though he say 'I have spoke'!

kissed Felt spoken held was found

Exercise 2d)

[12.4]
See SB, page 143 for the words of *I still haven't found what I'm looking for.*

Exercise 2e) Again this aims to reinforce concept and use.

No, we don't.

Exercise 3 Asks for SS' personal response to the song.

Present Perfect or Past Simple?

Exercise 4a) As you do the feedback for this exercise keep asking SS to say **why** they chose the verb form they did. Correct any mistakes immediately.

I've visited went were weren't had have had
have also stayed went were didn't have

Exercise 4b) and c) After SS have had time to look at the question forms in the grammar box, practise pronunciation. Encourage the use of weak and strong forms of the auxiliary *have* (see L). After they have done the interview roleplay, invite SS to ask you about your holidays. Then in a class mingle activity let them ask each other. You could pull this activity together by finding out how many countries have been visited by people in the class.

Exercise 5a), b) and c) Before SS begin the quiz, compare these questions; *Have you sailed a boat? Have you ever sailed a boat?* The difference is basically that of emphasis. *Ever* encompasses the idea of one's whole life, at any time in one's life. It might be helpful, therefore, to repeat, *Have you ever, in all your life, sailed a boat?* This might give the idea of emphasis. This idea can then be reflected in the difference between. *I haven't been to America.* v. *I've never been to America.* It's important that SS associate *ever* with questions and *never* with negative sentences. Ask them to form questions for the first section of the quiz before pair work and check these for accuracy. Expect continued difficulty with producing the past participle at this point in the learning curve. Feedback could result in some interesting personal stories so make sure you allow sufficient time for this to develop. If you have any interesting personal anecdotes, join in the feedback. Depending on the mood of the class, how tired they are etc. decide whether you'll deal with corrections during or immediately after the feedback, or whether it would be better to note the mistakes and use these for a correction warmer in the following lesson.

Exercise 5a)

1 Have you ever worn unusual clothes?
When did you wear ...?
2 Have you ever played/done a dangerous sport? When did you do/play it?

3 Have you ever eaten unusual food? When did you eat it?
4 Have you ever gone/been for a walk in a dangerous place? When did you go?
5 Have you ever had a date with someone you didn't know? When did you have it?
6 Have you ever asked a hairdresser for a very different hairstyle? When did you ask for it?
7 Have you ever slept in an unusual place? When did you sleep there?

Extra material and ideas

1 WB page 72, Exercises 1–3, page 74, Exercises 4–6, page 74, Exercises 7–9.

2 PRACTISE AND CHECK, page 123 for more work on the Present Perfect.

3 Class mingle Write the following on the board:
PLACES SPORTS/HOBBIES
SS write down three places they have been to and three places they haven't been to but would like to visit; three sports or hobbies they have tried and three they haven't tried but would like to. Then in a mingle activity they try to find someone who has been to places they haven't but would like to and someone who has done the things they haven't but would like to. If they find someone, they then try to get as much information as possible about the place, sport or hobby.

4 Is it true or not? This could be done with the whole class, in pairs or small groups. SS take it in turns to tell the others that they have done something e.g., *I've climbed in the Alps*. This can be true or not. The objective is for other SS to ask questions to ascertain whether they think it's true or not. They should look for hesitation, lack of knowledge about it etc.

5 Lady in red page 148, 12.1. *Lady in red* by Chris de Burgh is on Class Cassette B at the end of Unit 12. It provides good practice of the Present Perfect and Past Simple. There is a gapped and complete version. You may wish to pre-teach some vocabulary: *shine, ro'mance, chance, 'highlights, blind, wanna (= want to), 'gorgeous, a'mazing, 'utter.*

SKILLS

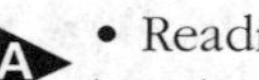

• Reading: prediction, reading for detail, reacting to a text.
• Vocabulary: dictionary work.
• Listening, speaking and writing: listening for detail, writing a paragraph, talking about families and childhood memories.

Reading

L • The texts will be quite challenging for this level. However, if sufficient attention is given to unfamiliar vocabulary before reading, SS should understand the key points and be able to answer the questions. Apart from the adjectives describing human characteristics which are dealt with in Exercise 2a) the following will probably be unfamiliar: *'full-time 'job, 'average, out'going, 'cleverer, 'recognise, fight, don't get on 'well.* Explore as many of these as you feel necessary. Remember to write them on the board so that SS can recognise their written form when they read it.

Students' Book (page 118)

Exercise 1a) As a warmer and prediction exercise ask SS to form groups according to whether they are an only child, the youngest child, the middle child or the oldest child in their family. Ask them to talk about the good and bad things about being such a child. This will then feed into the questions about only children and identical twins.

Exercise 1b) Assign different words to different SS to look up if your SS still take a long time to locate words and digest the information from a dictionary. You may want to preteach other vocabulary if you think it will increase confidence (see L).

spoilt = someone, often a child, who has always got everything he/she wanted
lonely = unhappy because you are alone
confident = sure that you can do something well and easily
different = not the same
grown-up = not a child
competitive = someone who wants to win or to be more successful than other people
successful = when you get the result you wanted

Exercise 1c) Divide the class into Groups A and B. You could set a time limit in an attempt to get the groups to finish at roughly the same time. Ask them to read quickly to see if their predictions were correct and assure them they will have time to read in more detail later. Emphasise that Group A are reading about an only child and Group B are reading about twins. Check their predictions.

Exercise 1d) and e) Allow SS to work at their own pace but give them a five-minute warning before you expect them to check their questions in groups. Let representatives from each group check their group's answers with you, or leave the answers where they can refer to them.

Group A's answers
1F 2T 3T 4F

Group B's answers
1F 2F 3F 4T 5F

Exercise 1f) Ask SS to write the questions down. This will allow you to walk around and monitor the question forms without having to interrupt the pairwork.

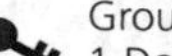

Group B's questions about Article A
1 Does she get a lot of things from her parents?
2 Are her parents strict?
3 Is Zoe lonely? Why/Why not?
4 Do 'only children' want to do well?
5 Are 'only children' competitive?

Group A's questions about Article B
1 Does Sue like being an identical twin?
2 Are Sue and Anne the same age?
3 What did they do when they were at school?
4 Do they get on well now?
5 Have Sue and Anne got identical twins?

Exercise 1g) Feed back to summarise the articles which will facilitate the next exercise.

Exercise 1h) This asks SS to give a personal response to the articles and you could join in.

Extra material and ideas

Poem You will need glue or sticky tape. Write on the board:

A good sister/brother is someone who
A bad sister/brother is someone who

Ask SS to tear a piece of paper into eight strips. They think of four things that they think make a good sibling and four which they associate with a bad sibling. They write these eight sentences on their strips of paper. In groups of four they pool their sentences, all the good ones together, all the bad ones together. Each group will have a total of 32 strips of paper. The objective is to compose two poems which begin with the sentences above use eight of the sixteen sentences they have pooled together for each poem. Give a few suggestions to show that it can be as simple as:

A good sister is someone who
is kind
makes me a cup of coffee in the morning, etc.

Listening, speaking and writing

L • Much of the vocabulary in the reading texts is recycled in the listening exercise. However, *'jealous, a'dore, 'funny* (strange) may cause comprehension difficulties.

Students' Book (page 119)

Exercise 2 To aid prediction, go over the gapped text establishing what information SS have to listen for. Tell them you will play the cassette through once; then you will play it again but you'll stop to let them fill in the information. Play it once and find out what information they can supply after the first listening. This will reduce the amount that they have to concentrate on when you play it again.

[12.5]
I'm the second in a family of four children. I've got an older brother. Tom – he's two years older than me. Then there's Steve, who's eighteen months younger and Rebecca, who's three years younger. When I was a child, I was very close to my sister and I got on OK with Steve – we weren't close, but we got on all right. But I hated my older brother. I always felt he was better than me – you know, more attractive, more confident. He did better at school. I suppose I was jealous. Everyone thought I'd be jealous of Steve – I was only eighteen months old when he was born – but I wasn't. And Rebecca – because she was the only girl and the youngest, everyone spoilt her – and I adored her, too. It's interesting because now I don't see her very often – she travels a lot and has different lifestyle. And Steve – I see him but not often either. But Tom and I are very close – we both have children now and we live quite near each other. Funny, isn't it?

Tom is **older** than him and Steve and Rebecca are **younger**. When Paul was a child he was very close to **Rebecca**, but he didn't get on with **Tom**. He was jealous of **Tom** because he was more attractive and **confident**. Steve was born when Paul was **eighteen** months old. He **wasn't** jealous of Steve and he **loved** Rebecca. Now he **doesn't see** her a lot. He **sometimes** sees Steve but he and Tom are now very **close**.

Exercise 2b) An alternative to having SS write about themselves would be for them to interview another SS and write about their partner. This has the added motivation of checking what their partner has written to see if it's an accurate description.

Extra material and ideas

P **Playlet** page 149, 12.2. If you used the first playlet in Unit 9 (see page 89), establish this is the same family but a different argument.
Scene round the dinner table. Mother and father are both in the kitchen cooking. Their teenage children are watching TV and reading magazines.
SS should be in groups of five for the sketch. One S is the director.
1 SS read sketch. Ask if they understand all the vocabulary. Then ask a few comprehension questions, e.g. *Who is in the kitchen? What are they doing? Where are the children?* etc.
2 SS choose which roles they want to play and who will direct the scene.
3 SS read out their parts giving eye contact to the person they're addressing. Monitor the groups' pronunciation, sentence stress and intonation. If you think they could all benefit from some guidance from you, stop the proceedings and focus on one aspect. Ask them to try again.
4 Tell the directors they now have to think about the environment: *Where's the kitchen? Where's the TV?* etc. The SS should now be acting as well as speaking their parts. The directors should get the group to repeat the conversation until they think it's the best it can be.
5 SS should then act out their scene for the other SS. Encourage the others to applaud after each group has performed.

REVIEW

L • Vocabulary: music and entertainment, adjectives describing shape, size colour, and materials.
• Grammar: verb patterns including modal auxiliaries, Present Perfect.

Students' Book (page 120)

Vocabulary

Exercise 1a) Check the answers before doing the pair work activity with As and Bs.

a) Student A: drums, guitar, trumpet
Student B: violin, flute, guitar

Exercise 1b) Monitor the pair work and make notes of any mistakes you hear. These could form the basis of a *Spot the Mistake* homework. Write sentences which include some of the mistakes you noted down. Give or dictate these to your SS who then correct them for homework.

Student A: There are drums, a guitar and a trumpet in my picture. It is a modern square concert hall, made of glass and wood. It is white and brown with red doors.
Student B: There is a violin, a flute and a guitar in my picture. It is an old round concert hall. It is made of grey stone. It has a green roof.

Using your grammar

Exercise 2 Make sure SS understand the scoring system before they begin. It might be better to illustrate the instructions by asking them a question they *will* know the answer to, one they would be *less sure* about and one they *won't* know and ask them to score them according to the scoring in the exercise. The more sure they are the higher number of points they should allocate. They must also understand that they lose this number if they are wrong. Ten is the minimum they can allocate.

1 Wrong – Why don't you go to the cinema? 2 Correct. 3 Correct. 4 Wrong – I can't understand this exercise. 5 Wrong – Can you give me some money? 6 Wrong – I've finished reading that book. 7 Correct. 8 Wrong – She's the girl who lives next door. 9 Wrong – I saw her yesterday. 10 Correct.

Exercise 3 Let SS go straight into the activity but monitor the question forms they produce. If there are a lot of mistakes of form, stop the activity and establish the correct questions before letting them continue. If there are only a few mistakes, correct them as they occur.

Have you ever lost any money? Where did you lose it? What did you do? Did you find it again?
Have you ever won a competition? When did you win it? What did you win?
Have you ever played an unusual musical instrument? What was it? Was it difficult? Was the sound nice?
Have you ever spoken to a famous person? Who did you speak to? Where were you? What did he/she say? Was he/she nice/friendly?
Have you ever travelled to a foreign country? Where did you go? When did you go? What did you do there?

There is a Test for Units 10–12 on pages 156 and 157.

Practise and check key (Units 10-12)

PRACTISE

1 Comparatives

(Suggested answers)
1 A mouse is smaller than a cheetah. 2 A fish risotto and salad is healthier/better for you than a lemon pudding and cream. 3 Playing chess is slower than snowboarding. Snowboarding is more exciting than playing chess. 4 Villages are friendlier/quieter than cities. 5 A Fiat Uno is slower than a Porsche. A Porsche is more expensive than a Fiat Uno.

2 Superlatives

a) the busiest, the tallest, the most expensive, the coldest, the fastest, the most popular, the oldest, the heaviest, the longest, the largest
b)
2 the coldest place 3 the busiest airport 4 the most expensive diamond 5 the tallest tower 6 the oldest woman 7 the fastest animal 8 the heaviest cake 9 the most popular record 10 the longest hair 11 the largest island

3 Modals and verbs with *-ing* or verbs *+/– to*

2 to find 3 doing 4 listening 5 cook 6 to meet 7 smoke 8 smoking 9 to join 10 to say 11 to write 12 send

4 Verbs + two objects

2 him (Tim) something for his computer
3 them (Brian and Norma) some chocolates
4 them (mum and dad) a present last week
5 her (Tina) some earrings 6 him (Alex) a video from the shop

5 The Present Perfect

a)
1 2 has never made 3 made
2 1 had 2 sang
3 1 has played 2 paid
4 1 worked 2 left 3 came 4 wrote
b)
2 hasn't sung, has never sung 3 hasn't played, has never played 4 hasn't written, has never written
c)
1 haven't 2 Did you sing, did 3 Did Liverpool pay, did
4 Have you worked, have 5 Did you write, did

CHECK

1 Verb forms

1 LIZ: Yes, I lived there when I was a child.
2 PAT: I'd like to go back to Mexico.
LIZ: Peter and I are going to have a holiday in Cancún next month. Do you want to come?
PAT: Yes, I'd love to! I've never been to Cancún.
3 LIZ: Do you speak Spanish well?
PAT: Yes, I studied it at university.
LIZ: Have you ever lived in Spain?
4 PAT: Where's Peter now?
LIZ: He's playing football. When he comes home he's going to cook a Thai meal. Have you ever eaten Thai food?
LIZ: Would you like to stay for dinner?
LIZ: I love Thai food. It's the most delicious food I've ever eaten.

2 Correct the mistakes

2 's it like? 3 by 4 'll pick 5 going 6 does it look like 7 saddest 8 bring it back 9 go

3 Prepositions

1 2 At 3 in 4 at 5 With
2 1 in 2 by 3 of 4 about
3 1 of 2 for 3 in

4 Vocabulary

a)
1 look after 2 try on 3 turn on 4 look for 5 take off 6 Hang up
b)
1 The house: carpets, close the curtains, wardrobe, make the bed, listen to a CD, a sink, turn off the tap
2 Shopping: they don't fit, I'm just looking..., receipt, what size is she?, cheque card
3 Music: classical, listen to a CD, play the piano, go to a concert
4 Adjectives to describe a thing: cotton, round, useful, wooden, square

Prepositions and everyday expressions

These are the most important prepositions and everyday expressions in the SB.

UNIT 1

Prepositions

go ***to*** *the theatre*
He's married ***to*** *Natasha Richardson.*
My birthday is ***in*** *September.*
on *the 1st of March*
on *Saturday*
at *five o'clock*
five ***past*** *two*
ten ***to*** *three*
He's got a flat ***in*** *New York.*
They come ***from*** *Britain.*
on *the east coast of Ireland*
at *the university of Glasgow*
near *the sea*
Dublin is famous ***all over*** *the world for its beer.*

Everyday expressions

Here you are.
I'm sorry.
I think so.
I don't know.

UNIT 2

Prepositions

on
behind
in front of *the desk*
next to
in
under
by *bus*
on *foot / the Underground*
She lives ***by*** *herself, not* ***with*** *her family.*
I sometimes work ***at*** *home.*
She spends money ***on*** *clothes.*
He gets the train ***from*** *London to Oxford.*
I work ***for*** *French TV.*
They go ***to*** *bed* ***at*** *eight o'clock.*
Do you ever listen ***to*** *music?*
What's the English ***for*** *the days* ***of*** *the week?*

Everyday expressions

Can I *have a tissue, please?*
Of course you can. Help yourself.
Could I *borrow your mug?*
I'm afraid it's dirty.
Whose *are those?*

UNIT 3

Prepositions

I have toast ***for*** *breakfast.*
I always drink wine ***with*** *my meals.*
I just have a sandwich ***at*** *lunchtime.*
I go to work ***by*** *car.*
I go on holiday ***by*** *plane or* ***by*** *train.*
I spend the day ***on*** *the beach.*
We usually stay ***in*** *a hotel or* ***at*** *a campsite.*
Would you like a cup ***of*** *tea?*
in *spring/summer/autumn/winter*

Everyday expressions

How much is *a cup of tea?*
Do you take *sugar?*
Can I help you?
That comes to *eighty pence.*
Would you like *some milk?*
I'd like *a biscuit, please.*
I'll have *a glass of orange juice.*

UNIT 4

Prepositions

My brother is ***in*** *this photograph.*
How do you say it ***in*** *English?*
At *the beginning* ***of*** *the film*
At *the end* ***of*** *the film*
He didn't see them ***until*** *the end of the war.*
I usually go ***to*** *bed* ***after*** *midnight.*
before *midnight.*
He's good ***at*** *languages.*
The film is ***about*** *James Bond.*

UNIT 5

Prepositions

opposite *the bank*
between *the bank and the shop*
walk ***up/down/along*** *the street*
on *the left/right*
go ***straight on***
on *the corner* ***of*** *the road*
come ***out of*** *the railway station*
I listened ***in*** *silence.*
I went ***to*** *England* ***for*** *a holiday.*
I stayed there ***for*** *a long time.*
I met her ***at*** *the seaside.*
She took her purse ***out of*** *her bag.*

UNIT 6

Prepositions

I'm interested ***in*** *birds.*
What does he think ***of*** *the food?*
I'm staying ***with*** *my friends this week.*
I never talk ***to*** *Jim.*
Can you ask the teacher ***about*** *it?*
He asked the policeman ***for*** *help.*
I want to pay ***for*** *this book.*
I met him ***for*** *the first time yesterday.*

UNIT 7

Prepositions

pay ***by*** *credit card*
Let's go away ***for*** *the weekend.*
We drove ***into*** *the country.*
It's an island ***in*** *the Pacific Ocean.*
Did you do well ***in*** *your exams?*
He works ***in*** *a bank.*
Look ***at*** *the map.*
Go ***across*** *the road to the other side.*

Everyday expressions

You ***can't*** *smoke here.*
Shall I *book a room for you?*

UNIT 8

Prepositions

apply ***for*** *a job*
work ***as*** *a cleaner.*
What can you see ***in*** *the picture?*
I live ***with*** *my parents.*
Take a photo ***of*** *me.*

Everyday expressions

for the first time

UNIT 9

Prepositions

Which platform does the train leave ***from?***
One ***of*** *my brothers is ill.*
That's nice ***of*** *you!*
Are you happy ***with*** *your new car?*
I have to go ***back to*** *your house. I left my coat there.*
Come ***in****! It's cold outside.*
I'm going ***out*** *for a walk.*
I spent a lot of money ***on*** *that car.*
It costs £1 ***for*** *a cup of tea!*
I've got an appointment ***with*** *the doctor.*
He was ***away from*** *work yesterday.*

Everyday expressions

You should
You'd better *go to the doctor.*
Why don't you

You shouldn't
You'd better not *go to work.*

What's the matter?
What's wrong?

UNIT 10

Prepositions

It is ***on*** *the other side of the town.*
We climbed ***to*** *the top of the mountain.*
At *the top we ate our picnic.*
At *the moment it is raining.*
The child ran ***in front of*** *the bus.*

Everyday expressions

make the bed

UNIT 11

Prepositions

Madonna is ***in*** *a new film* ***at*** *the Odeon cinema.*
We met ***at*** *the theatre* ***by*** *the river.*
It's difficult ***for*** *me to say.*
I never think ***about*** *work when I'm at home.*

Everyday expressions

Let's go *to the cinema.*
I'd love to. / That would be great.
Do you want to buy anything? No, ***I'm just looking****.*
*These shoes'****ll be fine****. I'll take them.*

UNIT 12

Prepositions

What's this made ***of****?*
He spends a lot of time ***with*** *his father.*
Can I have a cup of tea ***without*** *sugar?*
She ran ***through*** *the fields.*

Everyday expressions

What's it like?
It's a kind of ...
What does it look like?
What's it for?

Photocopiable material

P 1.1

policeman	morning	magazine
video	afternoon	question
telephone	tomorrow	letter
guitar	today	cheese
student	day	pizza
sandwich	from	oranges
Britain	later	first
waiter	London	mother
bus	apple	sister
tennis	dictionary	brother
alphabet	woman	wife
eleven	children	son
chairs	newspaper	daughter
taxi	address	country
excellent	street	America
pronounce	road	Brazil
English	phone	tomato
spell	number	desk
computer	person	clock
photograph	reading	river
pronunciation	eating	football
thanks	postcard	sea

P 1.2

Student A

a) Dictate this to your partner.

Jean is from Belgium. He's seventy-two and a half.

He's short and fat. He's got a pet snake called Lewis.

b) Write what your partner dictates.

....

....

....

Student B

a) Write what your partner dictates.

....

....

....

b) Dictate this to your partner.

Sonia's from

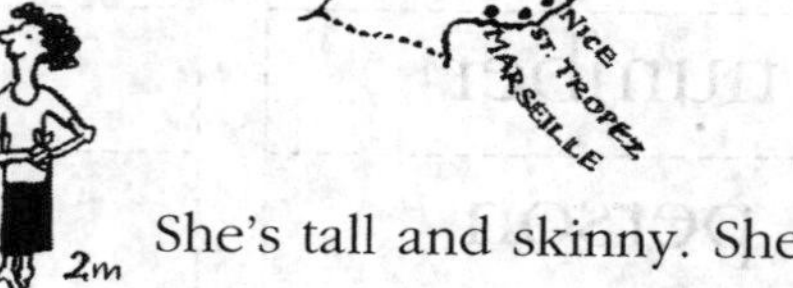

the South of France.

She's tall and skinny. She's got

a pet spider called Itsy.

P 1.4

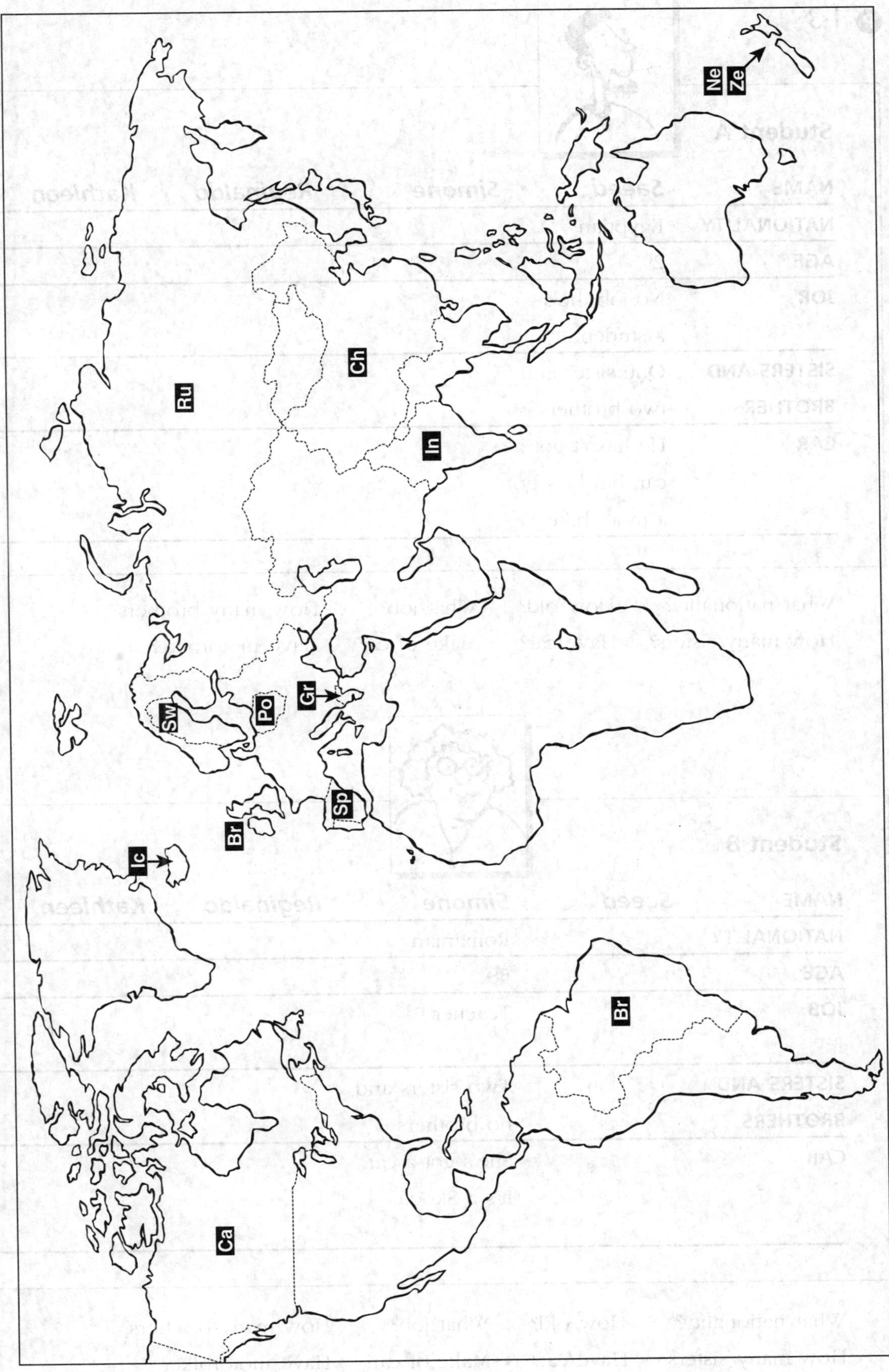

1.3

Student A

NAME	*Saeed*	*Simone*	*Reginaldo*	*Kathleen*
NATIONALITY	Egyptian			
AGE	29			
JOB	No job, he's a student.			
SISTERS AND BROTHERS	One sister and two brothers			
CAR	He hasn't got a car, but he's got a motorbike.			

What/nationality? How/old? What/job? How many/brothers?
How many/sisters? Have/car? Make of car? Have/motorbike?

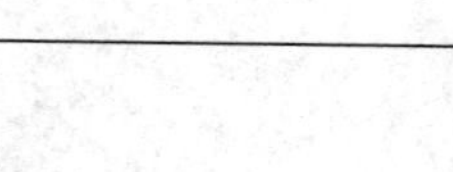

Student B

NAME	*Saeed*	*Simone*	*Reginaldo*	*Kathleen*
NATIONALITY		Romanian		
AGE		58		
JOB		Teacher		
SISTERS AND BROTHERS		Two sisters and no brothers		
CAR		She's got a car. It's a Skoda.		

What/nationality? How/old? What/job? How many/brothers?
How many/sisters? Have/car? Make of car? Have/motorbike?

Student C

NAME	*Saeed*	*Simone*	*Reginaldo*	*Kathleen*
NATIONALITY			Portuguese	
AGE			35	
JOB			Policeman	
SISTERS AND BROTHERS			Six brothers and four sisters	
CAR			He's got a car. It's a Ford.	

What/nationality? How/old? What/job? How many/brothers?
How many/sisters? Have/car? Make of car? Have/motorbike?

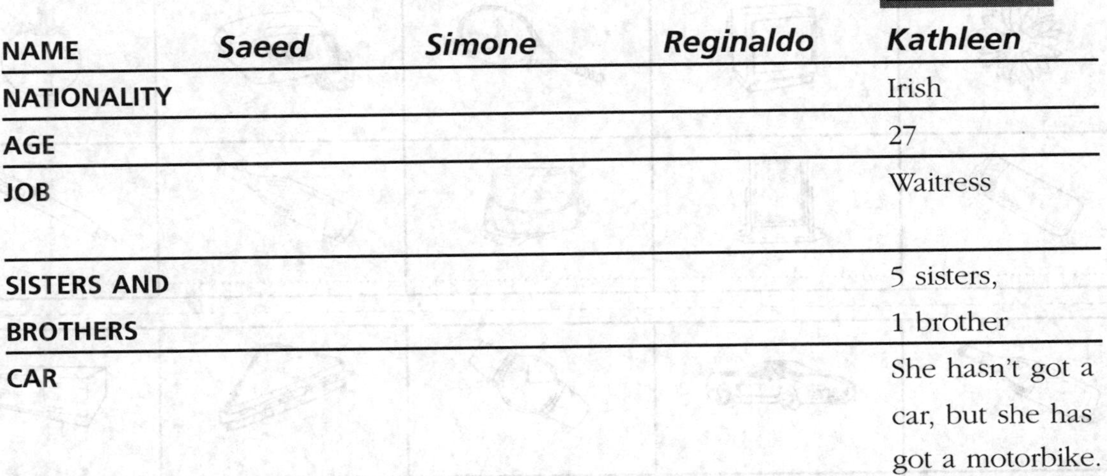

Student D

NAME	*Saeed*	*Simone*	*Reginaldo*	*Kathleen*
NATIONALITY				Irish
AGE				27
JOB				Waitress
SISTERS AND BROTHERS				5 sisters, 1 brother
CAR				She hasn't got a car, but she has got a motorbike.

What/nationality? How/old? What/job? How many/brothers?
How many/sisters? Have/car? Make of car? Have/motorbike?

P 1.5

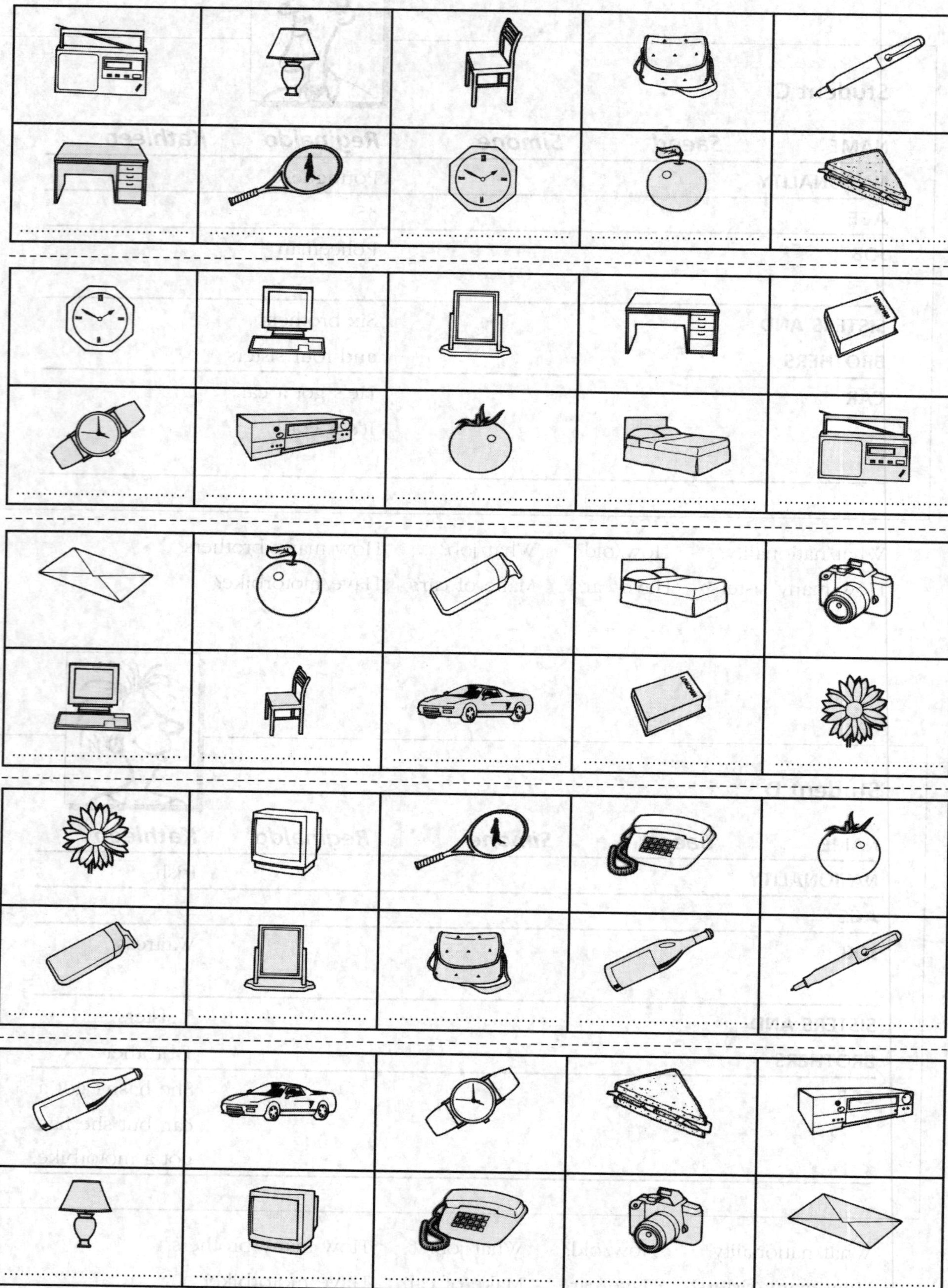

Ⓟ 1.6

999	15 March	83	210
21 Oct	54	607	20 May
47	484	20 June	1,000
175	984	12 Nov	13

10 April	33	293	22 Aug
25 Dec	17	564	90
614	4 July	210	666
18	85	72	12

13 Feb	3 May	27 June	285
867	56	32	614
45	36	1 Jan	31 Dec
5 Feb	13 Jan	268	17

234	856	912	4 Oct
15 June	31 Aug	216	987
25 Nov	22 April	478	101
31 July	497	12 Sept	562

27 Jun	126	42	16 Feb
3 Dec	10 Sept	593	28
18	193	1 Nov	27 March
6 Jan	21 May	28 Oct	49

164	11 June	832	79
123	634	9 May	27 Aug
423	910	451	7 Jan
128	1000	18 July	333

47	246	178	109
954	87	1 May	22 June
56	18 May	9 March	568
68	23	905	15 April

167	296	257	110
23 April	27 Jan	14 Nov	367
222	9 Oct	29 Dec	129
1 Aug	451	725	901

12 Aug	26 March	428	107
253	781	90	18 March
347	189	25	12 Jan
543	980	874	19 June

217	318	23 May	17 Oct
678	926	12	12 June
32	452	6 Sept	27 Nov
987	213	235	319

P 1.7

Sailing

I am sailing
I am sailing
Home again 'cross the sea.
I am sailing
Stormy waters,
To be near you, to be free.

I am flying
I am flying
Like a bird 'cross the sky.
I am flying passing high clouds,
To be with you, to be free.

Can you hear me,
Can you hear me,
Thro' the dark night far away?
I am dying
Forever trying,
To be with you, who can say.

We are sailing,
We are sailing,
Home again 'cross the sea.
We are sailing,
Stormy waters,
To be near you, to be free.
Oh Lord to be near you,
To be free.

Sailing

I .... sailing
I ....
Home again 'cross the sea.
I ....
Stormy waters,
To be near you, to be free.

I .... flying
I ....
Like a bird 'cross the sky.
I .... passing high clouds,
To be with you, to be free.

Can you hear ....,
Can you hear me,
Thro' the dark .... far away?
I .... dying
Forever trying,
To be with ...., who can say.

We ....,
We ....,
Home again 'cross the sea.
We ....,
Stormy waters,
To be near you, to be free.
Oh Lord to be near you,
To be free.

P 2.1

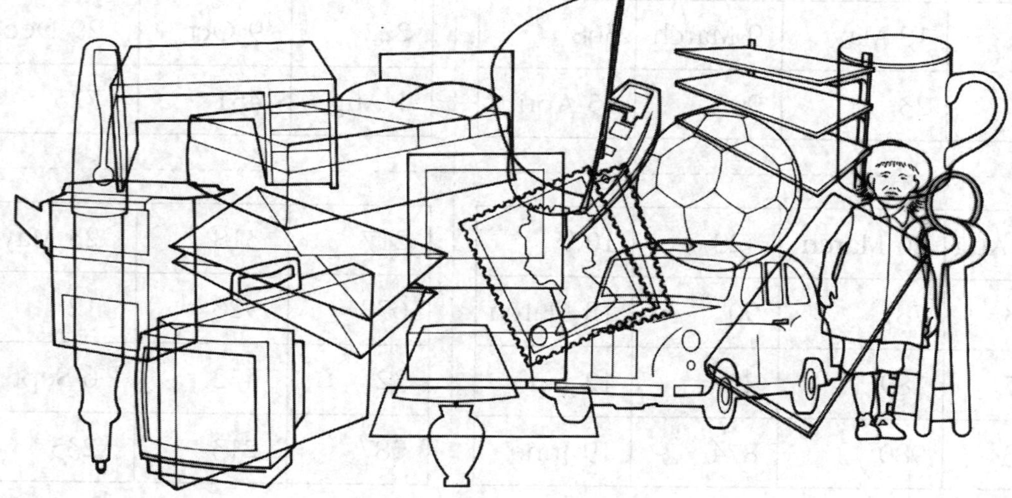

P 2.2

briefcase	tissues	shelf	desk	computer	diary	lamp	bag	door	window

P 2.4

Guess how your partner would finish these sentences.

He/She gets up at ________ and he/she eats ________ for breakfast and drinks ________. He/She often has lunch at ________ and he/she often eats ________ but he/she doesn't eat __________. In the evening he/she often ________ but he/she doesn't ________. He/She often goes to bed at ________ and he/she doesn't go to bed before ________. His/Her favourite colour is ________ and he/she doesn't like the colour ________. His/Her favourite sport is ________ but he/she doesn't like ________.

P 2.3

Student A

a) Write questions for these sentences about Susan Davidson.

1 ....?
Susan gets up at ....

2 ....?
Susan starts works at ....

3 ....?
Susan has lunch at ....

4 ....?
She usually eats .... for lunch.

5 ....?
In the evening she usually ....
or .... and she never ....

6 ....?
At the weekends she often ....

7 ....?
She usually goes to bed at ....

b) Read about Patrick Dean and be ready to answer your partner's questions about him.

Patrick Dean is a seventeen-year-old school boy. In the week he gets up at 7.15am and has a shower before he has breakfast. He goes to school at 8.40am. Classes begin at 9am. He finishes school at 3.45pm. In the evening Patrick always does his homework. It usually takes about two hours. After his homework he sometimes goes to play football with his friends or he watches TV or plays computer games. He usually goes to bed at 11pm. At the weekends he sometimes works in a supermarket. On Saturday and Sunday afternoons he plays a lot of sport with his friends.

c) Now ask your partner your questions about Susan Davidson and complete the sentences in Exercise a).

d) Answer your partner's questions about Patrick Dean.

Patrick Dean

Student B

a) Write questions for these sentences about Patrick Dean.

1 ....?

Patrick gets up at ....

2 ....?

School starts at ....

3 ....?

Patrick finishes school at ....

4 ....?

In the evening he ...., ...,

.... or ....

5 ....?

In the week he usually goes to bed at ....

6 ....?

At the weekends he ....

b) Read about Susan Davidson and be ready to answer your partner's questions about her.

Susan Davidson

Susan Davidson is thirty years old and she's a writer for a women's magazine. She usually gets up at 8am, has a bath and then has coffee and toast for breakfast. She leaves her house at 9.30am and arrives at her office at about 10am. She has lunch at 1.30pm and she usually has a cheese sandwich and an apple. She finishes work between 7 and 8pm and she usually goes out to restaurants or the cinema with her friends. She never watches TV. She doesn't like it. At the weekends she often visits her friends or she stays at home and works in the garden. She usually goes to bed at midnight.

c) Now answer your partner's questions about Susan Davidson.

d) Ask your partner your questions about Patrick Dean and complete the sentences in Exercise a).

3.1

ACROSS

2 

5 

8 

9 

11 

12 

DOWN

1 

3 

4 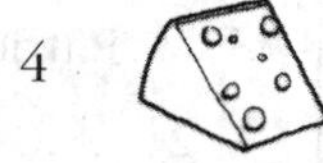

5 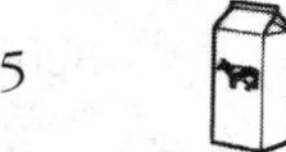

6 

7 

8 

10 

3.2

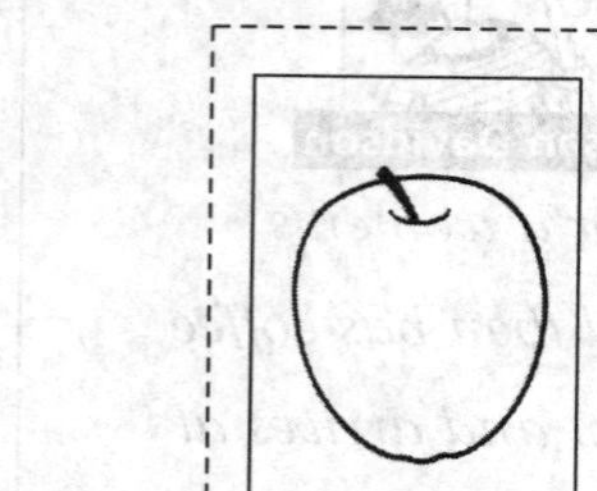

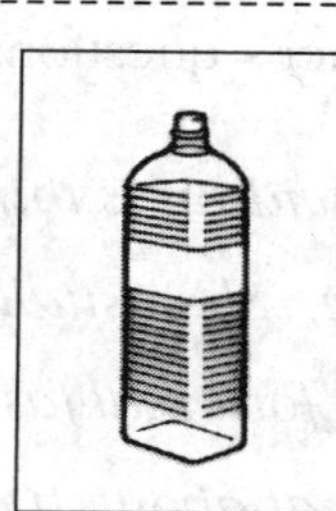

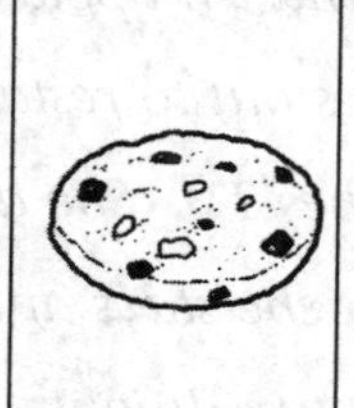

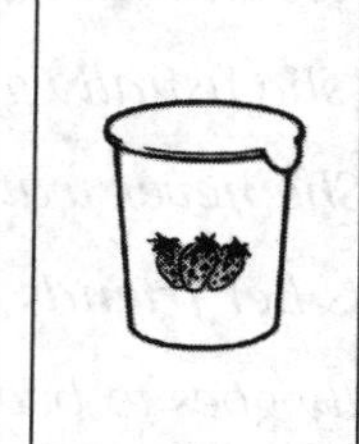

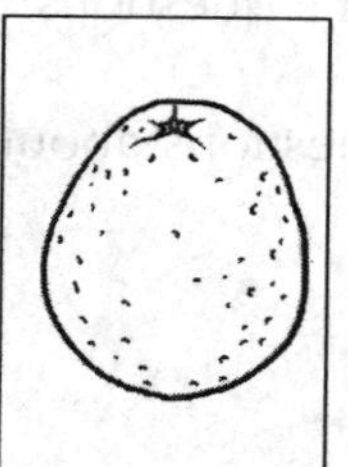

P 3.3

ACROSS

4 It's white and you can ski on it.
5 The opposite of *fast*.
8 Today's _________ is 30° Celsius.
9 You can't see in this weather.
11 The opposite of *expensive*.
12 The opposite of *sunny*.

DOWN

1 The opposite of *boring*.
2 There's a lot of this if it isn't quiet.
3 You can find campsites in the _________.
4 You can _________ in the sea.
6 The opposite of *early*.
7 A: What's the _________ like?
B: It's sunny.
10 The opposite of *new*.

P 3.5

fast
slow
expensive
cheap
good
bad

boring
exciting
hot
cold
love
hate
quiet

noisy
clean
dirty
happy
sad
correct
wrong

3.4

Student A

I'm having a very boring ________ holiday. The weather is hot ________ but I hate ________ it. The hotel is cheap ________ but it's noisy ______ and dirty ________. The restaurants are bad ________, the food is terrible ________. The bus to the seaside is very slow ________! This is an awful ________ holiday.

Mrs Smith
15, Green Road
Luton
England

Student B

I'm having a very exciting ________ holiday. The weather is cold ________ but I love ________ it. The hotel is expensive ________ but it's quiet ________ and clean ________. The restaurants are good ________, the food is excellent ________. The bus to the seaside is very fast ________! This is a wonderful ________ holiday.

John Clarke
11, Church Street
Wisbech
England

3.6

Currency	Country	Nationality
dollars		
pounds		
yen		
drachma		
peseta		
franc		
rouble		
ringgit		
schilling		
peso		
forint		
zloty		
lire		

4.1 *Questionnaire*

HOW MUCH DO YOU CARE ABOUT CLOTHES AND FASHION?

	STUDENT 1	STUDENT 2
1 Do you like shopping for clothes? (Yes/No)		
2 Do you spend a lot of money on clothes? (Yes/No)		
3 How many pairs of shoes have you got?		
4 How many pairs of trousers have you got?		
5 How many jackets have you got?		
6 How many coats have you got?		
7 How many hats have you got?		
8 How many sweaters have you got?		
9 How many shirts have you got?		
10 Do you buy or look at fashion magazines? (Yes/No)		
11 How often do you buy new clothes? (once a week/once a month/three times a year)		
12 Have you got any very expensive clothes? (Yes/No)		
13 Do you care what your boyfriend or girlfriend wears? (Yes/No)		
14 Do you look at what other people are wearing? (Yes/No)		

15 What clothes do you like? ________________

16 What clothes do you not like? ________________

4.2

Student A

1 He cans play the piano.
2 You don't can sing very well.
3 Are you good at tennis?
4 My brother walks quite slowly.
5 He comes never to class.
6 Can do you the splits?
7 She's a good swimmer.
8 You speak English good.
9 She works hard.
10 He runs fastly.
11 They speak English fluently.

Student B

1 He can play the piano.
2 You can't sing very well.
3 Are you good in tennis?
4 My brother walks quite slow.
5 He never comes to class.
6 Can you do the splits?
7 She's a well swimmer.
8 You speak English well.
9 She works hardly.
10 He runs fast.
11 They speak fluently English.

P 4.3

Student A

Complete the sentences with a word from the box below.

A: ________ you like to go to the ________ ________ ?

B: Yes, I'd like to go. What films are on?

A: ________ 's a new ________ film, *The Spider*.

B: I don't like horror films. Is there another film on?

A: Yes, a ________ story – *When Harry Met Sally* ________ it's an ________ film.

B: I'd like to see that.

A: OK. We ________ go now. It ________ in half an hour.

B: Oh. I haven't got any money and the bank is closed.

A: It doesn't matter. I've ________ a lot of money. I ________ pay for your ________.

B: Thank you. I'll give you the money tomorrow.

A: Take a coat. It's ________.

B: OK. Let's go.

but horror there love would ticket cold
'll old tonight cinema starts got can

Student B

Complete the sentences with a word from the box below.

A: Would you like to go to the cinema tonight ?

B: Yes, I'd like to ________. ________ films ________ on?

A: There's a new horror film, *The Spider*.

B: I ________ like horror films. Is there ________ film on?

A: Yes, a love story – *When Harry Met Sally* but it's an old film.

B: I'd ________ to ________ that.

A: OK. We can go now. It starts in half an hour.

B: Oh. I ________ got any money and the bank is ________.

A: It doesn't matter. I've got a lot of money. I'll pay for your ticket.

B: ________ you. I ________ give you the ________ tomorrow.

A: Take a coat. It's cold.

B: OK. Let's go.

what haven't thank are don't go another like closed see 'll money

5.1

saw	took	began
lit	spoke	smoked
woke	knew	wanted
came	thought	put

drank	left	heard
walked	spoke	hit
lit	woke	began
found	slept	knew

put	went	saw
helped	found	walked
was/were	put	knew
began	felt	did

married	killed	slept
hit	found	felt
lit	opened	drank
arrived	wanted	smoked

said	gave	opened
felt	tried	took
spoke	went	waited
listened	had	sat

listened	came	helped
thought	was/were	went
found	smoked	thought
hit	drank	knew

slept	began	walked
took	sat	listened
said	waited	left
lit	knew	woke

did	had	went
heard	knew	gave
found	slept	put
spoke	said	took

P 5.2

Student A

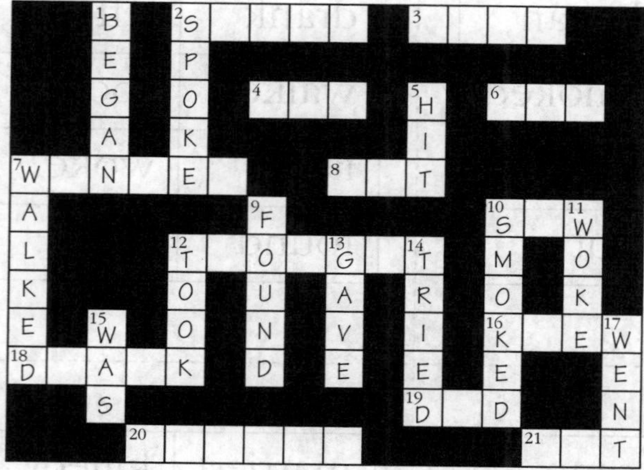

a) The verbs in your crossword are in the Past Simple. What is the infinitive of these verbs?

b) Give your partner clues for the words down.
Example: *One down is the Past Simple of begin.*

c) Check your answers with your partner's crossword.

Student B

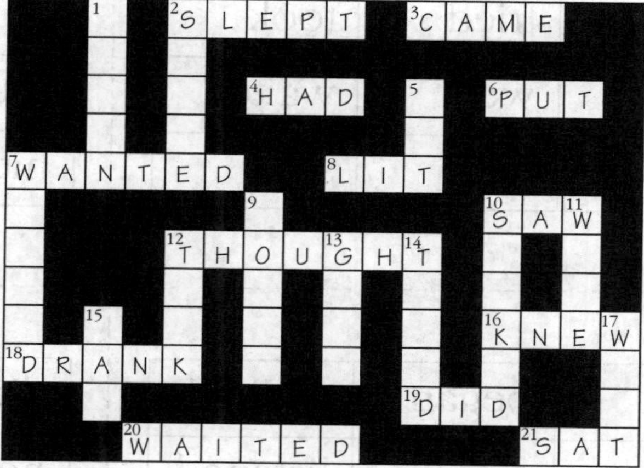

a) The verbs in your puzzle are in the Past Simple. What is the infinitive of these verbs?

b) Give your partner clues for the words across.
Example: *Two across is the Past Simple of sleep.*

c) Check your answers with your partner's crossword.

5.3

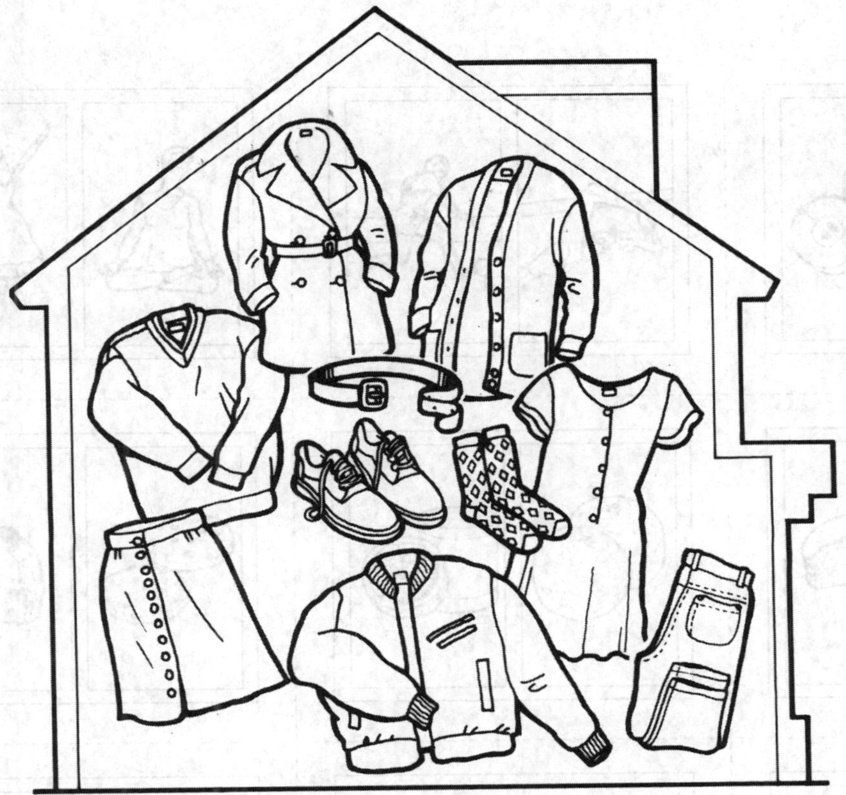

BISCUIT
ASSORTMENT
SUGAR
CRISPS
CHEESE & ONION
Mineral WATER
Soup
Yogurt

P 6.1

6.2

Ayrton Senna
BRAZIL'S FAMOUS RACING DRIVER

Born São Paulo, Brazil, 21st March, 1960

1964 began driving go-karts
1973 first go-kart race
1981 drove his first racing car
1988 Grand Prix World Champion for the first time
1990 and 1991 World Champion again
1994 1st May died in crash at the San Marino Grand Prix, Imola, Italy

Martin Luther King
AMERICA'S GREAT CIVIL RIGHTS LEADER

Born Atlanta, Georgia, USA, 15th January, 1929

1948 became a Minister in the Baptist Church
1953 married Coretta Scott
1956 went to prison to get equal rights for black people in the USA
1963 28th August made his famous speech "*I have a dream*" in Washington DC
1968 3rd April made his famous speech about the *"Promised Land"*
4th April a gunman shot him outside his hotel in Memphis, Tennessee

John Lennon
LIVERPOOL'S FAMOUS BEATLE

Born Liverpool, England, 9th October, 1940

1958 his mother, Julia, died in a road accident
1960 the Beatles pop group began
1962 married Cynthia Powell on 23 August
the Beatles made their first record *Love me do*
1968 met Yoko Ono. Cynthia divorced him
1969 married Yoko in Gibraltar
1970 the Beatles ended
1980 8 December Mark David Chapman shot John outside his flat in New York

James ("Jimmy") Dean
HOLLYWOOD'S ANGRY YOUNG MAN

Born Marion, Indiana, USA, 8th February, 1931

1936 went to live in Los Angeles
1939 his mother, Mildred, died of cancer
Jimmy went to live with his aunt and uncle in Fairmount, Indiana
Jimmy loved fast cars and motorbikes
1948 went to the University of California to study acting
after university Jimmy went to work in New York for a year
1954 got his first contract in Hollywood in the film of John Steinbeck's *East of Eden*
fell in love with Pier Angelli, a young Italian actress
1955 starred in *Rebel without a cause* and *Giant* with Rock Hudson and Elizabeth Taylor
bought a new silver Spyder Porsche
1955 30 September James Dean died in a car crash on the road between Los Angeles and Salinas

P 7.1

M O U N T A I N A X
B F C Y R D E O P F
G F R T E S G I A H
R I I L E K M S T S
M C P R E T T Y H T
T E E X L P A E K R
W O O D J B G L M E
N Z P Q Q U I E T E
S T L U X Y J N L T
F I E L D B D M T G
R F B K C I N E M A

P 7.3

Lynne Soames

- **MONDAY**
  8.30am Flight to Paris →
  9pm return from Paris.

- **TUESDAY**
  9 am– 1pm meeting with Dick Smith.
  1.30 pm Lunch with Dick and Jane Simmonds.
  3 pm– 6pm Visit South London office.

- **WEDNESDAY**
  12 am– 2 pm Visit North London Office.
  3 pm Phone Dick Smith in New York.
  4 pm Meeting with Paul Brown.
  5.30 pm Flight to Paris.

Peter Finlay

Monday
am Free
2pm → 4pm Lunch with Paul Brown.
4pm → 6pm Visit office in Piccadilly.

Tuesday
8.30am → 11 am Meeting with Mr Lennard.
12 midday Lunch with Gerry Barnes.
2.30 pm Visit South London Office.
Meeting with Lynne Soames at 3pm.
6pm Dentist

Wednesday
12.30pm Flight to Amsterdam,
meeting with Cristian.
6pm flight back to London.

Susan Lock

MONDAY
- am Free
- 1pm → 4pm Meeting with Dick Smith.
- 4pm Doctor's appointment.

TUESDAY
- 8am Flight to Paris to see new office.
- 3pm Flight back to London.

WEDNESDAY
- 11am → 1pm Meeting with Paul Brown.
- 1pm Lunch with Janet.
- Phone Dick Smith in New York between 2pm and 4pm
- 5.30 pm Flight to Berlin. Meeting with George Hawkins about the new office.

P 7.4

ACROSS

3 The adverb from the adjective *fast*.
4 The adjective from the verb *attract*.
5 The adjective from the noun *dirt*.
6 The adverb from the adjective *good*.
8 The noun from the verb *choose*.
10 The adverb from the adjective *beautiful*.
14 The adjective from the noun *correction*.
15 The adverb from the adjective *quick*.

DOWN

1 The adverb from the adjective *bad*.
2 The adjective from the noun *kindness*.
3 The adjective from the noun *friend*.
7 The noun from the verb *examine*.
9 The adjective from the noun *danger*.
11 The adverb from the adjective *slow*.
12 The adjective from the adverb *noisily*.
13 The verb from the noun *decision*.

P 8.1

P 8.2

FINISH 23	? 22	? 21	20
? 16	17	? 18	? 19
? 15	14	? 13	12
8	? 9	10	? 11
? 7	? 6	5	? 4
START	? 1	2	3

Have you got a brother?
(Yes = 1 place forward, No = 1 place back)

Can you count up to 40 in English?
(Yes = 2 places forward, No = 2 places back)

Did you go on holiday at Christmas?
(Yes = 1 place back, No = 1 place forward)

Have you got a pair of red shoes?
(Yes = 2 places forward, No = 2 places back)

Are you wearing yellow?
(Yes = 2 places forward, No = 1 place back)

Is it Monday today?
(Yes = 3 places forward, No = 1 place back)

Can you play the violin?
(Yes = 3 places forward, No = 2 places back)

Can you walk backwards in a straight line?
(Yes = 3 places forward, No = 2 places back)

Have you got brown eyes?
(Yes = 1 place forward, No = 1 place back)

Can you tell a joke in English?
(Yes = 2 places forward, No = 1 place back)

Is it raining today?
(Yes = 2 places back, No = 2 places forward)

Can you stand on your head?
(Yes = 3 places forward, No = 1 place back)

Have you got an English dictionary?
(Yes = 3 places forward, No = 2 places back)

Are you wearing glasses?
(Yes = 1 place back, No = 2 places forward)

Do you like salad?
(Yes = 2 places forward, No = 3 places back)

Do you go to the cinema once a week?
(Yes = 1 place forward, No = 1 place back)

8.3

milk +	ham –	rice –
water –	chicken +	mushrooms +
orange juice +	frozen peas ?	butter ?
sugar +	melon +	onions –
carrots ?	lamb ?	eggs +
jam –	apples +	grapes ?
pototoes +	oranges +	sandwiches –
wine ?	bananas ?	bread –

8.4

Student A
Words for doctor and teacher

patient homework mark pills teach a prescription student a classroom an appointment a nurse a surgery a board

TEACHER

Ask Student B for words for these jobs.

Student B
Words for actor and hairdresser

scissors a film a director a hairbrush a play a comb a theatre a client a tip cut act an audience a tip

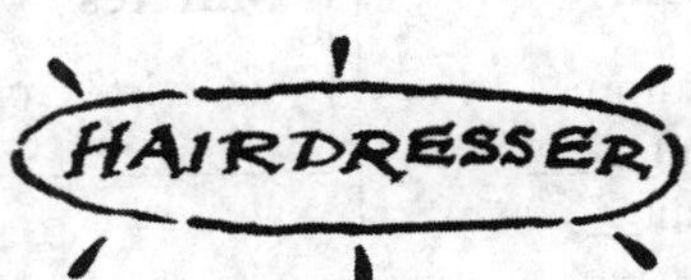

Ask Student A for words for these jobs.

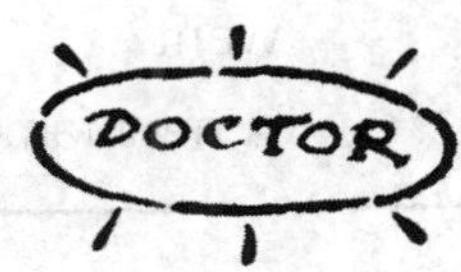

8.5

What's his/her job?

1 2 3

4 5 VOTE FOR ME! 6

7 8 9

Stem	Suffixes
drumm__	er ist cian
guitar__	
wait__	
garden__	
jewell__	
politi__	
scient__	
photograph__	
engine__	

9.1

NO FOOD IN THE HOUSE

MOTHER: Can you go to the shops for me, please?

TEENAGER 1: Sorry Mum, I have to do my homework.

MOTHER: You don't have to do it now, do you?

TEENAGER 1: Yes, I do because I'm going to meet David at 6 o' clock. We're going to watch the school football team play.

MOTHER: What about your dinner?

TEENAGER 1: Oh, I'm not hungry.

MOTHER: You have to eat something.

TEENAGER 1: OK. I'll take an apple.

MOTHER: Can you go to the shops for me, please?

TEENAGER 2: Sorry Mum, I have to go to Tom's and get my bike. I left it at his house.

MOTHER: Again?

TEENAGER 2: Yes. See you later, bye.

FATHER: I'm hungry. What's for dinner?

MOTHER: Nothing.

FATHER: Nothing? Why?

MOTHER: I have to go to the shops. We've got no food in the house.

FATHER: I'll go. What do you want?

MOTHER: A new family!!

9.2

Student A
Find someone who ...

1 likes cats ______
2 is frightened of spiders ______
3 had pets as a child ______
4 likes mice ______
5 likes dogs ______
6 is frightened of snakes ______
7 likes birds ______
8 has a pet now ______

Student B
Find someone who ...

1 doesn't like cats ______
2 isn't frightened of spiders ______
3 didn't have pets as a child ______
4 doesn't like mice ______
5 doesn't like dogs ______
6 isn't frightened of snakes ______
7 doesn't like birds ______
8 doesn't have a pet now ______

10.1

Questionnaire

Name: .... ***Country:*** ....

1 ***Who is your oldest relative?*** ....
2 ***Who is your youngest relative?*** ....
3 ***What was the furthest country you travelled to in the last 10 years?*** ....
4 ***What was the latest time you went to bed last week?*** ....
5 ***What was the earliest you got up last week?*** ....
6 ***What was the best thing you did last week?*** ....
7 ***What was the worst thing you did last week?*** ....
8 ***What was the biggest meal you ate yesterday?*** ....
9 ***What was the smallest thing you bought last week?*** ....
10 ***What was the most expensive thing you bought last week?*** ....
11 ***What was the cheapest thing you bought last week?*** ....
12 ***What was the best film you saw last year?*** ....
13 ***Who was the most interesting person you met last year?*** ....

P 10.2

	after	gym
/ə/	her	he
/ɜː/	furniture	cream
/I/	word	tree
/iː/	heard	field
/ʌ/	learn	please
police	early	people
better	him	hungry
telephone	chicken	under
address	dictionary	up
today	pretty	butter
comfort	ill	son

P 7.2

Barbara and Henry wanted to go ________ for the weekend. They ________ ________ early on their motorbike. It was a beautiful sunny ________. They took a ________ and something to eat and drink and ________ into the country. Then at about three o'clock they ________ a small bridge and stopped by a ________. It was very hot so Henry went for a ________ in the river. Barbara took a ________ of him. After that, they decided to ________ ________ the tent and and had something to eat. Then they fell ________. Some boys ________ Henry's clothes, Barbara's camera and the map. It started to ________ and Barbara and Henry ________ ________. They were ________ and they didn't have any money.

asleep	photo	set off	cross	swim	camping	put up	
steal	rode	river	rain	wake up	tent	day	lost

P 11.1

Student A

Read about Akio Morita and write six questions about him for Student B to answer.

1 ______________________________?
2 ______________________________?
3 ______________________________?
4 ______________________________?
5 ______________________________?
6 ______________________________?

AKIO MORITA

Akio Morita was born in Japan in 1921. When he was at school he made a very simple recorder which was the beginning of his interest in technology. He took an examination to work for the Tokyo-Shibaura Electric Company but he failed so he went to work for a film processing company. Then he left that company and went to university and studied physics. Morita and his partner Masaru Ibuka started to work together to repair broken radios and in 1949 they made the first Japanese cassette recorders. They worked very hard and later started the company called Sony, which is now world famous for video recorders, televisions, CD players, video cameras and other electronic machines for the home.

Student B

Read about Charles Schulz and write six questions about him for Student A to answer.

1 ______________________________?
2 ______________________________?
3 ______________________________?
4 ______________________________?
5 ______________________________?
6 ______________________________?

CHARLES SHULZ

Charles Shulz was born in America in 1922. In 1950 he sent his idea for a comic strip to a company that worked for different newspapers. The comic strip was about a group of children. A few newspapers used the comic strip and called it Peanuts. The most important character is Charlie Brown. He is a little boy who tries to do things but always fails. Lucy is another character. She is a little girl who always argues with Charlie Brown. Schulz didn't like the name Peanuts but the comic strip soon became very popular and Schulz became one of the richest men in America. Peanuts appears in 1,800 newspapers and magazines around the world.

P 10.3

Z	E	A	R	M	R	T	O	E	S
M	T	C	O	L	D	G	O	P	T
O	T	T	E	A	C	H	E	R	O
U	A	O	W	M	K	E	N	F	M
T	B	R	T	P	S	A	N	L	A
H	L	Y	N	B	E	D	T	U	C
L	E	Y	E	P	R	V	K	C	H
M	U	S	I	C	I	A	N	O	A
T	E	E	T	H	C	R	T	U	C
F	C	H	A	I	R	M	N	G	H
G	R	B	A	C	K	A	C	H	E
D	R	A	W	E	R	S	T	P	L

P 11.2

	I'm waiting	I will
I love	I forgot	I can't
I hate	I've decided	I would like
I want	I've finished	I've started
I enjoy	I'll stop	I began
I hope	I can	I refuse
I promise	I could	I learnt

11.3

Spot the mistakes

a) Which four pictures don't belong to the story?

b) Look at the fourteen underlined verb patterns. Correct the ten verb pattern mistakes.

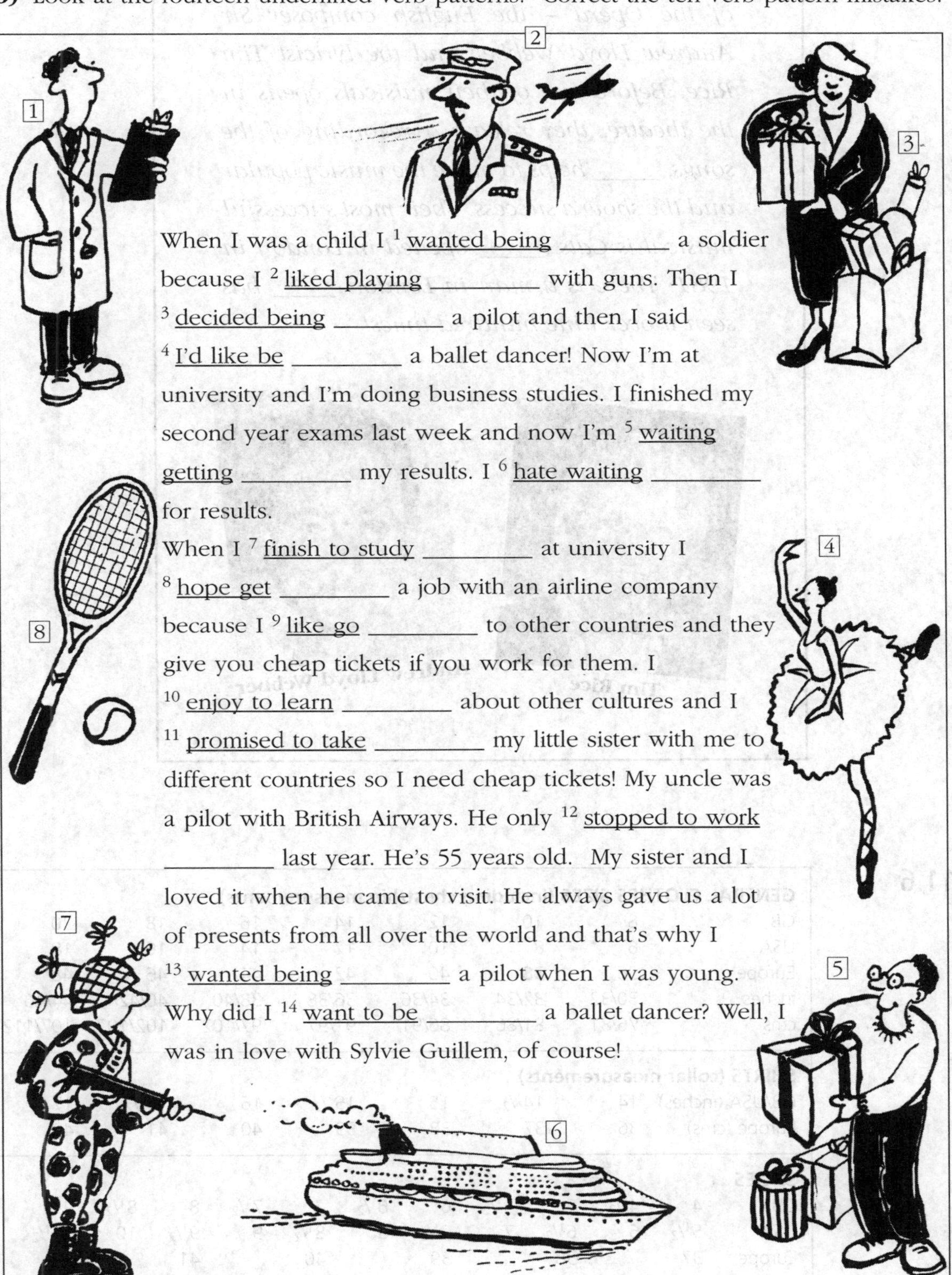

When I was a child I [1] wanted being ________ a soldier because I [2] liked playing ________ with guns. Then I [3] decided being ________ a pilot and then I said [4] I'd like be ________ a ballet dancer! Now I'm at university and I'm doing business studies. I finished my second year exams last week and now I'm [5] waiting getting ________ my results. I [6] hate waiting ________ for results.

When I [7] finish to study ________ at university I [8] hope get ________ a job with an airline company because I [9] like go ________ to other countries and they give you cheap tickets if you work for them. I [10] enjoy to learn ________ about other cultures and I [11] promised to take ________ my little sister with me to different countries so I need cheap tickets! My uncle was a pilot with British Airways. He only [12] stopped to work ________ last year. He's 55 years old. My sister and I loved it when he came to visit. He always gave us a lot of presents from all over the world and that's why I [13] wanted being ________ a pilot when I was young. Why did I [14] want to be ________ a ballet dancer? Well, I was in love with Sylvie Guillem, of course!

11.4 Complete the sentences with *who* or *which*.

These are the men _____ wrote the Phantom of the Opera – the English composer Sir Andrew Lloyd Webber and the lyricist Tim Rice. Before one of their musicals opens in the theatre, they release a recording of the songs, _____ helps to make the music popular and the show a success. Their most successful musical is Cats, _____ opened in London in 1981. There is a man in London _____ has seen it over nine hundred times!

Tim Rice

Andrew Lloyd Webber

11.6

GENERAL CLOTHES SIZES (including chest/hip measurements)

GB	8	10	12	14	16	18	20
USA	6	8	10	12	14	16	18
Europe	36	38	40	42	44	46	48
inches	30/32	32/34	34/36	36/38	38/40	40/42	44/46
cms	76/81	81/86	86/91	91/97	97/102	102/107	107/112

SHIRTS (collar measurements)

GB/USA (inches)	14	14½	15	15½	16	16½	17
Europe (cms)	36	37	38	39	40	41	42

SHOES

GB	4	4½	5	5½	6	6½	7	7½	8	8½	9
USA	5½	6	6½	7	7½	8	8½	9	9½	10	10½
Europe	37		38		39		40		41		42

11.5

belt tie skirt dress shoes socks
cardigan scarf trainers hat shirt trousers

P 12.1

The Lady in red

I've never seen you looking so lovely as you did tonight
I've never seen you shine so bright

I've never seen so many men ask you if you wanted to dance,
they're looking for a little romance, given half a chance,
and I have never seen that dress you're wearing,
or the highlights in your hair that catch your eyes,
I have been blind.

The lady in red is dancing with me, cheek to cheek,
there's nobody here, it's just you and me, it's where I wanna be,
but I hardly know this beauty by my side,
I'll never forget the way you look tonight.

I've never seen you looking so gorgeous as you did tonight
I've never seen you shine so bright
you were amazing
I've never seen so many many people want to be there by your side,
and when you turned to me and smiled, it took my breath away,
and I have never had such a feeling, such a feeling of complete and utter love,
as I do tonight.

I never will forget the way you look tonight.
The lady in red, my lady in red.

The Lady in red

I'............ .... you looking so lovely as you did tonight
I'............ .... you shine so bright

I'............ .... so many men ask you if you .... to dance,
they' .... for a little romance, given half a chance,
and I .... that dress you' ....,
or the highlights in your hair that catch your eyes,
I .... blind.

The lady in red .... with me, cheek to cheek,
there's nobody here, it's just you and me, it's where I wanna be,
but I hardly .... this beauty by my side,
I' .... the way you look tonight.

I' .... you looking so gorgeous as you did tonight
I' .... you shine so bright
you were amazing
I' .... so many many people want to be there by your side,
and when you .... to me and ...., it .... my breath away,
and I .... such a feeling, such a feeling of complete and utter love,
as I do tonight.

I never will forget the way you look tonight.
The lady in red, my lady in red.

forget	smile	look	wear	
dance	be	want	see(x7)	take
have	look	know	turn	

P 12.2

Dinner time

FATHER: We need knives and forks on the table, please.

TEENAGER 1: You do it.

TEENAGER 2: No. I did it last night.

MOTHER: Now, please. Do it immediately.

TEENAGER 2: I always do the housework. It's because I'm the youngest!

FATHER: Stop arguing.

TEENAGER 1: Can I go out tonight?

MOTHER: No. You have to go to school tomorrow.

FATHER: You can go out on Friday.

TEENAGER 1: My friends can go out in the week.

TEENAGER 2: Well, you can't!

MOTHER: Stop arguing. Come on let's eat now.

TEENAGER 1: I don't like salad.

TEENAGER 2: You don't like any food.

FATHER: Stop arguing!!

MOTHER: Oh, come on, dear. Let's go out to a restaurant. Let's leave these two to fight.

FATHER: Good idea. A quiet meal. Bye bye you two.

MOTHER: Don't forget to wash up.

TEENAGER 1: You wash up.

TEENAGER 2: No. You do it.

Mother and father leave.

Test 1 Units 1 - 3

GRAMMAR

A *To be*: questions and answers

Complete the sentences with the correct form of the verb *to be*. Use the contracted form where possible. (10 marks)

1 ______ you a student? Yes I ______.
2 ______ Maria from Spain? No, she ______.
3 ______ Jack your uncle? Yes, he ______.
4 ______ these your books? No, they ______.
5 ______ we late? No, it _____ only 8.45.

___ / 10 marks

B *Have/has* got

Tim, Pat and Jenny are friends. They're having coffee in a café. Complete their conversation with *have got* or *has got*, positive and negative. Use contracted forms where possible. (20 marks)

TIM: Pat, (*you*) (1) _________ a pen, please?

PAT: No, I'm sorry I (*not*) (2) _________ one but Jenny (3) _________ two.

JENNY: Here you are.

TIM: Thanks. (*you*) (4) _________ any paper?

JENNY: Yes, I (5) _________ a lot. Do you want some?

TIM: Yes please. (*you or Jenny*) (6) _________ got a Spanish dictionary?

PAT: No, we (7) _________ one, but look, Sam and Peter (8) _________ one.

TIM: Oh, good. (*they*) (9) _________ a car?

JENNY: No they (10) _________ one. Why?

TIM: I (11) _________ a Spanish examination at 10 am. I'm late!

PAT: Get a taxi.

TIM: I can't. I (*not*) (12) _________ any money.

JENNY: I (*not*) (13) _________ any money. (*you*) (14) _________ any Pat?

PAT: I (15) _________ £5, but I need it.

JENNY: Peter (16) _________ his bike here.

Tim: OK. Oh, I (*not*) (17) _________ my watch.

PAT: I (18) _________ one. Here, take it.

TIM: Thank you Pat. Goodbye. See you later.

PAT: Bye. Good luck in your Spanish exam.

PAT: (*you*) (19) _________ a pen, Jenny?

JENNY: No, Tim (20) _________ it.

___ / 20 marks

C The Present Simple

a) Read the paragraph about Penny Larson. Then write questions and short answers about her life. (10 marks)

Penny Larson teaches English in a language school in Hastings. She works every morning from 9.30 am to 1 pm but she doesn't work in the afternoons. She has lunch with her students at a restaurant near the school. After lunch she usually walks home but sometimes she goes home by bus. In the afternoon she always reads the newspaper and then she visits her parents.

1 Penny/teach English?
Question _______________________________?
Answer _______________________________.

2 she/have lunch with other teachers?
Question _______________________________?
Answer _______________________________.

3 she/teach in the afternoons?
Question _______________________________?
Answer _______________________________.

4 she/always walk home?
Question _______________________________?
Answer _______________________________.

5 she/visit her parent at the weekend?
Question _______________________________?
Answer _______________________________.

___ / 10 marks

b) Put the words in the correct order. (5 marks)

1 n't (not) does she usually work afternoon the in
_______________________________.

2 you to music often do listen?
_______________________________?

3 n't (not) we drink in do coffee morning the
_______________________________.

4 speak do Portuguese they?
_______________________________.

5 never a big eat I lunch

______________________________________.

___ / 5 marks

c) Correct the underlined verb mistakes in the sentences. (5 marks)

1 They <u>likes</u> football and tennis. ____________
2 I <u>eat not</u> chicken. ____________
3 <u>Do he</u> get up at 8 am? ____________
4 We <u>not smoke</u>. ____________
5 <u>Do you wants</u> a mineral water? ____________

___ / 5 marks

D The Present

Write the correct form of the verb in brackets. Use contracted forms. (10 marks)

1 Peter and Mike (*like*) ________ TV but I (*not do*) ________.

2 Linda (*work*) ________ in a bank. It (*be*) ________ near the station.

3 Jim (*have got*) ________ two sisters. They (*be*) ________ students.

4 A: (*John play*) ____________ tennis?
B: I (*know not*) ________________.

5 A: (*you like*) ____________ your teacher?
B: Yes, she (*be*) ____________ good.

6 Mr and Mrs Lewis (*not be*) ________ at home. They (*visit*)________ their daughter in Hull.

7 A: (*you be*) ____________ English?
B: Yes, I (*be*) ________.

8 A: (*you have got*) ____________ a pen?
B: No, I (*not have*) ________.

9 A: (*you want*) ____________ a small ham roll?
B: No I (*want*) ____________ a big one, please.

10 Joan (*not be*) ____________ here. She (*play*) ________ tennis with Gillian.

___ / 10 marks

E Object and possessive pronouns

Write the correct pronouns in the sentences. (10 marks)

1 That's Kelly's cousin. I like (*she*) ________.
2 Is this book (*you*) ________?
3 That dictionary is (*I*) ________.
4 Harry lives near (*we*) ________.
5 This is my desk. That's (*they*)________.
6 I know his name. I don't know (*she*) _______.
7 I think this wine is (*we*) ________.
8 I phone (*he*) ________ every day.
9 This is my house but I don't like (*it*) ______.
10 A: Is this Paul's book?
B: No, that's (*he*) ________ on the desk.

___ / 10 marks

F *A, an* and *some*

Complete the sentences with *a, an* or *some*. (10 marks)

1 Would you like _____ apple?
2 I've got _____ cheese in the fridge.
3 I'd like _____ pot of tea, please.
4 Do you want _____ sandwich?
5 I want _____ computer.
6 I'd like _____ grapes, please.
7 He's got _____ glass of orange juice.
8 David wants _____ egg sandwich.
9 June would like _____ water.
10 I want _____ office near London.

___ / 10 marks

VOCABULARY

G The family, food and drink, the weather, and the office

a) Which word is the odd one out? (5 marks)

1 sunny desk telephone computer diary
2 wife daughter mug brother son
3 chicken ham bread aunt yogurt
4 raining niece cold cloudy windy
5 water tea bacon coffee beer

___ / 5 marks

b) Wordsearch. (15 marks)
Find the five words for the family, three words for weather, three words for the office and four words for food and drink in the puzzle.

```
W M P N F A T H E R
D F G S U N N Y X T
N M U N C L E Y N E
S O K O Z L P F B L
D R A W E R H R I E
S A D R F Q E A S P
H N S A N D W I C H
E G P S O U P N U O
L E S I S T E R I N
F B C O U S I N T E
```

___ / 15 marks

Total ___ / 100 marks

Test 2 Units 4-6

GRAMMAR

A *Can* and *can't*

Correct the underlined verb form mistakes in these sentences. (5 marks)

1 I <u>can to speak</u> Polish. ________
2 <u>Do</u> you <u>can drive</u>? ________
3 Harry <u>can plays</u> the guitar. ________
4 We <u>don't can come</u> tomorrow. ________
5 <u>Can I leaving</u> class at 4, please? ________

___ / 5 marks

B Adjectives and adverbs

a) Complete the sentences with the adverb of the adjective in brackets. (5 marks)

1 She sings (*beautiful*) ________.
2 He answered all the questions (*easy*) ________.
3 Mary speaks very (*quiet*) ________.
4 Simon plays the piano (*good*) ________.
5 You're speaking very (*fast*) ________.

___ / 5 marks

b) Underline the correct word in the sentences. (5 marks)

1 Lenny is a *good/ well* driver.
2 My grandmother walks very *slow/ slowly.*
3 Julie isn't a very *interesting/ interestingly* person but I like her.
4 Billy understands English but he doesn't speak it very *fluent/ fluently.*
5 They did their homework *quick/ quickly.*

___ / 5 marks

C Past Simple

a) Write the Past Simple form for these verbs. (10 marks)

give	
speak	
arrive	
open	
put	
have	
see	
say	
look	
wait	

___ / 10 marks

b) Complete the conversation with the correct form of the verb. (20 marks)

TOM: I (*phone*) (1)________ you yesterday. Where (*be*) (2)________ you?

CATHY: I (*go*) (3)________ to see my parents. It (*be*) (4)________ my mother's birthday. My sister and I (*cook*) (5)________ lunch.

TOM: (*she have*) (6)________ a birthday cake?

CATHY: Yes, I (*take*) (7)________ her one. She really (*like*) (8)________ it.

TOM: What (*you do*) (9)________ after lunch?

CATHY: We (*sit*) (10)________ and (*talk*) (11)________. I (*want*) (12)________ to go for a walk but my mother (*not want*) (13)________ to. In the evening we (*listen*) (14)________ to music. It (*be*) (15)________ a nice day.

TOM: (*you sleep*) (16)________ there or (*you come*) (17)________ home?

CATHY: I (*not stay*) (18)________. I (*come*) (19)________ home at 10 pm. What (*you do*) (20)________ yesterday, Tom?

___ / 20 marks

c) Read about President Kennedy (1917-1963). Then write questions and short answers about his life. (10 marks)

John F Kennedy was the President of America from 1961–63. He married Jacqueline Bouvier in 1953 and they had two children. He went to Dallas on November 22 1963 and he died there. He was 46 years old.

1 (*be*) John Kennedy born in 1917?

________________?

Yes, he ________.

2 (*he marry*) Jacqueline in 1952?

________________?

No, he ________. He married her in 1953.

3 (*they have*) four children?

________________?

No, they ________. They had two.

4 (*he die*) in Dallas?

________________?

Yes, he ____________.

5 (*be*) he 40 years old when he died?

______________________________?

No, he ____________. He was 46 years old.

___ / 10 marks

d) Read about Pablo Picasso. Then write questions with the words in brackets. (5 marks)

Pablo Picasso was born in Málaga in 1881 and he died in 1973. He studied art in Barcelona when he was 15. He visited Paris in 1900 and went to live there in 1904. He had four children, two wives and twelve houses.

1 Where/born?

______________________________?

2 When/die?

______________________________?

3 What/do in Barcelona?

______________________________?

4 When/live in Paris?

______________________________?

5 How many/houses/have?

______________________________?

___ / 5 marks

D *A(n), the* or no article

Write *a, an, the* or nothing in the sentences. (10 marks)

I'm (1)____ English teacher and I went to (2)____ China last year. It's (3)____ very big country. I stayed in (4)____ very good hotel in (5)____ Beijing. I stayed there for (6)____ two weeks. I love (7)____ restaurants and I had (8)____ dinner every evening in (9)____ beautiful restaurant near (10)____ hotel.

___ / 10 marks

E Prepositions

Correct the preposition mistakes. There is **one** in each sentence. (10 marks)

1 I live to 12 Hills Road. The house is between a shop and a school. ________

2 I went to a restaurant and I paid of lunch. ________

3 I went in holiday last week and I stayed in a hotel for two weeks. ________

4 What do you think at this dictionary? I got it from the shop on the corner. ________

5 I'm very interested in football and I watch it on TV at Saturdays. ________

6 My birthday is on May and I want to have dinner with Sue in the evening. ________

7 I usually drink coffee after lunch but I always have a cup with tea for breakfast. ________

8 A: Is John in home? B: No. He went to work.

9 I talked at him about my homework.

10 Go straight up this street and the bank is at the right near the station. ________

___ / 10 marks

F VOCABULARY

a) Odd ones out. There are **two** words in each column which are in the wrong place. Write them in the correct column. (8 marks)

Clothes	**Town**	**Leisure**	**Describing people**
yoga trousers cardigan trainers quiet skirt	traffic lights socks church kind railway station garage	swimming tennis ballroom dancing hat supermarket motocross	stamp-collecting intelligent sad attractive hospital interesting

___ / 8 marks

b) Complete the sentences with a word from the box below. (12 marks)

friendly	grey	garage	opera	games
quiet	cinema	swimming	trainers	
dangerous	coat	watch		

1 I like playing computer ________.

2 People go to the ________ to see films.

3 The car is in the ________.

4 I don't like ________ in the sea.

5 Put your ________ on. It's cold today.

6 I want to play tennis. Where are my ________?

7 I've got a new ________ jacket.

8 I think motocross is a ________ sport.

9 I haven't got a ________. What time is it?

10 Kay doesn't talk much. She's very ________.

11 Sue's got a new boyfriend. He's very ________.

12 Do you like listening to ________?

___ / 12 marks

Total ___ / 100 marks

Test 3 Units 7 - 9

GRAMMAR

A *Going to*

Complete the sentences with *going to*. (12 marks)

1 (*we play*) __________ tennis tonight?
2 (*you cook*) __________ dinner this evening?
3 (*Helen not buy*) __________ a new table.
4 (*they eat*) __________ at about 9 pm.
5 (*Richard take*) __________ some photos.
6 (*I not pay*) __________ for lunch today.
7 I can't see you this evening. I (*visit*) __________ my uncle.
8 (*my mother and father arrive*) __________ in ten minutes and we haven't got any coffee.
9 (*your children start*) __________ school in September?
10 (*Paula and Simone study*) __________ English in Britain or Australia?
11 (*they not come*) __________ to the party.
12 (*Gordon not bring*) __________ wine. He likes beer.

__ / 12 marks

B *Going to, if* or *when*

Underline the correct answer in the three brackets in each sentence. (8 marks)

1 (*I have/I'm going to have*) a shower (*if/when*) (*I finish/I'm going to finish*) my breakfast.
2 (*If/When*) (*John finishes/John's going to finish*) that book (*he gives/he's going to give*) it to me.
3 (*If/When*) (*you buy/you're going to buy*) those jeans for me (*I wear/I'm going to wear*) them tonight.
4 (*If/When*) (*they leave/they're going to leave*) the office early (*I tell/I'm going to tell*) the manager.
5 (*Do we walk/Are we going to walk*) to work tomorrow (*if/when*) (*it's/it's going to be*) sunny?
6 What (*does Jo do/is Jo going to do*) (*if/when*) (*he fails/he's going to fail*) his exams?
7 (*Do you watch/Are you going to watch*) the video (*if/when*) (*you finish/are going to finish*) writing that letter?
8 (*If/When*) it snows tomorrow, (*I don't drive/I'm not going to drive*) to school.

__ / 8 marks

C *A(n), some* or *any*

Complete the conversation with *a(n), some* or *any*. (15 marks)

JANE: Are you going to the shop?
CAROL: Yes, I am. We haven't got (1)______ bread and I want (2)_____ bottle of mineral water.
JANE: We need (3)______ cheese.
MONA: Oh good, you're going to the shop, Jane. I'm going to cook dinner tonight. Can you buy (4)________ melon, (5)________ rice, (6)______ tin of tuna fish, (7)________ tomatoes and have we got (8)_______ onion?
JANE: We've got one.
MONA: Good. Don't buy (9)______ onions.
CAROL: Can I have (10)________ money?
MONA: I haven't got (11)_______ money but I'm going to go to the bank tomorrow.
JANE: Oh Mona! You never have (12)_______ money. I've got (13)________ money, Carol. How much do you want?
MONA: I don't know. About £20, I think.
JANE: Are there (14)________ good films on TV?
CAROL: I don't know. I'll buy (15)______ newspaper. See you later girls.

__ / 15 marks

D *How much* or *how many?*

Underline the correct sentence. (10 marks)

1 How much hours do you work in a week?
How many hours do you work in a week?
2 How much homework did you have?
How many homework did you have?
3 How much does that bottle of wine cost?
How many does that bottle of wine cost?
4 How much sandwiches do you want?
How many sandwiches do you want?
5 How much coffee does Susan drink in a day?
How many coffee does Susan drink in a day?
6 How much sugar do you want in your tea?
How many sugar do you want in your tea?
7 How much photographs did you take?
How many photographs did you take?

8 How much money have you got?

How many money have you got?

9 How much garlic did you put in the pasta?

How many garlic did you put in the pasta?

10 How much English books has Anna got?

How many English books has Anna got?

___ / 10 marks

E *Have* and *has to*

Complete the sentences with *(do/does) have to* and *has to* or *don't/doesn't have to*. (10 marks)

1 A: Can you come for lunch?

B: Sorry I __________ finish this before 2.

2 A: Janet __________ get up early tomorrow.

B: No, she doesn't. Her plane leaves at 3 pm.

3 A: ____ you __________ drive your husband to the station?

B: No. He can get a taxi.

4 A: Tom can't go out. He ________ work.

B: He __________ do it tonight. He can do it tomorrow, it's Saturday.

5 A: ____ your children _________ to have tea?

B: No. They can have milk.

6 Irene wants that job in Germany so she ________ learn German.

7 I *(not)* ________ cook tonight. My husband is going to make dinner.

8 A: ______ Pamela ________ buy a dictionary?

B: No. The teacher gave her an old one.

9 A: _____ your parents _________ leave now?

B: No. Their plane doesn't leave until 10.

___ / 10 marks

F Prepositions

Correct the preposition mistakes. There is **one** in each sentence. (5 marks)

1 I spoke to John yesterday for the holiday.

2 The plane leaves on Monday and arrives at 6 am at the morning. _____

3 I saw Beth at town this morning. She talked for an hour about her new job. _____

4 Hello. Come in and sit in. I'm afraid I can't talk for very long. I have to leave soon. _____

5 I bought this pen to you from the shop. _____

___ / 5 marks

G Verb forms: past, present and future

Complete the sentences with the correct verb form. (20 marks)

Sometimes I *(not like)* (1)__________ my sister. Last week she *(take)* (2)________ my car but she *(not ask)* (3)________ me. I *(be)* (4)________ very angry with her. She never *(think)* (5)__________ about other people. Next month our parents *(visit)* (6)__________ my grandmother and they *(ask)* (7)________ me and my sister to go with them. Last night she *(say)* (8)________, 'I *(not visit)* (9)__________ grandmother with you because I *(want)* (10)__________ to go out with my friends.' My sister isn't very nice.

___ / 20 marks

H VOCABULARY

a) Odd ones out. There are **two** words in each column that are in the wrong place. Write them in the correct column. (10 marks)

The body	Jobs	The country	Illness	Food
melon	hairdresser	field	headache	peas
finger	carrots	face	cough	banana
toe	musician	wood	actor	cold
gate	doctor	earache	flu	stomach
mouth	forest	mountain	electrician	lamb

___ / 10 marks

b) Complete with the correct word. (10 marks)

1 Verb: **decide** Noun: __________.

2 Noun: **danger** Adjective: __________.

3 Noun: **friend** Adjective: __________.

4 Verb: **attract** Adjective: __________.

5 Noun: **rain** Adjective: __________.

6 Adjective: **dirty** Noun: __________.

7 Noun: **beauty** Adjective: __________.

8 Verb: **drink** Noun: __________.

9 Verb: **examine** Noun: __________.

10 Noun: **cloud** Adjective: __________.

___ / 10 marks

Total ___ / 100 marks

Test 4 Units 10 - 12

GRAMMAR

A Comparative and superlative adjectives

a) Complete the table with comparative and superlative adjectives. (20 marks)

Adjective	Comparative	Superlative
big		
small		
dirty		
beautiful		
attractive		
nice		
good		
cheap		
quiet		
short		

___ / 20 marks

b) Complete the sentences with the **comparative** adjective. (5 marks)

1 I thought the last test was (*difficult*) ________ than this one.
2 Can you carry this bag, please? It's (*heavy*) ________ than that one.
3 Is your brother (*young*) ______ than you?
4 A: Your hair looks (*good*) ________ today.
B: Yes. I washed it last night.
5 My father is (*old*) ________ than my mother.

___ / 5 marks

c) Complete the sentences with the **superlative** adjective. (10 marks)

1 Nelly is the (*kind*) ________ person I know.
2 This is the (*expensive*) ________ wine in the restaurant.
3 Who's the (*tall*) ________ boy in class?
4 This is the (*dirty*) ________ hotel I've ever stayed in.
5 Jacqueline is the (*interesting*) ________ person I've ever met.
6 When was the (*happy*) ________ time of your life?
7 Motocross is the (*danger*) ________ sport I've done.
8 Laura is the (*popular*) ________ student here.
9 I'm sorry I can't talk to you now. This is the (*busy*) ________ time in the office.
10 I think question 3 is the (*difficult*) ________ one to answer.

___ / 10 marks

B Verbs with *-ing* or *to*

Underline the correct answer. (10 marks)

1 I enjoy to meet/meeting people from China.
2 She wants going/to go to Egypt this year.
3 My doctor told me to stop to smoke/smoking.
4 I'm waiting to talk/talking to the policeman.
5 I hope to finish/finishing this book tomorrow.
6 Jack finished watching/to watch TV at 10 pm.
7 You can to go/go now.
8 I decided to leave/leaving my job.
9 I'd like to go out/going out for a meal.
10 They should relax/relaxing.

___ / 10 marks

C Verbs + two objects

Put the words in the correct order. (5 marks)

1 gave book her a her birthday for I
________________________________.
2 him showed Fred's painting we
________________________________.
3 me she your told address
________________________________.
4 you can me newspaper a buy
________________________________?
5 Maria her gave him dictionary
________________________________.

___ / 5 marks

D *Who* or *which*

Complete the sentences with *who* or *which*. (5 marks)

1 I have never met the man ______ lives next door.
2 I don't like people ______ drive very fast.
3 I can't find my pen ______ was on the table.
4 Have you seen the woman ______ took the letter off my desk?
5 I think the books ______ have the answer key are more expensive.

___ / 5 marks

E Present Perfect or Past Simple?

a) Complete the conversation with the Present Perfect or Past Simple. (15 marks)

SANDRA: You look wonderful!

PETER: Yes. Last week I (*be*) (1)______ in Greece. (*you ever be*) (2)______ there?

SANDRA: Yes. I (*go*) (3)______ there with my parents when I (*be*) (4)______ about four. (*your wife go*) (5)______ with you?

PETER: No. She hates planes. She (*never travel*) (6)______ by plane. We (*go*) (7)______ to France in 1995 but we (*take*) (8)______ the train and (*drive*) (9)______ to Marseilles. But Greece (*be*) (10)______ really nice. I love Greek food. (*you ever eat*) (11)______ their cheese? Oh, what's it called?

SANDRA: Feta cheese.

PETER: Yes. I (*eat*) (12)______ it every day when I (*be*) (13)______ on holiday.

SANDRA: (*you drink*) (14)______ the Greek wine, *ouzo*, when (*you be*) (15)______ there?

PETER: Every day with the feta cheese. Lovely.

___ / 15 marks

F Mixed grammar points

Complete the text with words from the boxes. (10 marks)

Do you know a famous person?

some is going to would be for met meet finish if

I have never met a famous person but I (1)______ like to (2)______ one. I want to (3)______ a journalist when I (4)______ studying. My mother is a photographer. She works (5)______ a newspaper and she has (6)______ a lot of famous people. (7)______ I pass my exams in June, my mother (8)______ introduce me to (9)______ important people in the newspaper business.

studying at in finishes him when a the an any going to

My brother is (10)______ doctor and he works at (11)______ University Hospital. My sister is (12)______ to be (13)______ actress. She doesn't know (14)______ famous people (15)______ the moment but she says she's (16)______ work (17)______ Hollywood (18)______ she (19)______ studying. My father says we all know a famous person because we know (20)______!

___ / 10 marks

G VOCABULARY

a) Odd ones out. There are two words in each table in the wrong place. Write them in the correct table. (8 marks)

The house	Shopping	Describing things	Music
leather	cheque	refund	violin
curtains	to try on	oblong	exchange
wardrobe	round	square	armchair
drums	receipt	beautiful	flute
cooker	jazz	microwave	pop/rock

___ / 8 marks

b) Find the four words for music, one word for shopping, two words to describe a thing and five words for the house in the puzzle. (12 marks)

M C O T T O N R L F
W S R F G W O O D C
A N X W W T C R T L
S P T J L B V C W A
H F R I D G E H X S
B B U D R A W E R S
A L M O G H M S J I
S A P N U K O T C C
I K E S I N K R G A
N Q T O T P U A J L
E X C H A N G E N P
L M I C R O W A V E

___ / 12 marks

Total ___ / 100 marks

Key

TEST 1 Units 1-3

(Total marks 100)

A *To be*: questions and answers

1 mark for each correct answer. (10 marks)

1 Are, am 2 Is, isn't 3 Is, is 4 Are, aren't 5 Are, 's

B *Have/has got*

1 mark for each correct answer. (20 marks)

1 have you got 2 haven't got 3 's got 4 have you got 5 have got 6 Have you or Jenny got 7 haven't got 8 have got 9 Have they got 10 haven't got 11 've got 12 haven't got 13 haven't got 14 Have you got 15 've got 16 's got 17 haven't got 18 've got 19 Have you got 20 's got

C The Present Simple

1 mark for each correct answer. (20 marks)

a)

1 Does Penny teach English? Yes, she does.
2 Does she have lunch with other teachers? No, she doesn't.
3 Does she teach in the afternoons? No, she doesn't.
4 Does she always walk home? No, she doesn't.
5 Does she visit her parents at the weekend? No, she doesn't.

b)

1 She doesn't usually work in the afternoon.
2 Do you often listen to music?
3 We don't drink coffee in the morning.
4 Do they speak Portuguese?
5 I never eat a big lunch.

c)

1 like 2 don't eat 3 Does he 4 don't smoke 5 Do you want

D The Present

1 mark for each correct answer. (10 marks)

1 like, don't 2 works, 's 3 's got, 're 4 Does John play, don't know 5 Do you like, 's 6 aren't, 're visiting 7 Are you, am 8 Have you got, haven't 9 Do you want, want 10 isn't, 's playing

E Object and possessive pronouns

1 mark for each correct answer. (10 marks)

1 her 2 yours 3 mine 4 us 5 theirs 6 hers 7 ours 8 him 9 it 10 his

F *A, an* and *some*

1 mark for each correct answer. (10 marks)

1 an 2 some 3 a 4 a 5 a 6 some 7 a 8 an 9 some 10 an

G The family , food and drink, the weather and the office

1 mark for each correct answer. (5 marks)

a)

1 sunny 2 mug 3 aunt 4 niece 5 bacon

b) Wordsearch

1 mark for each correct answer. (15 marks)

TEST 2 Units 4-6

A *Can* and *can't*

1 mark for each correct answer. (5 marks)

1 can speak 2 Can you drive? 3 can play 4 can't come 5 Can I leave

B Adjectives and adverbs

1 mark for each correct answer. (10 marks)

a)

1 beautifully 2 easily 3 quietly 4 well 5 fast

b)

1 good 2 slowly 3 interesting 4 fluently 5 quickly

C Past Simple

1 mark for each correct answer. (45 marks)

a) gave, spoke, arrived, opened, put, had, saw, said, looked, waited

b)

1 phoned 2 were 3 went 4 was 5 cooked 6 Did she have 7 took 8 liked 9 did you do 10 sat 11 talked 12 wanted 13 didn't want 14 listened 15 was 16 Did you sleep 17 did you come 18 didn't stay 19 came 20 did you do

c)

1 Was John Kennedy born in 1917? Yes, he was.
2 Did he marry Jacqueline in 1952? No he didn't.
3 Did they have four children? Yes, they did.
4 Did he die in Dallas? Yes, he did.
5 Was he 40 years old when he died? No, he wasn't.

d)

1 Where was he born? 2 When did he die?
3 What did he do in Barcelona? 4 When did he live in Paris? 5 How many houses did he have?

D *A(n), the* or no article

1 mark for each correct answer. (10 marks)

1 an 2 - 3 a 4 a 5 - 6 - 7 - 8 - 9 a 10 the

E Prepositions

1 mark for each correct answer. (10 marks)

1 in 2 for 3 on 4 of 5 on 6 in 7 of 8 at 9 to 10 on

F Vocabulary

1 mark for each correct answer. (20 marks)

a)

Clothes: socks, hat Town: supermarket, hospital
Leisure: yoga, stamp-collecting
Describing people: kind, quiet

b)

1 games 2 cinema 3 garage 4 swimming 5 coat 6 trainers 7 grey 8 dangerous 9 watch 10 quiet 11 friendly 12 opera

TEST 3 Units 7-9

A *Going to*

1 mark for each correct answer. (12 marks)

1 Are we going to play 3 Are you going to cook 3 Helen isn't going to buy 4 They're going to eat 5 Richard's going to take 6 I'm not going to pay 7 'm going to visit 8 My mother and father are going to arrive 9 Are your children going to start 10 Are Paula and Simone going to study 11 They are not going to come 12 Gordon's not going to bring

B *Going to, if* and *when*

1 mark for each correct answer. (8 marks)

1 I'm going to, when, I finish
2 When, John finishes, he's going to give
3 If, you buy, I'm going to wear
4 If, they leave, I'm going to tell
5 Are we going to walk, if, it's
6 is Jo going to do, if, he fails
7 Are you going to watch, when, you finish
8 If, I'm not going to drive

C *A(n), some* or *any*

1 mark for each correct answer. (15 marks)

1 any 2 a 3 some 4 a 5 some 6 a 7 some 8 an 9 any 10 some 11 any 12 any 13 some 14 any 15 a

D *How much* or *how many*

1 mark for each correct answer. (10 marks)

1 How many 2 How much 3 How much
4 How many 5 How much 6 How much
7 How many 8 How much 9 How much
10 How many

E *Have* and *has to*

1 mark for each correct answer. (10 marks)

1 have to 2 has to 3 Do you have to 4 has to, doesn't have to 5 Do your children have 6 has to 7 don't have to 8 Does Pamela have to 9 Do your parents have to

F Prepositions

1 mark for each correct answer. (5 marks)

1 about 2 in 3 in 4 down 5 for

G Verb forms: past, present and future

2 marks for each correct answer. (20 marks)

1 don't like 2 took 3 didn't ask 4 was 5 thinks 6 are going to visit 7 asked/are going to ask 8 said 9 'm not going to visit 10 want

H Vocabulary

1 mark for each correct answer. (20 marks)

a)

The body: face, stomach Jobs: actor, electrician
The country: gate, forest Illness: cold, earache
Food: melon, carrots

b)

1 decision 6 dirt
2 dangerous 7 beautiful
3 friendly 8 drink
4 attractive 9 examination
5 rainy 10 cloudy

TEST 4 Units 10-12

A Comparative and superlative adjectives

1 mark for each correct answer. (20 marks)

a)

bigger, the biggest
smaller, the smallest
dirtier, the dirtiest
more beautiful, the most beautiful
more attractive, the most attractive
nicer, the nicest
better, the best
cheaper, the cheapest
quieter, the quietest
shorter, the shortest

b)

One mark for each correct answer. (15 marks)

1 more difficult 2 heavier 3 younger 4 better 5 older

c)

1 kindest 2 most expensive 3 tallest 4 dirtiest 5 most interesting 6 happiest 7 most dangerous 8 most popular 9 busiest 10 most difficult

B Verbs with *-ing* or *to*

1 mark for each correct answer. (10 marks)

1 meeting 2 to go 3 smoking 4 to talk 5 to finish 6 finished watching 7 go now 8 to leave 9 to go out 10 relax

C Verb + two objects

1 mark for each correct answer. (5 marks)

1 I gave her a book for her birthday.
2 We showed him Fred's painting.
3 She told me your address.
4 Can you buy me a newspaper?
5 Maria gave him her dictionary.

D *Who* or *which*

1 mark for each correct answer. (5 marks)

1 who 2 who 3 which 4 who 5 which

E Present Perfect or Past Simple?

1 mark for each correct answer. (15 marks)

a)

1 was 2 Have you ever been 3 went 4 was 5 Did you wife go 6 has never travelled 7 went 8 took 9 drove 10 was 11 Have you ever eaten 12 ate 13 was 14 Did you drink 15 you were

F Mixed grammar points

½ mark for each correct answer. (10 marks)

1 would 2 meet 3 be 4 finish 5 for 6 met 7 If 8 is going to 9 some 10 a 11 the 12 studying 13 an 14 any 15 at 16 going to 17 in 18 when 19 finishes 20 him

G Vocabulary

1 mark for each correct answer. (8 marks)

a)

The house: armchair, microwave Shopping: refund, exchange Describing things: leather, round Music: drums, jazz

b) Wordsearch

1 mark for each correct answer (12 marks)

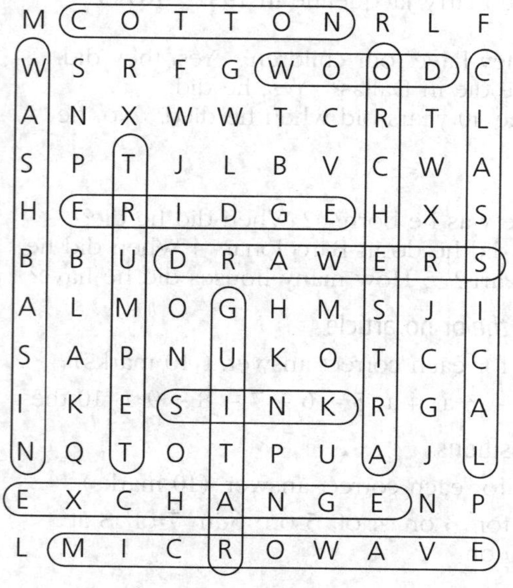